The Transitional Program

The Death Agony of Capitalism and the Tasks of the Fourth International

by Leon Trotsky

edited by the International Bolshevik Tendency, with a new introduction and a selection of related materials

Bolshevik Publications London~Toronto

First published 1998 by
Bolshevik Publications
BCM Box 4771, London WC1N 3XX
PO Box 332, Adelaide St. Station, Toronto M5C 1J0

Introduction: International Bolshevik Tendency
Web page: www.bolshevik.org
e-mail: ibt@babeuf.actrix.gen.nz

Typeset by voluntary labor
Printed and bound in Great Britain by St Edmundsbury Press,
Bury St Edmunds

British Library Cataloguing in Publication Data
A catalogue record for this book is available from the British Library

ISBN 0 9534367 0 5

Cover photo: Institut Léon Trotsky

Contents

Preface

On 25 March 1935, in an entry to his private diary, the great Russian revolutionary Leon Trotsky observed:

> "...I think that the work in which I am engaged now, despite its extremely insufficient and fragmentary nature, is the most important work of my life—more important than 1917, more important than the period of the Civil War or any other.
>
> "For the sake of clarity I would put it this way. Had I not been present in 1917 in Petersburg, the October Revolution would still have taken place....
>
> "Thus I cannot speak of the 'indispensability' of my work, even about the period from 1917 to 1921. But now my work is 'indispensable' in the full sense of the word....There is now no one except me to carry out the mission of arming a new generation with the revolutionary method over the heads of the leaders of the Second and Third International[s]....I need at least about five more years of uninterrupted work to ensure the succession." [1]

Trotsky, who was assassinated a little more than five years later, considered the adoption of the *Transitional Program* (officially entitled *The Death Agony of Capitalism and the Tasks of the Fourth International*) by the founding conference of the Fourth International in 1938 to be a critical step in "ensuring the succession" of Bolshevism. In his salute to the new international he wrote:

> "The acceptance of this program, prepared and assured by a lengthy previous discussion—or rather, a whole series of discussions—represents our most important conquest. The Fourth International is now the only international organization which not only takes clearly into account the driving forces of the imperialist epoch, but is armed with a system of transitional demands capable of uniting the masses for a revolutionary struggle for power."[2]

Sixty years after its original publication, the International Bolshevik Tendency (IBT) is pleased to reissue the text that Trotsky considered the Fourth International's "most important conquest." To provide historical context, as well as demonstrate the continuing relevance of this document, we have included an extensive new introduction. In the concluding chapter we trace the connection between the demands contained in the *Transitional Program* and those advocated by the revolutionary Communist International in Lenin's time.

We have also reprinted a number of related items. These include a 1987 interview with Howard Keylor, a well-known supporter of the International Bolshevik Tendency, in which he describes his experience over three decades

1 Leon Trotsky, *Trotsky's Diary in Exile—1935* (New York: Atheneum, 1963), p 46–7

2 Leon Trotsky, "A Great Achievement," *Writings of Leon Trotsky (1937–38)* (New York: Pathfinder Press, 1976), p 439

in the American dockers' union and, in particular, his participation in an attempt to forge a class-struggle opposition to the labor bureaucracy. Keylor, a former Communist Party cadre, was won to Trotskyism in the mid-1970s by the then-revolutionary Spartacist League/U.S. (SL).

During the 1960s and 1970s the Spartacist League represented the living continuity of Trotsky's Fourth International. Among its most important political contributions was its exemplary work in building class-struggle caucuses in a variety of unions on the basis of a full transitional program. Trotsky had written the 1938 program as a tool for intervention in the unions, but to the best of our knowledge the SL was the only ostensibly Trotskyist organization to have ever fully grounded its trade-union work on the *Transitional Program*.

In the early 1970s, as part of the SL's turn to the unions, Chris Knox, then the group's trade-union director, wrote a series of important articles in the SL's newspaper, *Workers Vanguard* (*WV*), that traced the history of communist, and particularly Trotskyist, work in the mass organizations of the American working class. We have reprinted these articles, two of which were co-signed by Len Meyers.

The SL's trade-union work in the 1970s was not only principled, but also flexible and effective. To demonstrate this we have included a selection of contemporary articles from the SL's press that give some indication of how the various class-struggle caucuses intervened among phone-workers, autoworkers, dockers and sailors on the basis of a full transitional program. (A more complete picture of this work can be obtained by consulting other articles in the SL's public press and internal bulletins, as well as the various newsletters, leaflets, minutes and other materials produced by the caucuses themselves.)

During the later 1970s and early 1980s, the rightward drift of American society, and the downturn in the level of class struggle, was paralleled by a qualitative political degeneration of the Spartacist League and its affiliates in the international Spartacist tendency (iSt). (We described this process in "The Road to Jimstown," *Bulletin of the External Tendency of the iSt*, May 1985.) After a series of debilitating internal purges, the SL leadership liquidated what remained of its trade-union work, thereby throwing away the precious toeholds in the labor movement that had been established through years of self-sacrifice and hard work by dozens of dedicated cadres. The External Tendency of the iSt (the progenitor of the IBT) fought this betrayal at the time (see "Stop the Liquidation of the Trade Union Work!," 25 June 1983).

The Spartacist League is widely regarded today as an irrelevant and introverted organization, best known for its sectarian semi-hysterics. Yet despite its political degeneration, the sustained and serious attempt of the SL of the 1970s to intervene in the organizations of the American proletariat on the basis of the *Transitional Program* is an important chapter in the history of Trotskyism. It is an experience containing many valuable lessons that revolutionaries today must assimilate in order to prepare for the struggles of tomorrow.

Introduction

Leon Trotsky, co-leader of the October Revolution and founder of the Red Army, wrote the *Transitional Program* in March and April 1938 while living in exile in Mexico. It was adopted as the program of the Fourth International at its founding conference in September 1938.

Prior to finishing the draft, Trotsky participated in a series of discussions in late March 1938 with four leaders of the American Socialist Workers Party (SWP): James P. Cannon, Vincent Dunne, Rose Karsner and Max Shachtman. The SWP was the most substantial section of the fledgling Fourth International in terms of size, political capacity and mass influence. Trotsky's discussions with the SWPers helped to clarify certain aspects of the program and to refine his ideas about how it should be presented. In a 15 April 1938 letter to Cannon, Trotsky wrote:

> "Without your visit to Mexico, I could never have written the program draft because I learned during the discussions many important things which permitted me to be more explicit and concrete." [1]

The *Transitional Program* remains relevant today because it addresses the central task of our epoch: the mobilization of the working class for power. To be sure, the world has changed a great deal since 1938. Accordingly, in applying the program, revolutionaries must distinguish between those passages containing its core programmatic conceptions and the more descriptive passages that reflect the specific historical period in which it was written.

By 1938 the world order established at Versailles in 1919 was in shreds. The enormous social devastation of the Great Depression, the rise of fascism and other events preparing the way for a cataclysmic inter-imperialist bloodbath provided the context for the rather categorical (and even apocalyptic) tone of some passages in the *Transitional Program.* Trotsky wrote:

> "The economic prerequisite for the proletarian revolution has already in general achieved the highest point of fruition that can be reached under capitalism. Mankind's productive forces stagnate. Already, new inventions and improvements fail to raise the level of material wealth.
>
> . . .
>
> "International relations present no better picture. Under the increasing tension of capitalist disintegration, imperialist antagonisms...must inevitably coalesce into a conflagration of world dimensions. The bourgeoisie, of course, is aware of the mortal danger to its domination represented by a new war. But that class is now immeasurably less capable of averting war than on the eve of 1914."

Trotsky expected that World War II would end in a wave of revolutionary explosions just as World War I had. Moreover, he was by no means alone in

1 Leon Trotsky, "Letter to James P. Cannon," *Writings of Leon Trotsky (1937–38)* (New York: Pathfinder Press, 1976), p 317

anticipating this. On 25 August 1939, a few days before the outbreak of hostilities, the French ambassador told Hitler: "as a result of the war, there would be only one real victor—Mr. Trotsky."[2]

World War II was a catastrophe that cost tens of millions of lives and wreaked unprecedented destruction. In its aftermath, potentially revolutionary situations arose in a number of European countries. In France and Italy these were defused, largely as a result of the treachery of the Moscow-loyal Communist Parties, whose cadres disarmed the partisans and propped up the post-war "anti-fascist" bourgeois regimes. Maurice Thorez, leader of the French Communist Party, advanced the slogan: "One police, one army, one state!" In Greece, the Kremlin tacitly supported the British Army, monarchists and Nazi collaborators in brutally crushing the leftist National Liberation Front (EAM).

The Nazi occupation of Western Europe generated intense hostility toward the indigenous bourgeoisie (who overwhelmingly collaborated with the fascists), but it also revived illusions in the "anti-fascist" imperialists. The Stalinists used the authority they accrued through their central role in the anti-Nazi resistance and their association with the victorious Red Army in pursuit of global reconciliation with imperialism. In 1943 Stalin went so far as to dissolve the Comintern in a demonstration of goodwill toward British and American imperialism. The New York *Herald Tribune* observed:

> "So far as the present Russian government is concerned, there is no reason to suspect that the dissolution of the Comintern is merely a gesture. Instead, it appears far more probable that it is the climax of the process that began when Stalin won his duel with Trotsky for leadership in Russia—the organization of that country into a national state run on Communist lines, rather than a center of world revolution."[3]

By the end of the war, only the Fourth International laid claim to the heritage of the Leninist Comintern. Yet so many key Trotskyist cadres had been murdered during the war (by both Stalinists and Nazis) that the Fourth International had ceased to function as a coherent organization. Individuals and small groups of militants remained active and carried out some exemplary interventions, but the International was far too weak to take advantage of the post-war revolutionary opportunities.

The social-democratic organizations, which had ceased to operate during the Nazi occupation, were revived by the British and Americans as pro-capitalist counterweights to the influence of the Communists in the European labor movement. Having successfully contained the upheavals of 1945–46, Western European capitalism, with the support of the American colossus, went on to enjoy over 20 years of relative stability and prosperity. During this period, in stark contrast to the 1930s, the reformist leaders of the working

2 Leon Trotsky, "The Twin Stars: Hitler-Stalin," *Writings of Leon Trotsky (1939-40) (New York: Pathfinder Press, 1973), p 122*

3 *Herald Tribune* (New York), 23 May 1943

class were able to win some limited but real material concessions from the bourgeoisie—concessions which had a conservatizing effect upon their base.

Post-War Expansion and the Transitional Program

The rather categorical nature of some of Trotsky's formulations in his 1938 draft and their apparent refutation by subsequent developments have led some ostensible Marxists to draw the conclusion that the *Transitional Program* lost its relevance and applicability in the post-war period. Yet the system of revolutionary transitional demands that constitutes the core of the program did not flow from Trotsky's conjunctural prognoses of 1938. The performance of the capitalist economy at a given historical moment conditions the framework within which the class struggle takes place, and thus the immediate political possibilities, but such conjunctural factors do not affect the revolutionary Marxist assessment of the objective historic necessity for human society to make the leap to socialism.

This necessity flows from the qualitative intensification of the global contradictions of capitalism in what Lenin and Trotsky called the "imperialist" stage of its development. Imperialism is characterized by attempts on the part of the most advanced countries to resolve the crisis tendencies inherent in the capitalist accumulation process through mechanisms which transfer wealth from weaker to stronger regions of the global economy and produce extremely uneven patterns of development. In addition to endless military adventures in the neo-colonies, inter-imperialist competition leads inexorably to world war.

There is clearly a sense in which the advent of the imperialist epoch marked the end of capitalism's historically progressive role in developing the forces of production, defined broadly as "global human capacities." The intensified contradictions of the capitalist mode of production in the metropolitan imperialist regions set the stage for periodic military conflicts that destroy productive forces on a massive scale. Moreover, imperialism blocks the diffusion of advanced technologies to more backward regions, thereby retarding the development of labor productivity on a world scale. On the eve of the 21st century, capitalism has failed to completely uproot pre-capitalist economic forms in much of the "Third World." It has "succeeded" in creating a reserve army of the unemployed and under-employed that comprises more than 30 percent of the global workforce. The inability of the market to promote qualitative growth in "macro-economic productivity" (even as it retains a remarkable capacity to stimulate the "micro-productivity" of individual enterprises) confirms the continuing validity of the long-standing Leninist-Trotskyist proposition that capitalism constitutes an obstacle to human progress.

It is with these considerations in mind that we should evaluate Trotsky's comment in the *Transitional Program* regarding the "stagnation" of the productive forces in the inter-war period. This characterization was one-sided and therefore inaccurate to the extent that it failed to register the continuing potential for advances in technology and labor productivity *at the level of the capitalist enterprise*—although if there was ever a time in the 20th century that this appeared to be in doubt, it was certainly during the 1930s. Over the past 50 years, we have witnessed enormous growth in the productivity of that segment of the global workforce that remains involved in directly productive activity within capitalist industry, and a massive expansion of material wealth. In this sense the "economic prerequisites" for the creation of a planned economy stand at a far higher level today than in the 1930s.

In spite of the one-sided character of the formulation of the question in the *Transitional Program*, it would be unfair to impute to Trotsky the notion that capitalism, even in the epoch of its "death agony," posed an absolute barrier to further advances in productive technique. In his last major programmatic document, the May 1940 "Manifesto of the Fourth International on the Imperialist War and the Proletarian World Revolution," he remarked (albeit off-handedly) that, "technology is infinitely more powerful now than at the end of the war of 1914–18...."[4]

Despite the new material basis for renewed capital accumulation created by World War II, post-war capitalist expansion eliminated neither political and social crises nor real opportunities for the working class to struggle for power. The colonial and semi-colonial world witnessed a series of major upheavals, from mass struggles for national independence in Africa and Asia, to successful anti-capitalist social revolutions in China, Vietnam and Cuba. While potentially revolutionary situations were less common in the advanced capitalist countries in the post-war than the inter-war period, sharp class struggles continued to erupt in several European countries long after the working-class upsurges of the mid-1940s. The May–June 1968 events in France, Italy's "hot autumn" in 1969, and the Portuguese crisis of 1974–75 were clearly all pre-revolutionary situations. A number of other major class battles of the 1960s and 1970s also demonstrated the potential vulnerability of the capitalist order even during a period which was generally characterized by rising working-class living standards and relatively dynamic economic growth. These included the Belgian general strike of 1961, the Chilean *cordones industriales* (workers' councils) of 1972–73, Quebec's 1972 general strike and the 1974 showdown between the British miners and the Tory government. Many of the demands included in the *Transitional Program* were every bit as relevant in these struggles as they had been in comparable situations in the 1920s and 1930s.

The past two decades have seen falling real wages, declining living standards and growing social inequality and insecurity throughout the "developed" (i.e., imperialist) world. Working people are told to get used to the idea that life for their children will be harder than their own lives are today. In the

4 Leon Trotsky, "Manifesto of the Fourth International on the Imperialist War and the Proletarian World Revolution," *Writings of Leon Trotsky (1939–40)* (New York: Pathfinder Press, 1973), p 184

"Third World," hundreds of millions of human beings are consigned to short and brutal lives of hopeless and desperate poverty. Those lucky enough to get employment in low-wage "newly industrializing" neo-colonies are subject to conditions reminiscent of the horrors of the Industrial Revolution. Today's brave new world of instantaneous communication, "flexible" production and global financial markets is also one in which tens of thousands of children starve to death daily, and in which the destruction of the biosphere proceeds inexorably.

'Can Capitalism Survive?'

The tendency for capitalist economic rivalry to escalate into military conflict produced two world wars in the 20th century. These were not random events or natural disasters. They derive from an inner logic of capitalist competition, a logic that compels each bourgeoisie to continually attempt to improve its position at the expense of its rivals. In the Fourth International's 1940 manifesto, Trotsky posed the following alternatives for humanity:

> "The question is whether, as a result of the present war, the entire world economy will be reconstructed on a planned scale, or whether the first attempt of this reconstruction will be crushed in a sanguinary convulsion, and imperialism will receive a new lease on life until the third world war, which can become the tomb of civilization."[5]

Imperialism did indeed receive a new lease on life after World War II. But today's sharpening economic competition between the major capitalist trading blocs reminds us that, sooner or later, a third inter-imperialist conflict is inevitable. Today, as in 1938, "nothing short of the overthrow of the bourgeoisie can open a road out."

Contrary to the insistence of capitalist ideologues that "communism is dead," and that Marx's analysis of capitalism is no longer "relevant," a growing number of studies by leftist scholars in recent years have demonstrated a remarkable conformity between the real dynamics of capital accumulation since World War II and Marx's description of the "laws of motion" of the capitalist mode of production.[6] A long-term fall in the average rate of profit, associated with a rise in the "organic composition of capital" (the ratio of "dead" to living labor in production), was evident in a number of advanced

5 Leon Trotsky, "The World Situation and Perspectives," *Writings of Leon Trotsky (1939–40)* (New York: Pathfinder Press, 1973), p 147

6 See: Gerard Dumenil and Dominique Levy, *The Economics of the Profit Rate: Competition, Crises and Historical Tendencies in Capitalism* (Brookfield, Vermont: Elgar Publishing Co., 1993); Fred Moseley, *The Falling Rate of Profit in the Postwar United States Economy* (London: Macmillan, 1991); Anwar Shaikh and Ahmet Tonak, *Measuring the Wealth of Nations: The Political Economy of National Accounts* (Cambridge: Cambridge University Press, 1994); Murray E.G. Smith, *Invisible Leviathan* (Toronto: University of Toronto Press, 1994); Union for Radical Political Economics, *Empirical Work in Marxian Crisis Theory*, special double issue of *Review of Radical Political Economics*, Vol. 18 Nos. 1–2, 1986; Michael J. Webber and David L. Rigby, *The Golden Age Illusion: Rethinking Postwar Capitalism* (New York: Guildford Press, 1996)

capitalist countries up to at least the late 1970s. Just as Marx anticipated, the bourgeoisie responded to this profitability crisis with aggressive efforts to jack up the rate of exploitation of the labor force, and with attempts to resolve the "internal contradiction" by "extending the external field of production"[7]—that is, through heightened inter-imperialist competition for markets and arenas of profitable investment.

The economic malaise of the past two decades is the direct result of a classical profitability crisis resulting from the contradiction between the labor-displacing imperatives of capitalist accumulation/competition and the structural necessity of capitalism to continuously measure material wealth in terms of abstract labor time (i.e., the contradictions of the law of value). The only "medicine" that the capitalist class can dispense to alleviate such a crisis, short of a new world war and the massive destruction of the "dead labor" embodied in capitalist means of production, is a relentless assault on working-class living standards and trade-union rights. The "real history" of the capitalist mode of production in recent decades strikingly confirms Marx's fundamental insights that the accumulation of capital must give rise over time to ever greater class antagonisms, and that these heightened antagonisms present the working class with the opportunity and the challenge to end the rule of capital and inaugurate a new social order.

Marxists are not alone in viewing capitalism as an unstable and transitory moment in human history. The few bourgeois theorists who have thought seriously about the future of capitalism have tended to conclude that a profit-driven system cannot survive over the long term. In his 1942 opus, *Capitalism, Socialism and Democracy*, Joseph Schumpeter asked "Can capitalism survive?" and answered: "No, I do not think it can." In an interview promoting his influential 1993 tome, *Twenty-First Century Capitalism*, Robert Heilbroner, a leading American bourgeois economist, asked:

> "Why do none of our philosophers, not even [Adam] Smith or Schumpeter who are surely partisans of the order, foresee a long untroubled future for capitalism?
>
> "The obvious answer is the sheer difficulty of successfully maintaining capitalist order....
>
> "The crucial difficulty for maintaining economic order takes on many forms—the indeterminacy of the outlook for investment and for technology; the unequal distribution of incomes[;]...the technological displacement of labour and the technological impetus toward cartelization; the inflationary tendencies of a successful economy and the depressive tendencies of an unsuccessful one. Capitalism's uniqueness in history lies in its continuously self-generated change, but it is this very dynamism that is the system's chief enemy. The system will sooner or later give rise to unmanageable problems and will have to make way for a successor."[8]

The fundamental problem with capitalism is that everything is subordinated to the predatory struggle to maximize private profit—to measure human

7 Karl Marx, *Capital*, Vol. 3 (London: Penguin Books, 1981), p 353
8 *Globe and Mail Magazine* (Toronto), May 1993

wealth in terms of "surplus labor appropriated" even as capitalist production requires less and less living labor as a technical input to production. The full promise of labor-saving technology cannot be realized by a system governed by the logic of the class exploitation of living labor. To resolve these problems in a historically progressive manner, a "successor" system must provide humanity with the ability to consciously control its social environment and gear production to the satisfaction of human needs rather than to the perpetuation of class inequality.

The Role of the Conscious Factor

The capitalist class conquered political power after first establishing its economic domination. For the working class this process is reversed. A planned economy will not emerge semi-spontaneously from capitalist anarchy, as capitalism did from feudalism; it must be created through extending conscious human control over the production and distribution of the goods and services necessary for society to develop and reproduce itself. The revolutionary transformation of all existing social relations can only be initiated on the basis of a high level of political consciousness within the proletariat.

The centrality of the "subjective factor" in the struggle for socialism (i.e., a disciplined political vanguard of the proletariat) lies at the heart of Trotskyism:

> "The new parties and the new International must be built upon a new foundation: that is the key with which to solve all other tasks. The tempo and the time of the new revolutionary construction and its consummation depend, obviously, upon the general course of the class struggle, the future victories and defeats of the proletariat. Marxists, however, are not fatalists. They do not unload upon the 'historical process' those very tasks which the historical process has posed before them. The initiative of a conscious minority, a scientific program, bold and ceaseless agitation in the name of clearly formulated aims, merciless criticism of all ambiguity—those are some of the most important factors for the victory of the proletariat. Without a fused and steeled revolutionary party a socialist revolution is inconceivable."[9]

Trotsky, like Lenin, rejected as objectivist nonsense the notion that capitalism must inevitably or automatically collapse:

> "There is no crisis that can be, by itself, fatal to capitalism. The oscillations of the business cycle only create a situation in which it will be easier, or more difficult, for the proletariat to overthrow capitalism. The transition from a bourgeois society to a socialist society presupposes the activity of living people who are the makers of their own history. They do not make history by accident, or according to their caprice, but under the influence of objectively determined causes. However, their own actions—their initiative, audacity, devotion, and likewise their stupidity and cowardice—are necessary links in the chain of historical development.

9 Leon Trotsky, "Open Letter for the Fourth International," *Writings of Leon Trotsky (1935–36)* (New York: Pathfinder Press, 1977), p 27

"The crises of capitalism are not numbered, nor is it indicated in advance which one of these will be the 'last.' But our entire epoch and, above all, the present crisis imperiously command the proletariat: 'Seize power!' If, however, the party of the working class, in spite of favorable conditions, reveals itself incapable of leading the proletariat to the seizure of power, the life of society will continue necessarily upon capitalist foundations—until a new crisis, a new war, perhaps until the complete disintegration of European civilization."[10]

While the Fourth International was established to struggle to resolve the "crisis of revolutionary leadership," Trotsky was acutely aware of the enormous difficulties it faced:

"...shall we succeed in preparing in time a party capable of leading the proletarian revolution? In order to answer this question correctly it is necessary to pose it correctly. Naturally, this or that uprising may end and surely will end in defeat owing to the immaturity of the revolutionary leadership. But it is not a question of a single uprising. It is a question of an entire revolutionary epoch.

"The capitalist world has no way out, unless a prolonged death agony is so considered. It is necessary to prepare for long years, if not decades, of war, uprisings, brief interludes of truce, new wars, and new uprisings. A young revolutionary party must base itself on this perspective. History will provide it with enough opportunities and possibilities to test itself, to accumulate experience and to mature....[T]he great historical problem will not be solved in any case until a revolutionary party stands at the head of the proletariat. The question of tempos and time intervals is of enormous importance; but it alters neither the general historical perspective nor the direction of our policy."[11]

A rise in working-class militancy will often be met by court injunctions prohibiting mass pickets, plant seizures, "hot-cargoing," sympathy strikes and any other effective tactics. If this proves insufficient, police pressure is stepped up: pickets and demonstrators are attacked, union assets seized and workers' leaders detained. The mass media, which normally operates as the ideological police of the ruling class, works overtime to confuse, divide and demoralize the workers and their potential allies.

Such measures are often sufficient for the capitalists to reassert control, but sometimes repression can backfire and result in new layers of the population being drawn into struggle. A deep-going crisis in the bourgeois social order inevitably manifests itself in division and a loss of self-confidence in the ruling class, and in uncertainty, confusion and hesitation within the repressive apparatus itself. In such circumstances the capitalists often come to rely more heavily on fascists and gangs of strikebreakers and thugs recruited from the

10 Leon Trotsky, "Once Again, Whither France?" *Leon Trotsky On France* (New York: Monad Press, 1979), p 79

11 Leon Trotsky, "Manifesto of the Fourth International on the Imperialist War and the Proletarian World Revolution," *Writings of Leon Trotsky (1939–40)* (New York: Pathfinder Press, 1973), pp 217–18

"patriotic" petty bourgeoisie, the lumpenproletariat and backward elements of the working class.

An effective leadership of the workers' movement must anticipate such developments and be prepared to act swiftly and decisively to neutralize reactionary formations before they grow. While proper technical preparations for this sort of intervention are essential, the most important task is the continuing political mass mobilization of the working class as it awakens to its historic interests through the course of the struggle. The *Transitional Program* is an algebraic codification of the essential measures with which the proletarian vanguard can broaden the scope of struggle and counter the attacks of the class enemy in a pre-revolutionary or revolutionary situation:

> "The basic conditions for the victory of the proletarian revolution have been established by historical experience and clarified theoretically: (1) the bourgeois impasse and resulting confusion of the ruling class; (2) the sharp dissatisfaction and striving towards decisive changes in the ranks of the petty bourgeoisie without whose support the big bourgeoisie cannot maintain itself; (3) the consciousness of the intolerable situation and readiness for revolutionary actions in the ranks of the proletariat; (4) a clear program and a firm leadership of the proletarian vanguard—these are the four conditions for the victory of the proletarian revolution."[12]

Program and Party 'Of a New Type'

In the late 19th century, the leaders of the Second International anticipated that as the working class grew in social weight, internal cohesion and political maturity, it would gradually lose its connections to the peasantry and urban petty bourgeoisie and embrace the socialist project (the "maximum" component of the classical social-democratic program). In the meantime, they sought to draw the working class into a unitary party of "the whole class" by focusing on the "minimum" needs of working people within the framework of capitalism.

The social-patriotic capitulation of the Second International during World War I forced Lenin to conclude that a bribed layer of pro-capitalist "labor aristocrats" were actively promoting false consciousness within the proletariat. This dictated a decisive break from the conception of a "party of the whole class" in favor of a "party of a new type"—a revolutionary combat party capable of leading the working class in a fight for power. Lenin's recognition of the necessity of organizing a party of the most advanced workers separately from the more backward layers was his single most important contribution to Marxism.

The Leninist "party of a new type" naturally required a new sort of program. The parties of the Second International claimed to be Marxist, and even "revolutionary," but they considered the "maximum" program as something for the indefinite future. The Communist International (Comintern),

12 *Ibid.*, pp 216–17

by contrast, actively sought to address the immediate struggles of the class in ways that led to revolutionary modes of consciousness and action. The Comintern under Lenin explicitly advocated the use of "transitional demands" that would unite the proletariat across its sectional divisions while also prefiguring the economic, social and political content of the future workers' state, thereby posing, at least implicitly, the necessity of socialist revolution.

The use of transitional demands does not imply an abandonment of struggles for more limited objectives. The Fourth International would not:

> "...discard the program of the old 'minimal' demands to the degree to which these have preserved at least part of their vital forcefulness. Indefatigably, it defends the democratic rights and social conquests of the workers. But it carries on this day-to-day work within the frame-work of the correct actual, that is, revolutionary perspective....The old 'minimal program' is superseded by the *transitional program*, the task of which lies in systematic mobilization of the masses for the proletarian revolution."[13]

Reformists have no use for transitional demands because their activity does not go beyond the "practical" task of reforming bourgeois society; indeed, reformism seeks only to win reforms that are compatible with maintaining the conditions of bourgeois rule, in particular, rates of profit deemed to be "reasonable" by the capitalist class. By contrast, revolutionaries are not constrained to operate within the bounds established by the imperatives of capitalist profitability:

> "If capitalism is incapable of satisfying the demands, inevitably arising from the calamities generated by itself, then let it perish. 'Realizability' or 'unrealizability' are in the given instance a question of the relationship of forces...."[14]

Marxists have long observed that the greatest gains for working people tend to come as by-products of revolutionary struggle:

> "If we say that we will only demand what they can give, the ruling class will give only one-tenth or none of what we demand. When we demand more and can impose our demands, the capitalists are compelled to give the maximum. The more extended and militant the spirit of the workers, the more is demanded and won. They are not sterile slogans; they are means of pressure on the bourgeoisie, and will give the greatest possible material results immediately."[15]

Reformists are not alone in their rejection of transitional demands. Sectarian ultra-lefts also have no use for them. Having already rhetorically embraced the most extreme formulas, they reject all tactical maneuvers, compromises or partial struggles, and content themselves with striking poses and issuing

13 Leon Trotsky, *The Transitional Program*, see p 37

14 *Ibid.*, see p 38–9

15 Leon Trotsky, "The Political Backwardness of the American Workers," *The Transitional Program for Socialist Revolution* (New York: Pathfinder Press, 1974), p 129

fearsomely radical-sounding declamations, while patiently waiting for the great day when the masses will seek them out.

Bourgeois 'Recess' and Proletarian 'Strategic Retreat'

In discussing the *Transitional Program* with the SWP/U.S. leaders, Trotsky noted that some of his followers seemed to have, "the impression that some of my propositions or demands [in the draft program] were opportunistic, and others...were too revolutionary, not corresponding to the objective situation."[16] Pointing to the fact that the U.S. was in the grip of "a social crisis without precedent," Trotsky proposed that the SWP should be "more optimistic, more courageous, more aggressive in our strategy and tactics":

> "What is the sense of the transitional program? We can call it a program of action, but for us, for our strategic conception, it is a transitional program—it is a help to the masses in overcoming the inherited ideas, methods, and forms and of adapting themselves to the exigencies of the objective situation. This transitional program must include the most simple demands. We cannot foresee and prescribe local and trade union demands adapted to the local situation of a factory, the development from this demand to the slogan for the creation of a workers' soviet.
>
> "These are both extreme points, from the development of our transitional program to find the connecting links and lead the masses to the idea of revolutionary conquest of power. That is why some demands appear to be very opportunistic—because they are adapted to the actual mentality of the workers. That is why other demands appear too revolutionary—because they reflect more the objective situation than the actual mentality of the workers. It is our duty to make this gap between objective and subjective factors as short as possible. That is why I cannot overestimate the importance of the transitional program."[17]

Trotsky was well aware that there are downturns, as well as upturns, in the class struggle. He even raised the possibility that capitalism might emerge intact from the impending world war:

> "You can raise the objection that we cannot predict the rhythm and tempo of the development and that possibly the bourgeoisie will find a political recess—that is not excluded—but then we will be obliged to realize a strategic retreat. But in the present situation we must be oriented for a strategic offensive, not a retreat."[18]

This is an interesting passage because, of course, the bourgeoisie did indeed "find a political recess" after World War II. Consequently, revolutionaries in the imperialist heartlands had little choice but to "retreat" from a perspective of imminent mass revolutionary struggle in order to prepare for the future through propagandistic activities: patiently recruiting and training

16 Leon Trotsky, "A Summary of Transitional Demands," *The Transitional Program for Socialist Revolution* (New York: Pathfinder Press, 1974), p 232
17 *Ibid.*, p 235
18 *Ibid.*, pp 235–36

a new generation of cadres, while sinking roots in the organizations of the working class. But, for Trotsky, such a reorientation would not involve abandoning the transitional program in favor of a reformist minimal/democratic program:

> "...we proceed from the inevitability and imminence of the international proletarian revolution. This fundamental idea, which distinguishes the Fourth International from all other workers' organizations, determines all our activities....This does not mean, however, that we do not take into account the conjunctural fluctuations in the economy as well as in politics, with the temporary ebbs and flows. If one proceeds only on the basis of the overall characterization of the epoch, and nothing more, ignoring its concrete stages, one can easily lapse into schematism, sectarianism, or quixotic fantasy. With every serious turn of events we adjust our basic tasks to the changed concrete circumstances of the given stage. Herein lies the art of tactics." [19]

Transitional Demands and the Communist Manifesto

It is often taken for granted by both Trotsky's supporters and his detractors that the idea of "transitional demands" was first introduced in the 1938 draft. For example, in a footnote explaining Trotsky's use of the term "transitional demands" during the first of the series of discussions he held with the SWP leaders in March 1938, the Pathfinder Press editors assert:

> "One of Trotsky's most important contributions to Marxist theory and practice was his development in 1938 of the concept of **transitional demands and slogans**, which became the central feature of the programmatic document he wrote in April for the [Fourth International's] founding conference."[20]

In fact, Trotsky specifically addressed this very misconception during these same discussions:

> "This program is not a new invention of one man. It is derived from the long experience of the Bolsheviks. I want to emphasize that it is not one man's invention, that it comes from long collective experience of the revolutionaries. It is the application of old principles to this situation. It should not be considered as fixed like iron, but flexible to the situation."[21]

At its Fourth Congress in 1922, the Communist International passed a motion explicitly endorsing the concept of transitional demands. Most of the transitional demands included in the 1938 program had previously been adopted, in one form or another, in various resolutions of the first four con-

19 Leon Trotsky, "On the Question of Workers' Self-Defense," *Writings of Leon Trotsky (1939–40)* (New York: Pathfinder Press, 1973), p 103

20 *Writings of Leon Trotsky (1937–38)* (New York: Pathfinder Press, 1976), note 290, p 488

21 Leon Trotsky, "The Political Backwardness of the American Workers," *The Transitional Program for Socialist Revolution* (New York: Pathfinder Press, 1974), p 129

gresses of the Communist International (see "Transitional Demands: From the Comintern to the Fourth International," p 203).

The advocacy of transitional measures can be traced right back to the *Communist Manifesto* of 1848. The ten "pretty generally applicable" demands advanced in that document included the abolition of landed property and inheritance; a heavily progressive taxation system; confiscation of property of "rebel" capitalists; nationalization of transport and communication; "Extension of factories...owned by the state;" and "Equal liability of all to labor." Marx and Engels raised these demands as a means to make "despotic inroads on the rights of property, and on the conditions of bourgeois production." They were not advanced as a means of reforming capitalism, but rather as measures:

> "...which appear economically insufficient and untenable, but which, in the course of the movement, outstrip themselves, necessitate further inroads upon the old social order, and are unavoidable as a means of entirely revolutionising the mode of production."[22]

In his 1938 essay commemorating "Ninety Years of the Communist Manifesto," Trotsky commented:

> "Calculated for a revolutionary epoch the *Manifesto* contains...ten demands, corresponding to the period of direct transition from capitalism to socialism. In their Preface of 1872, Marx and Engels declared these demands to be in part antiquated....The reformists seized upon this evaluation to interpret it in the sense that transitional revolutionary demands had forever ceded their place to the Social Democratic 'minimum program,' which, as is well known, does not transcend the limits of bourgeois democracy. As a matter of fact, the authors of the *Manifesto* indicated quite precisely the main correction of their transitional program, namely, 'the working class cannot simply lay hold of the ready-made state machinery, and wield it for its own purposes.' In other words the correction was directed against the fetishism of bourgeois democracy. Marx later counterposed to the capitalist state, the state of the Commune. This 'type' subsequently assumed the much more graphic shape of soviets. There cannot be a revolutionary program today without *soviets* and without *workers' control.* As for the rest, the ten demands of the *Manifesto*, which appeared 'archaic' in an epoch of peaceful parliamentary activity, have today regained completely their true significance. The Social Democratic 'minimum program,' on the other hand, has become hopelessly antiquated."[23]

Rosa Luxemburg made remarkably similar observations in December 1918, at the founding of the German Communist Party:

> "We are faced with a position similar to that which was faced by Marx and Engels when they wrote the *Communist Manifesto* seventy years ago. As you

22 Karl Marx and Frederick Engels, "Manifesto of the Communist Party," *Karl Marx and Frederick Engels Selected Works in One Volume* (New York: International Publishers, 1969), p 52

23 Leon Trotsky, "Ninety Years of the Communist Manifesto," *Writings of Leon Trotsky (1937–38)* (New York: Pathfinder Press, 1976), pp 23–24

all know, the *Communist Manifesto* dealt with socialism, with the realization of the aims of socialism, as the immediate task of the proletarian revolution. This was the idea represented by Marx and Engels in the revolution of 1848; it was thus, likewise, that they conceived the basis for proletarian action in the international field."[24]

The defeat of the 1848 revolutions compelled Marx and Engels to reassess their earlier projection of an imminent European socialist revolution. The adoption of the Erfurt Program in 1891 by the German Social Democratic Party made explicit the division between the minimum and maximum programs:

> "The socialist program was thereby established upon an utterly different foundation, and in Germany the change took a peculiarly typical form. Down to the collapse of August 4, 1914, the German social democracy took its stand upon the Erfurt program, and by this program the so-called immediate minimal aims were placed in the foreground, while socialism was no more than a distant guiding star."[25]

In rejecting the minimum/maximum programmatic dichotomy, Luxemburg called for a return to the original conception of the *Manifesto*: "It has become our urgent duty today to replace our program upon the foundations laid by Marx and Engels in 1848."[26] She forthrightly asserted:

> "Our program is deliberately opposed to the leading principle of the Erfurt program; it is deliberately opposed to the separation of the immediate and so-called minimal demands formulated for the political and economic struggle, from the socialist goal regarded as the maximal program."[27]

Workers' Control and Factory Committees

Many critical developments in Marxism have come as a direct result of the experience of mass working-class struggle. Prior to the Paris Commune of 1871, Marx and Engels had assumed that the conquest of political power by the working class was a matter of gaining control of the existing (capitalist) state apparatus. But the experience of the Commune demonstrated that, "the working class cannot simply lay hold of the ready-made state machinery, and wield it for its own purposes."[28] The Commune was, in Marx's words, "the political form at last discovered under which to work out the economic emancipation of labour."[29]

Workers' councils or "soviets" (which Trotsky saw as "crowning" the program of transitional demands) first appeared in the course of the Russian

24 Rosa Luxemburg, "Speech to the Founding Convention of the German Communist Party," *Rosa Luxemburg Speaks* (New York: Pathfinder Press, 1970), p 405

25 *Ibid.*, pp 407–8

26 *Ibid.*, p 408

27 *Ibid.*, p 413

28 Karl Marx, "The Civil War in France," *Karl Marx and Frederick Engels Selected Works in One Volume* (New York: International Publishers, 1969), p 288

29 *Ibid.*, p 294

Revolution of 1905. Two other key transitional demands—"workers' control" and "factory committees"—derived from the experience of the Russian Revolution of 1917. Like the soviets in 1905, they had not been advocated by any leftist party or theoretician, but arose from the logic of the class struggle itself.

After the Tsar was toppled in February 1917, factory committees sprouted up in many enterprises. They were organized as delegated bodies embracing workers from every department, from every union and also unorganized workers. Trotsky described these bodies as an example of "the realization of the united front of the working class."[30] Initially concerned with issues of wages, conditions of employment and the length of the workday, as the factory committees gained authority and influence, they began to take up broader social questions. The more militant of them gradually established a veto over management decisions, and began to probe company accounts and check financial records. These are the main elements of a regime of "workers control":

> "Workers' control through factory councils is conceivable only on the basis of sharp class struggle, not collaboration. But this really means dual power in the enterprises, in the trusts, in all the branches of industry, in the whole economy.
>
> "What state regime corresponds to workers' control of production? It is obvious that the power is not yet in the hands of the proletariat....What we are talking about is workers' control under the capitalist regime, under the power of the bourgeoisie. However, a bourgeoisie that feels it is firmly in the saddle will never tolerate dual power in its enterprises. Workers' control, consequently, can be carried out only under the condition of an abrupt change in the relationship of forces unfavorable to the bourgeoisie and its state. Control can be imposed only by force upon the bourgeoisie, by a proletariat on the road to the moment of taking power from them...."[31]

Factory committees and workers' control arise at moments of sharp social crisis, as the workers come to realize that to defend their interests they must go beyond simple trade unionism, and begin to challenge bourgeois property rights and management prerogatives.

Workers' control is not a necessary stage in the development of revolutionary consciousness, but it can play an important role in certain circumstances:

> "Under the influence of crisis, unemployment, and the predatory manipulations of the capitalists, the working class in its majority may turn out to be ready to fight for the abolition of business secrecy and for control over banks, commerce, and production before it has come to understand the necessity of the revolutionary conquest for power.
>
> "After taking the path of control of production, the proletariat will inevitably press forward in the direction of the seizure of power and of the means of

30 Leon Trotsky, "Workers Control of Production," *The Struggle Against Fascism in Germany* (New York: Pathfinder Press, 1971), p 80

31 *Ibid.*, p 78

> production. Questions of credits, of raw materials, of markets, will immediately extend control beyond the confines of individual enterprises."[32]

Factory committees arose in both Germany and Italy following World War I, but in the absence of effective revolutionary leadership, the capitalists were able to regroup and reassert their authority:

> "The contradictions, irreconcilable in their essence, of the regime of workers' control will inevitably be sharpened to the degree that its sphere and its tasks are extended, and soon will become intolerable. A way out of these contradictions can be found either in the capture of power by the proletariat (Russia) or in the fascist counterrevolution, which establishes the naked dictatorship of capital (Italy)."[33]

In "What Next? Vital Questions for the German Proletariat," written in January 1932, Trotsky posed the question of workers' control from a somewhat different angle:

> "The campaign for workers' control can develop, depending on the circumstances, not from the angle of production but from that of consumption. The promise of the Bruening government to lower the price of commodities simultaneously with the decrease in wages has not materialized. This question cannot but absorb the most backward strata of the proletariat, who are today very far from the thought of seizing power. Workers' control over the outlays of industry and the profits of trade is the only real form of the struggle for lower prices. Under the conditions of general dissatisfaction, workers' commissions with the participation of worker-housewives for the purpose of checking up on the increased cost of margarine can become very palpable beginnings of workers' control over industry."[34]

The *Transitional Program* carefully distinguishes between workers' control (a form of "dual power") and the expropriation of the bourgeoisie. The former represents a school for the latter: "On the basis of the experience of control, the proletariat will prepare itself for direct management of nationalized industry when the hour for that eventuality will strike." With the expropriation of the means of production, the essential economic content of the dictatorship of the proletariat is established.

Lenin's Transitional Program of 1917

During the middle of 1917, under the rule of Kerensky's bourgeois Provisional Government, the economic situation in war-weary Russia deteriorated at an alarming rate. Lenin placed the blame for the "impending catastrophe" squarely on the bourgeoisie:

32 *Ibid.*, p 81
33 *Ibid.*, p 82
34 Leon Trotsky, "What Next? Vital Questions for the German Proletariat," *The Struggle Against Fascism in Germany* (New York: Pathfinder Press, 1971), pp 241–42

"The capitalists are deliberately and unremittingly sabotaging (damaging, stopping, disrupting, hampering) production, hoping that an unparalleled catastrophe may mean the collapse of the republic and democracy, and of the Soviets and proletarian and peasant associations generally, thus facilitating the return to a monarchy and the restoration of the unlimited power of the bourgeoisie and the landowners.

"The danger of a great catastrophe and of famine is imminent. All the newspapers have written about this time and again....

. . .

"Yet the slightest attention and thought will suffice to satisfy anyone that the ways of [combating] catastrophe and famine are available, that the measures required to combat them are clear, simple, perfectly feasible, and fully within reach of the people's forces, and that these measures are *not* being adopted *only* because, *exclusively* because, their realization would affect the fabulous profits of a handful of landowners and capitalists."[35]

Lenin did not call on Kerensky to pass a law against capitalist sabotage. Nor did he content himself with abstract reflections about how all problems would one day be solved by a future socialist revolution. Instead he addressed the burning issues of the moment with a series of concrete proposals to revive economic activity, counteract bourgeois sabotage and broaden the intervention of the masses in economic decision-making. The "principal measures" he advocated were:

"1. Amalgamation of all banks into a single bank and state control over its operations, or nationalization of the banks.

"2. Nationalization of the syndicates, i.e., the largest, monopolistic capitalist associations (sugar, oil, coal, iron and steel, and other syndicates).

"3. Abolition of commercial secrecy.

"4. Compulsory syndication (i.e., compulsory amalgamation into associations) of industrialists, merchants and employers generally.

"5. Compulsory organization of the population into consumers' societies, or encouragement of such organization, and the exercise of control over it."[36]

Taken together these measures represented the same kind of "despotic inroads on the rights of property" advocated in the *Communist Manifesto*. Lenin was quite clear about the revolutionary implications of his proposals:

"There is no way of effectively [combating] financial disorganization and inevitable financial collapse except that of revolutionary rupture with the interests of capital and that of the organization of really democratic control, i.e., control from 'below,' control by the workers and poorest peasants *over* the capitalists...."[37]

35 Vladimir I. Lenin, "The Impending Catastrophe and How to Combat It," *V.I. Lenin Selected Works in Three Volumes* (Moscow: Progress Publishers, 1970), Vol. 2, pp 241–42

36 *Ibid.*, p 246

37 *Ibid.*, p 266

Lenin's program was a "transitional" one (although it does not seem that the term had yet been coined) because it connected the immediate problems faced by the workers' movement to the question of proletarian state power.

Transitional Demands and the Left Opposition

In the statement of "fundamental principles" adopted at its first international gathering, in February 1933, the International Left Opposition (ILO) declared that it stood "on the ground of the first four congresses of the Comintern."[38] Denouncing the sterile ultimatism of Third Period Stalinism, the ILO reiterated the importance of both the united-front tactic and of transitional demands. It called for:

> "Recognition of the necessity to mobilize the masses under *transitional slogans* corresponding to the concrete situation in each country, and particularly under *democratic slogans* insofar as it is a question of struggle against feudal relations, national oppression, or different varieties of openly imperialist dictatorship...."[39]

The next year, in the aftermath of an armed fascist attack on the French parliament, the French section of the ILO published a "Program of Action for France" drafted by Trotsky. It called for "Abolition of 'Business Secrets'," "Workers' and Peasants' Control over Banks, Industry and Commerce," a shorter workweek with a pay raise "at the expense of the magnates," "Nationalization of Banks, Key Industries, Insurance Companies and Transportation" and the institution of a "Monopoly of Foreign Trade." It also advocated the "Defense of the Soviet Union," the "Disbanding of the police," "Arming of the proletariat, arming of the poor peasants!" and the preservation of public order by workers' militias directed by a "Workers' and Peasants' Commune."[40]

In March 1935, at a meeting of the CGT (the General Federation of Labor—the largest union federation in France) Alexis Bardin[41] delivered a speech written for him by Trotsky that criticized the union leadership's uto-

38 "The International Left Opposition, Its Tasks and Methods," *Documents of the Fourth International* (New York: Pathfinder Press, 1973), p 23

39 *Ibid.*, p 24

40 Leon Trotsky, "A Program of Action for France," *Writings of Leon Trotsky (1934–35)* (New York: Pathfinder Press, 1971), pp 21–32

41 **Alexis Bardin** is mentioned by Jean van Heijenoort in his book *With Trotsky in Exile* (Harvard University Press, 1978), p 74:

> "In Grenoble there was a young teacher, Alexis Bardin, who had strong Trotskyite sympathies; he even had two brothers in the Trotskyite group in Paris, one of whom, Boitel, played a leading role there. Alexis Bardin and his wife, Violette, were soon authorized by the Isère prefect to visit Trotsky and Natalia. Bardin, who was a member of the Socialist party, was involved in Grenoble's political and trade union life. The conversations between Trotsky and him revolved around local politics. Trotsky was interested in the smallest details, enjoying the chance to immerse himself in practical day-to-day activities. Bardin was becoming more and more active in local affairs, and some of his speeches at trade union meetings were written by Trotsky."

pian/reformist schemes for combating the ravages of the capitalist economic crisis. To the officials' vague talk of using credit as an economic "lever," the young militant counterposed ripping the banking system "out of the hands of the capitalist exploiters in order to make it a lever of social transformation, that is of socialist construction." Starting from the CGT leadership's own pronouncement that 90 plutocrats "own and control the economy of our country," Bardin proposed: "The response should be clear: we must expropriate them, unseat them, to return to the plundered people what belongs to them."[42] At each point where the bureaucrats' plan blurred the line between class struggle and class collaboration, Trotsky's text sharpened the distinctions.

How to Utilize Transitional Demands

Bardin's speech provides an example of how transitional demands should be used to connect the necessity of social revolution with the immediate practical concerns of an assembly of trade-union delegates. In a similar vein, during his discussion with the SWP leaders, Trotsky explained how to relate the demand for the opening of the capitalists' books to other political issues:

> "...you have millions of unemployed and the government claims it cannot pay more and the capitalists say that they cannot make more contributions—we want to have access to the bookkeeping of this society. The control of income should be organized through factory committees. Workers will say: We want our own statisticians who are devoted to the working class. If a branch of industry shows that it is really ruined, then we answer: We propose to expropriate you. We will direct better than you....This transitional demand is also a step for the workers' control of production as the preparatory plan for the direction of industry. Everything must be controlled by the workers who will be the masters of society tomorrow. But to call for conquest of power—that seems to the American workers illegal, fantastic. But if you say: The capitalists refuse to pay for the unemployed and hide their real profits from the state and from the workers by dishonest bookkeeping, the workers will understand that formula. If we say to the farmer: The bank fools you. They have very big profits. And we propose to you that you create farmers' committees to look into the bookkeeping of the bank, every farmer will understand that. We will say: The farmer can trust only himself; let him create committees to control agricultural credits—they will understand that. It presupposes a turbulent mood among the farmers; it cannot be accomplished every day. But to introduce this idea into the masses and into our own comrades, that's absolutely necessary immediately."[43]

42 Leon Trotsky, "From the CGT's Plan to the Conquest of Power," *Writings of Leon Trotsky (1934–35)* (New York: Pathfinder Press, 1971), p 223

43 Leon Trotsky, "How to Fight for a Labor Party in the U.S.," *The Transitional Program for Socialist Revolution* (New York: Pathfinder Press, 1974), pp 120–21

The masses cannot be mobilized for struggle around transitional demands "every day," but the job of revolutionaries is to seek to introduce these ideas into the working class, even in periods of relative quiescence. The proletarian vanguard must seek to lead, not follow, popular opinion.

Trotsky sought to train the cadres of the Fourth International to address the particular manifestations of capitalist crisis and economic dislocation—factory closures, wage cuts, layoffs, inflation, bank foreclosures, etc.—in ways that pointed toward the necessity of proletarian revolution:

> "Workers' militia and workers' control of production are only two sides of the same question. The worker is not a bookkeeper. When he asks for the books, he wants to change the situation, by control and then by direction. Naturally, our advancing slogans depends on the reaction we meet in the masses. When we see the reaction of the masses we [will] know what side of the question to emphasize. We will say, Roosevelt will help the unemployed by the war industry; but if we workers ran production, we would find another industry, not one for the dead but for the living. The question can become understandable even for an average worker who never participates in a political movement."[44]

Trotsky also proposed that the SWP seek to popularize the call for a sliding scale of wages and hours:

> "Then we have the question, how to present the program to the workers? It is naturally very important. We must combine politics with mass psychology and pedagogy, build the bridge to their minds. Only experience can show us how to advance in this or that part of the country. For some time we must try to concentrate the attention of the workers on one slogan: sliding scale of wages and hours.
>
> . . .
>
> "Naturally this is only one point. In the beginning this slogan is totally adequate for the situation. But the others can be added as the development proceeds....What is this slogan? In reality...[a sliding scale of wages and hours] is the system of work in socialist society. The total number of workers divided into the total number of hours. But if we present the whole socialist system it will appear to the average American as utopian, as something from Europe. We present it as a solution to this crisis which must assure their right to eat, drink, and live in decent apartments. It is the program of socialism, but in very popular and simple form."[45]

When asked, "Can we actually realize this slogan?," Trotsky replied:

> "It is easier to overthrow capitalism than to realize this demand under capitalism. Not one of our demands will be realized under capitalism. That is why we are calling them transitional demands. It creates a bridge to the mentality of the workers and then a material bridge to the socialist revolution. The whole question is how to mobilize the masses for struggle. The question

44 *Ibid.*, pp 121–22

45 Leon Trotsky, "The Political Backwardness of the American Workers," *The Transitional Program for Socialist Revolution* (New York: Pathfinder Press, 1974), pp 127–28

of the division between the employed and unemployed comes up. We must find ways to overcome this division."[46]

'Not a Complete Program'

In his conversations with the SWP leadership, Trotsky noted that the *Transitional Program* was not comprehensive:

> "The draft program is not a complete program. We can say that in this draft program there are things which are lacking and there are things which by their nature don't belong to the program. Things which don't belong to the program are the comments....A complete program should have a theoretical expression of the modern capitalist society at its imperialist stage....The beginning of the program is not complete. The first chapter is only a hint and not a complete expression. Also the end of the program is not complete because we don't speak here about the social revolution, about the seizure of power by insurrection, the transformation of capitalist society into the dictatorship, the dictatorship into socialist society. This brings the reader only to the doorstep. It is a program for action from today until the beginning of the socialist revolution. And from the practical point of view what is now the most important is how can we guide the different strata of the proletariat in the direction of the social revolution."[47]

The program was "incomplete" in another sense as well—it did not address the specific social and historical circumstances that play an important role in the political life of each country. Trotsky expected each section of the Fourth International to use the international program as the basis for elaborating one tailored to the specific requirements of the local political terrain:

> "The program is only the first approximation. It is too general in the sense in which it is presented to the international conference in the next period. It expresses the general tendency of development in the whole world....It is clear that the general characteristics of the world situation are common because they are all under the pressure of the imperialist economy, but every country has its peculiar conditions and real live politics must begin with these peculiar conditions in each country and even in each part of the country."[48]

Not only would the program have to be elaborated somewhat differently for each national section, but the demands advanced in each union would vary according to the specific situation confronting the workers it represented. The text of the *Transitional Program* notes that it would be impossible "to enumerate here those separate, partial demands which time and again arise on the basis of concrete circumstances—national, local, professional."[49] This is not because revolutionaries are indifferent to such issues: "The

46 *Ibid.*, pp 128–29

47 Leon Trotsky, "Completing the Program and Putting It to Work," *The Transitional Program for Socialist Revolution* (New York: Pathfinder Press, 1974), p 138

48 *Ibid.*, p 138

49 Leon Trotsky, *The Transitional Program*, see p 38

Bolshevik-Leninist stands in the front-line trenches of all kinds of struggles, even when they involve only the most modest material interests or democratic rights of the working class."[50]

To gain a hearing for their ideas, revolutionaries must do more than simply stand up and recite passages from the program. As Trotsky explained:

> "It is necessary to interpret these fundamental ideas by breaking them up into more concrete and partial ones, dependent upon the course of events and the orientation of the thought of the masses."[51]

The program must be applied flexibly and adapted in accordance with concrete circumstances:

> "The relative weight of the individual democratic and transitional demands in the proletariat's struggle [in the colonial and neo-colonial countries], their mutual ties and their order of presentation, is determined by the peculiarities and specific conditions of each backward country and to a considerable extent—by the *degree* of its backwardness."[52]

Moreover, in the course of any serious struggle, the key demands and their relative emphasis can vary from one place to another and from one day (or even hour) to the next:

> "During a transitional epoch, the workers' movement does not have a systematic and well-balanced but a feverish and explosive character. Slogans as well as organizational forms should be subordinated to the indices of the movement."[53]

Programmatic Extensions Since 1938

The *Transitional Program* is essentially a distillation of the lessons of the Bolshevik Revolution—a program for the mobilization of the proletariat for power. As such it remains a document of profound relevance today. Yet it does not, and could not, provide permanent, engraved-in-stone answers to all questions for all time. The world has changed a great deal since 1938. The section on "The Program of Transitional Demands in Fascist Countries" is obviously less crucial than it was when Germany and Italy were under fascist rule. Similarly, the nominal "decolonization," as well as the uneven industrialization and urbanization of much of the "Third World" has considerably changed the global framework within which the program of permanent revolution is advanced today as compared to 1938.

The post-war expansion of Soviet power into Eastern Europe was not anticipated by the founders of the Fourth International. Nor had they foreseen the creation of deformed workers' states in Vietnam, Yugoslavia and China through the agency of peasant-based guerrilla armies led by insurrectionary Stalinists.

50 *Ibid.*, see p 39
51 *Ibid.*, see p 50
52 *Ibid.*, see p 58
53 *Ibid.*, see p 40

Undoubtably the most important change in world politics since 1938 has been the counter-revolutionary destruction of the degenerated Soviet workers' state, an event that *was* anticipated in the *Transitional Program*:

> "The political prognosis [for the USSR] has an alternative character: either the bureaucracy, becoming ever more the organ of the world bourgeoisie in the workers' state, will overthrow the new forms of property and plunge the country back to capitalism; or the working class will crush the bureaucracy and open the way to socialism."[54]

In the former Soviet bloc Marxists today call for a social revolution to expropriate the emergent bourgeoisies and their imperialist patrons. In the remaining deformed workers' states (Cuba, China, Vietnam and North Korea) revolutionaries must combine their defense of collectivized property with a perspective of proletarian political revolution to shatter the ruling bureaucracies and establish the direct political rule of the working class.

A variety of important political issues are not addressed in the *Transitional Program*. For example, while struggles for national liberation and the right of nations to self-determination are upheld, the program does not address the difficult problems posed when "interpenetrated" peoples claim a single piece of territory, as for example in Cyprus, Northern Ireland, Bosnia or Israel/Palestine.

The dynamics and social function of racial, sexual and other forms of special oppression under capitalism are also barely touched on in the program. There is a call for the organization of working-class women, but no demands for free contraception, free and unrestricted access to abortion, free 24-hour childcare or equal access to all jobs. The defense of democratic rights for lesbians and gays is not mentioned, and neither is the necessity to oppose state interference in consensual sexual activities and other forms of victimless "crimes." Other important social issues not specifically addressed in the 1938 text include healthcare, housing and education, and the rights of immigrants and political refugees.

'Trotskyist' Critics of the Transitional Program

One section of the 1938 program that is clearly in need of updating is the one dealing with "opportunism and unprincipled revisionism." All the organizations mentioned have long-since disappeared, and in most cases their ecological niches have been occupied by various groupings misleadingly claiming some political affinity with Trotskyism. Naturally one of the common characteristics of these "opportunist and unprincipled revisionists" is their tendency to view the *Transitional Program* as an irrelevant relic from a bygone era.

An early, and influential, critic of the Fourth International and its program was Isaac Deutscher, Trotsky's biographer. A former leader of the Polish section

54 *Ibid.*, see p 62

of the Left Opposition, Deutscher had opposed launching the new international in 1938. In *The Prophet Outcast*, the third volume of his monumental biography of Trotsky, Deutscher dismissed the *Transitional Program* with a single sentence:

> "...the Draft Programme, which [Trotsky] wrote for the International, was not so much a statement of principles as an instruction on tactics, designed for a party up to its ears in trade union struggles and day-to-day politics and striving to gain practical leadership immediately."[55]

Deutscher's differences with Trotsky involved fundamental questions of Marxist principle and revolutionary strategy. Rejecting the struggle to forge a "world party of socialist revolution," Deutscher projected that, under the pressure of "the broad scheme of revolutionary development," the Stalinist bureaucracy would eventually be compelled not only to acknowledge Trotsky's greatness, but also to implement essential elements of his program.

Deutscher's projection has been definitively refuted by history. But his attitude toward the Fourth International and its founding program is echoed by a good many contemporary "Trotskyists," including the International Socialist current (IS) headed by Tony Cliff centered around the British Socialist Workers Party. In his book entitled *Trotsky's Marxism*, Duncan Hallas, a long-time IS leader, takes the opposite approach to Deutscher, suggesting that the *Transitional Program* was a product of Trotsky's detachment from the class struggle:

> "Inevitably, his enforced isolation from effective participation in the workers' movement, in which he had once played so big a part, affected to some extent his understanding of the ever-changing course of the class struggle. Not even his vast experience and superb tactical reflexes could substitute entirely for the lack of feedback from the militants engaged in the day to day struggle that is possible only in a real communist party. As the period of isolation lengthened, this became more apparent. Compare his 'Transitional Programme' of 1938 with its prototype, the 'Programme of Action' for France (1934). In freshness, relevance, specificity and concreteness in relation to an actual struggle, the latter is clearly superior."[56]

It perhaps did not occur to comrade Hallas that the "prototype" could be more "specific and concrete" precisely because it addressed a particular concrete situation faced by French workers in 1934. The program of the Fourth International, on the other hand, had to deal with the general situation of the *international* working class for an entire historical period. It therefore had to be presented in a more abstract manner. But Hallas has a more fundamental objection:

> "Whether or not it is possible to find slogans or 'demands' that meet these exacting specifications [a bridge from present consciousness to recognition of the necessity for socialism] depends, very obviously, on circumstances. If at a given time 'today's consciousness of wide layers' is decidedly

55 Isaac Deutscher, *The Prophet Outcast* (New York: Vintage Books, 1965), pp 425–26
56 Duncan Hallas, *Trotsky's Marxism* (London: Bookmarks, 1979), pp 96–97

> non-revolutionary, then it will not be transformed by slogans. Changes in actual conditions are needed. The problem at each stage is to find and advance those slogans which not only strike a chord in at least some sections of the working class...but which are also capable of leading to working class *actions*. Often they will not be transitional in terms of Trotsky's very restricted definition.
>
> "Of course Trotsky cannot be held responsible for the tendency of most of his followers to fetishise the notion of transitional demands, and even the specific demands of the 1938 Programme—most obviously the 'sliding scale of wages.' The emphasis he gave to this matter was, however, excessive and encouraged the belief that 'demands' have some value independent of revolutionary organisation in the working class."[57]

Here we have an attempt to obscure the fact that revolutionary organizations are distinguished from centrist and left-reformist ones by their program—i.e., what "demands" they fight for. The question of a group's size and influence in the working class will largely determine its ability to influence events, but has no bearing on the question of its fundamental political character. Trotsky had only a handful of supporters in Spain during that country's civil war, while Andres Nin's centrist Workers Party of Marxist Unification (POUM), which had broken with Trotsky precisely over his "sectarian" opposition to class-collaborationism, had thousands of members. To avoid "isolation" from the masses, the POUM leaders first blunted their criticisms of the popular front, and then ended up joining it—an act that Trotsky aptly described as a "crime" against the working class.

In an earlier series of articles on the history of the Fourth International, published in *International Socialism* between 1969 and 1973, Hallas, then Political Secretary of the British IS, argued that the *Transitional Program* was responsible for many of the problems of the Fourth International after World War II:

> "Unfavorable circumstances played a part in the decline in the Fourth Internationalist movement. More important were the fundamental weaknesses of the 1938 programme, especially its quite wrong analysis of Stalinism."[58]

This refers to Trotsky's rejection of the absurd notion, promoted by the Cliffites, that the economic system of the USSR was "state capitalist," i.e., qualitatively the same as Britain, the U.S. and other imperialist countries. Another "weakness," according to Hallas, was the assertion that capitalism remains subject to periodic economic crises stemming from the tendency of the rate of profit to fall. During the 1960s, the Cliffites decided that the capitalists had successfully overcome this problem by creating a "permanent arms economy." Hallas cited Michael Kidron (a leading IS intellectual at the time) who explained how "a leak" of capital intensive goods would mean that the rate of growth of the organic composition of capital:

57 *Ibid.*, p 104
58 *International Socialism* No. 60, July 1973

> "...'would be slower...[and] could even stop or be reversed. In such a case there would be no decline in the average rate of profit, no reason to expect increasingly severe slumps, and so on'. Such a leak had been found in the permanent arms economy.
>
> "The consequences of this fact, the contradictions of neo-capitalism, its prospects and limits; those are the basic problems to be faced by Western revolutionaries today. The difficulty for orthodox Trotskyists is to accept that these are the problems. For if they are, Trotsky's economic catastrophism must be rejected. And with it goes one of the two pillars upon which the FI was founded. The tiny grouplets of the FI expected to be swept forward in the tide of economic catastrophe, instead they found themselves stranded on the ebb tide produced by the 20 years of boom. Hence the irrelevance of the whole pretentious apparatus of 'World Leadership', 'World Congresses', 'International Executive Plenums', and all the rest of the paraphernalia borrowed from the Comintern."[59]

The impressionistic notion that capitalism was no longer subject to significant economic crises was widespread among petty-bourgeois New Leftists in the 1960s. But today the IS criticisms of those "orthodox Trotskyists" who argued that capitalism remained subject to periodic slumps can only be an embarrassment for those Cliffites who take Marxist theory at all seriously.

The "permanent arms economy" theory may now be out of fashion, but Cliff's attitude toward the *Transitional Program* has not changed. In 1993 he wrote:

> "These transitional demands fitted a situation of general crisis, of capitalism in deep slump. But under conditions of a massive expansion of capitalism, as took place after the Second World War, these demands were at best meaningless, and at worst reactionary. To limit wage rises to the rise in the cost of living was a demand of the capitalists and against the aspirations of the workers who wanted to improve their living standards. And in conditions of more or less full employment, a 'sliding scale of hours' is really meaningless."[60]

In fact it is Cliff's critique which is "meaningless." Trotsky explicitly indicated that transitional demands are not put forward as structural reforms to the operations of capitalism. They are demands which, if raised skillfully at appropriate junctures and taken up by the mass of workers, challenge the whole logic of the profit system. A "sliding scale of hours" is not something that revolutionaries would make a focus of popular agitation year in and year out—it is a demand appropriate in situations of mass unemployment. The call for a "sliding scale of wages," outside the context of a reduction in the workday, is only appropriate when inflation poses a threat to working-class living standards. It would make no sense in periods of deflation. Nor does the demand

59 *International Socialism* No. 40, October/November 1969

60 Tony Cliff, *Trotsky: The Darker the Night the Brighter the Star* (London: Bookmarks, 1993), p 300

to index wages to inflation in any way preclude fighting for improvements in the wage scale.

Cliff's criticisms presume that any program advocated by socialists must be a minimal (i.e., reformist) one. He appears unable to comprehend the idea of raising demands that are directed not at reforming capitalism, but at transforming the consciousness of the exploited and oppressed. Accordingly, his critique proceeds from the erroneous view that the *Transitional Program* is simply a "minimum program" composed of impractical or "at worst reactionary" reforms.

> "Similarly, other demands in Trotsky's *Transitional Programme*, such as the establishment of 'workers' defence guards', 'workers' militia', and 'the arming of the proletariat', certainly did not fit a non-revolutionary situation. Sadly many Trotskyists dogmatically repeated these slogans.
>
> "The basic assumption behind Trotsky's Transitional Demands was that the economic crisis was so deep that the struggle for even the smallest improvement in workers' conditions would bring conflict with the capitalist system itself. When life disproved the assumption the ground fell from beneath the programme."[61]

Cliff's "basic assumption" seems to be that capitalism is here to stay and that the job of socialists is to celebrate the struggle for small improvements. Cliff breezily dismisses the "arming of the proletariat" and "workers' defense guards" as slogans that do not "fit a non-revolutionary situation." In place of such "dogmatic" revolutionary slogans the Cliffites limit themselves to advancing demands that reflect the existing (bourgeois) consciousness of the masses. The only inconsistency in the IS approach is their persistence in continuing to identify themselves as "revolutionaries." After all, if the "arming of the proletariat" and the creation of a "workers' militia" are no longer on the historical agenda, then neither is "socialist revolution."

Alex Callinicos, currently the leading political theorist of the International Socialist tendency, is somewhat more guarded in his formulations, but he too rejects the *Transitional Program*. In a recent book he asserted that, after World War II, the attempt:

> "...to immunize Trotsky's theories from refutation carried with it the danger of transforming them into a set of dogmas. All too frequently this danger was realized. The Transitional Programme drafted by Trotsky and adopted at the First Congress of the FI in 1938 became an especial object of veneration. This document was thus named because it contained a set of 'transitional demands'—for example, the indexation of wages to prices ('the sliding scale of wages'). These were intended to bridge the old division in the Second International before 1914 between the minimum programme of limited reforms attainable within a capitalist context and the maximum programme whose implementation would require the establishment of worker's power. Trotsky argued that the economic crisis was so acute that the struggle for

61 *Ibid.*, p 300

even the most modest improvement in working-class conditions would come into conflict with the capitalist system itself."[62]

Callinicos is not particularly concerned about finding a bridge between the minimal and maximal programs. Like Cliff, he dismisses transitional demands as useless, unless, at some hypothetical point in the future, capitalism were to completely exhaust all possibility of further growth. In the meantime, according to Callinicos, the job of socialists is to leaven the workers' immediate demands with occasional references to the ultimate desirability of socialism.

In the final analysis all the criticisms of the *Transitional Program*'s "fetishism," "dogmatism" and "catastrophism" boil down to advocacy of a return to the minimum-maximum program of the Second International—that is to say, reformism now and socialism "later" (i.e., never). Trotsky was very familiar with this brand of "socialism":

> "The reformists have a good smell for what the audience wants....But that is not serious revolutionary activity. We must have the courage to be unpopular, to say 'you are fools,' 'you are stupid,' 'they betray you,' and every once in a while with a scandal launch our ideas with a passion."[63]

Callinicos and Cliff regard this as just so much "sectarianism," a charge that no one could level at the International Socialists, at least in terms of program. Their history is one of an endless series of political zig-zags driven by adaptations to the existing prejudices of the strata from which they hope to recruit. Often what seems "smart" (i.e., popular) today turns out to be an embarrassment tomorrow. A classic example of this was their initial support for British troops in Northern Ireland:

> "The breathing space provided by the presence of British troops is short but vital. Those who call for the immediate withdrawal of the troops...are inviting a pogrom which will hit first and hardest at socialists."[64]

While the IS stock-in-trade is "rank and file" trade-union economism, their opportunist appetites sometimes find expression in political adaptation to non-proletarian elements as well. In recent years the "revolutionary" IS offered electoral support to several openly *bourgeois* candidates (e.g., South Korea's president Kim Dae Jung in the 1992 election, and Nelson Mandela's African National Congress in 1994).

The Cliffites have also long exhibited an unhealthy enthusiasm for the 1979 "Islamic Revolution" led by Iran's arch-reactionary Ayatollah Khomeini. Reflecting on the significance of Khomeini's triumph almost a decade later, Callinicos argued that the Iranian left should have been:

> "...demanding that the mullahs wage a *revolutionary* war against the US and its allies, that, as I wrote at the beginning of the war [with Iraq], they 'make Teheran the beacon of *genuine* revolution throughout the region—granting

62 Alex Callinicos, *Trotskyism* (Minneapolis: University of Minnesota Press, 1990), p 40
63 Leon Trotsky, "Completing the Program and Putting It to Work," *The Transitional Program for Socialist Revolution* (New York: Pathfinder Press, 1974), p 145
64 *Socialist Worker*, 11 September 1969

> the right of self-determination to the Kurds, Arabs and other national minorities, establishing organs of popular power, fighting for the liberation of women from the Islamic yoke' (*Socialist Worker*, 4 October 1980)."[65]

The rather stark contrast between the Cliffites' rejection of Trotsky's transitional demands as meaningless and unrealizable and their willingness to call on the Iranian theocracy to carry out a "*genuine* revolution" reveals that the flip-side of their craven opportunism is a breath-taking capacity for self-delusion.

'We Must Tell the Workers the Truth'

Although some critics of the *Transitional Program* characterize it as "opportunist" because it contains demands aimed at intersecting the immediate concerns of the working class, most criticisms boil down to the complaint that it is too far ahead of the present consciousness of the class. In discussion with his American supporters in 1938, Trotsky addressed this objection:

> "The program must express the objective tasks of the working class rather than the backwardness of the workers. It must reflect society as it is and not the backwardness of the working class. It is an instrument to overcome and vanquish the backwardness."

He expanded on this later in the discussion:

> "We must tell the workers the truth, then we will win the best elements. Whether these best elements will be capable of guiding the working class, leading it to power, I don't know. I hope that they will be able, but I cannot give the guarantee. But even in the worst case, if the working class doesn't sufficiently mobilize its mind and its strength at present for the socialist revolution—even in the worst case, if this working class falls victim to fascism, the best elements will say, 'We were warned by this party; it was a good party.' And a great tradition will remain in the working class.
>
> "This is the worst variant. That is why all the arguments that we cannot present such a program because the program doesn't correspond to the mentality of the workers are false. They express only fear before the situation. Naturally if I close my eyes I can write a good rosy program that everybody will accept. But it will not correspond to the situation; and the program must correspond to the situation. I believe that this elementary argument is of the utmost importance. The mentality of the class of the proletariat is backward but the mentality is not such a substance as the factories, the mines, the railroads, but is more mobile and under the blows of the objective crisis, the millions of unemployed, it can change rapidly."[66]

Today, 60 years after the *Transitional Program* was written, the Bolshevik tradition which the Left Opposition carried forward remains just as relevant as ever. And that political tradition, codified in the founding programmatic document of the Fourth International, remains central to a historically progressive resolution of the "crisis of proletarian leadership."

65 *Socialist Worker Review*, September 1988

66 Leon Trotsky, "The Political Backwardness of the American Workers," *The Transitional Program for Socialist Revolution* (New York: Pathfinder Press, 1974), pp 126–27

Part One

The Transitional Program

The Death Agony of Capitalism and the Tasks of the Fourth International[1]

The Objective Prerequisites for a Socialist Revolution

The world political situation as a whole is chiefly characterized by a historical crisis of the leadership of the proletariat.

The economic prerequisite for the proletarian revolution has already in general achieved the highest point of fruition that can be reached under capitalism. Mankind's productive forces stagnate. Already, new inventions and improvements fail to raise the level of material wealth. Conjunctural crises under the weight of the social crisis affecting the whole capitalist system weigh ever heavier deprivations and sufferings upon the masses. Growing unemployment, in its turn, deepens the financial crisis of the State and undermines the unstable monetary systems. Democratic regimes, as well as fascist, stagger on from one bankruptcy to another.

The bourgeoisie itself sees no way out. In countries where it has already been forced to stake its last upon the card of fascism, it now toboggans with closed eyes toward an economic and military catastrophe. In the historically-privileged countries, i.e., in those where the bourgeoisie can still for a certain

1 The final draft of this document, adopted by the founding conference of the Fourth International in September 1938, was first published by the Socialist Workers Party (SWP) in *Socialist Appeal*, 22 October 1938. Trotsky's draft of the program had appeared in the May/June 1938 issue of the Russian-language *Biulleten Oppozitsii*. Louis Sinclair's 1972 bibliography of Trotsky's works also lists contemporary British, Chinese, French and Spanish editions of the program. In January 1939, the SWP reprinted the program and resolutions in *The Founding Conference of the Fourth International* with a foreword by Max Shachtman ("M.S."). Shachtman had presided over the conference, and, according to the minutes as published in *Documents of the Fourth International* (New York: Pathfinder Press, 1973), had moved a resolution (which carried) that the resident leadership of the International (to which he was subsequently elected), "revise the draft of the Transitional Program, improving the style, incorporating any factual amendments, etc."

There are minor discrepancies (mostly in subheads and subtitles) between the version of the program in *Socialist Appeal* in October 1938 and that published in January 1939. We have reproduced the text of the latter version (with one important exception—see note 12 below), including punctuation and style. We have corrected spelling throughout the document. At several points where words are omitted, or there are other obvious typographical errors, we have inserted corrections within square brackets.

We have also noted 16 places where Luciano Dondero has identified discrepancies between the Russian-language draft and the English version. The first of these is in the title itself—the Russian draft speaks of the "Agony" of world capitalism while the subsequent English-language editions use the phrase "Death Agony." The Russian draft has a subtitle under the main headline that generally does not appear in other versions: "The mobilization of the masses on the basis of transitional demands as preparation for the seizure of power." The *Biulleten Oppozitsii* also included a note describing the text as an: "Action program, submitted for the attention of the sections of the IV International by the International Secretariat."

period permit itself the luxury of democracy at the expense of national accumulations (Great Britain, France, United States, etc.) all of capital's traditional parties are in a state of perplexity, bordering on a paralysis of will. The "New Deal,"[2] despite its first period [of] pretentious resoluteness, represents but a special form of political perplexity,[3] possible only in a country where the bourgeoisie succeeded in accumulating incalculable wealth. The present crisis, far from having run its full course, has already succeeded in showing that "New Deal" politics, like Popular Front politics in France,[4] opens no new exit from the economic blind-alley.

International relations present no better picture. Under the increasing tension of capitalist disintegration, imperialist antagonisms reach an impasse at the height of which separate clashes and bloody local disturbances (Ethiopia, Spain, the Far East, Central Europe) must inevitably coalesce into a conflagration of world dimensions. The bourgeoisie, of course, is aware of the mortal danger to its domination represented by a new war. But that class is now immeasurably less capable of averting war than on the eve of 1914.

All talk to the effect that historical conditions have not yet "ripened" for socialism is the product of ignorance or conscious deception. The objective prerequisites for the proletarian revolution have not only "ripened;" they have begun to get somewhat rotten. Without a socialist revolution, in the next historical period, at that—a catastrophe threatens the whole culture of mankind. The turn is now to the proletariat, i.e., chiefly to its revolutionary

2 The **New Deal** was a program of reforms introduced by U.S. President Franklin Delano Roosevelt in March 1933. It was designed to ameliorate some of the worst effects of the Great Depression, while also heading off working-class radicalization.

3 The Russian draft reads "of perplexity" rather than "of political perplexity."

4 **"Popular Front politics in France"** refers to the election in 1936 of an overtly class-collaborationist coalition government of the Socialist Party (SFIO), the Communist Party (PCF) and the petty-bourgeois Radical Party. The term "popular front" was introduced by the Stalinized Communist International to describe its 1935 turn toward trying to create a multi-class alliance against fascism in the aftermath of the Nazi victory in Germany. This strategy of class collaboration is premised on the theory of a "two-stage" struggle for socialism, in which the socialist stage is postponed to the indefinite future after some other, more immediate, reformist objective is first achieved. The "first stage" inevitably involves the creation of "anti-fascist," "anti-monopoly" or "anti-imperialist" unity with a supposedly progressive wing of the capitalist class. Achieving this "unity" in turn requires the workers' parties to renounce the struggle for independent proletarian class interests.

The election of the popular-front government in France in 1936 sparked a mass general strike involving two million workers. It was ultimately demobilized by the joint efforts of the Stalinist and social-democratic participants in the government. When the Popular Front was elected in 1936 in Spain, the capitalists responded with a military coup and initiated a civil war to overthrow the government and crush the workers' movement.

Popular frontism has always spelled defeat for the workers' movement. The capitalists will only participate in such blocs when forced to do so to contain a restive working class. In France 1936, the government granted some initial concessions to demobilize the massive strike wave, but as the experience of the popular front in power gradually sapped the combativeness of the workers, the "reforms" were systematically reversed. In many other situations (e.g., Spain 1936–39, Indonesia 1965 and Chile 1973) the popular front has led directly to bloody defeats for the working class.

vanguard. The historical crisis of mankind is reduced to the crisis of the revolutionary leadership.

The Proletariat and Its Leadership

The economy, the state, the politics of the bourgeoisie and its international relations are completely blighted by a social crisis, characteristic of a pre-revolutionary state of society. The chief obstacle in the path of transforming the pre-revolutionary into a revolutionary state is the opportunist character of proletarian leadership; its petty bourgeois cowardice before the big bourgeoisie and its perfidious connection with it even in its death agony.

In all countries the proletariat is wracked by a deep disquiet. In millions, the masses again and again move onto the road of the revolutionary outbreaks. But each time they are blocked by their own conservative bureaucratic apparatus.

The Spanish proletariat has made a series of heroic attempts since April, 1931, to take power in its hands and guide the fate of society. However, its own parties (Social Democrats, Stalinists, anarchists, POUMists)—each in its own way—acted as a brake and thus prepared Franco's triumphs.

In France, the great wave of "sit-down" strikes, particularly during June, 1936, revealed the whole-hearted readiness of the proletariat to overthrow the capitalist system. However, the leading organizations (Socialists, Stalinists, Syndicalists) under the label of the Popular Front succeeded in canalizing and [damming], at least temporarily, the revolutionary stream.

The unprecedented wave of sit-down strikes and the amazingly rapid growth of industrial unionism in the United States (the CIO)[5] is most indisputable expression of the instinctive striving of the American workers to raise themselves to the level of the tasks imposed on them by history. But here, too, the leading political organizations, including the newly-created CIO, do everything possible to keep in check and paralyze the revolutionary pressure of the masses.

The definite passing over of the Comintern[6] to the side of the bourgeois

5 The **CIO** (Congress of Industrial Organizations) was established as an independent labor federation in 1938. It successfully organized production workers in the United States on an industrial, rather than a craft, basis. Much of the CIO's success derived from its use of militant tactics, particularly sit-down strikes where workers occupied their factories, thus ensuring that production ceased. Sit-down strikes spread from auto to rubber, steel, oil refining, shipbuilding and other industries. The CIO's initial organizing drives were spearheaded by thousands of Communist Party members and other leftist cadres. With the onset of the Cold War and the red purges of the late 1940s, the CIO moved sharply to the right, and in 1955, merged with the conservative, craft-unionist American Federation of Labor (AFL) to form the AFL-CIO.

6 The **Comintern** is the short form for the Third, or Communist, International. It was founded in 1919 by Lenin as an agency of world revolution in the wake of the betrayals by the parties of the Second (or Socialist) International, almost all of which supported their own bourgeoisies during World War I. By the mid-1920s, the Third International had itself undergone a profound political degeneration as a result of the consolidation of power by the conservative, nationalist Stalinist bureaucracy.

order, its cynically counter-revolutionary role throughout the world, particularly in Spain, France, the United States and other "democratic" countries, created exceptional supplementary difficulties for the world proletariat. Under the banner of the October Revolution, the conciliatory politics practiced by the "People's Front" dooms the working class to impotence and clears the road for fascism.

"People's Fronts" on the one hand—fascism on the other; these are the last political resources of imperialism in the struggle against the proletarian revolution. From the historical point of view, however, both these resources are stop-gaps. The decay of capitalism continues under the sign of the Phrygian cap[7] in France as under the sign of the swastika in Germany. Nothing short of the overthrow of the bourgeoisie can open a road out.

The orientation of the masses is determined first by the objective conditions of decaying capitalism, and second, by the treacherous politics of the old workers' organizations. Of these factors, the first, of course, is the decisive one: the laws of history are stronger than the bureaucratic apparatus. No matter how the methods of the social-betrayers differ—from the "social" legislation of Blum[8] to the judicial frame-ups of Stalin—they will never succeed in breaking the revolutionary will of the proletariat. As time goes on, their desperate efforts to hold back the wheel of history will demonstrate more clearly to the masses that the crisis of the proletarian leadership, having become the crisis in mankind's culture, can be resolved only by the Fourth International.

The Minimum Program and a Transitional Program

The strategic task of the next period—a pre-revolutionary period of agitation, propaganda and organization—consists in overcoming the contradiction between the maturity of the objective revolutionary conditions and the immaturity of the proletariat and its vanguard (the confusion and disappointment of the older generation; the inexperience of the younger generation). It is necessary to help the masses in the process of the daily struggle to find the bridge between present demands and the socialist program of the revolution. This bridge should include a system of *transitional demands*, stemming from today's conditions and from today's consciousness of wide layers of the working class and unalterably leading to one final conclusion: the conquest of power by the proletariat.

Classical Social Democracy, functioning in an epoch of progressive capital-

7 A "**Phrygian cap**" is a conical cloth hat with the peak turned over in the front. Also known as a "liberty cap," it has been a symbol of republicanism in France since the 1790s.

8 **Léon Blum** led the SFIO (French Socialist Party) and became prime minister after the electoral victory of the Popular Front in 1936. Blum, along with Communist Party leader Maurice Thorez, played a central role in demobilizing the massive general strike that erupted in June 1936 in response to the election of the Popular Front. The "social" legislation enacted by Blum's government, like other concessions made by the employers, proved transitory.

ism, divided its program into two parts, independent of [one] another; the *minimum program* which limited itself to reforms within the framework of bourgeois society, and the *maximum program*, which promised substitution of socialism for capitalism in the indefinite future. Between the minimum and the maximum program no bridge existed. And indeed Social Democracy has no need of such a bridge, since the word Socialism is used only for holiday speechifying. The Comintern has set out to follow the path of Social Democracy in an epoch of decaying capitalism; when, in general, there can be no discussion of systematic social reforms and the raising of the masses' living standards;[9] when every serious demand of the proletariat and even every serious demand of the petty-bourgeoisie inevitably reaches beyond the limits of capitalist property relations and of the bourgeois state.

The strategical task of the Fourth International lies not in reforming capitalism but in its overthrow. The political aim, the conquest of power by the proletariat for the purpose of expropriating the bourgeoisie. However, the achievement of this strategic task is unthinkable without the most considered attention to all, even small and partial questions of tactics. All sections of the proletariat, all its layers, professions and groups should be drawn into the revolutionary movement. The present epoch is distinguished not for the fact that it frees the revolutionary party from day-to-day work but because it permits this work to be carried on indissolubly with the actual tasks of the revolution.

The Fourth International does not discard the program of the old "minimal" demands to the degree to which these have preserved at least part of their vital forcefulness. Indefatigably, it defends the democratic rights and social conquests of the workers. But it carries on this day-to-day work within the frame-work of the correct actual, that is, revolutionary perspective. Insofar as the old, partial "minimal" demands of the masses clash with the destructive and degrading tendencies of decadent capitalism—and this occurs at each step—the Fourth International advances a system of *transitional demands*, the essence of which is contained in the fact that ever more openly and decisively they will be directed against the very bases of the bourgeois regime. The old "minimal program" is superseded by the *transitional program*, the task of which lies in systematic mobilization of the masses for the proletarian revolution.

Sliding Scale of Wages and Sliding Scale of Hours

Under the conditions of disintegrating capitalism, the masses continue to live the meagerized life of the oppressed, threatened now more than at any

9 The following passage: "when the bourgeoisie always takes away with the right hand twice what it grants with the left (taxes, tariffs, inflation, 'deflation,' high prices, unemployment, police supervision of strikes)" appeared at this point in the Russian language text, but was omitted from the editions published by the SWP in 1938, 1939 and 1946. Pathfinder Press did not include it in the text of its 1970 pamphlet or in either the 1973 or 1974 editions of *The Transitional Program for Socialist Revolution*. It does, however, appear in the version of the program reprinted in *Documents of the Fourth International*, published by Pathfinder in 1973.

other time with the danger of being cast to the pit of pauperism. They must defend their mouthful of bread, if they cannot increase or better it. There is neither the need nor the opportunity to enumerate here those separate, partial demands which time and again arise on the basis of concrete circumstances—national, local, professional. But two basic economic afflictions, in which is summarized the increasing absurdity of the capitalist system: that is *unemployment* and *high prices*, demand generalized slogans and methods of struggle.

The Fourth International declares uncompromising war on the politics of the capitalists which, to a considerable degree, like the politics of their agents, the reformists, aims to place the whole burden of militarism, the crisis, the disorganization of the monetary system and all other scourges stemming from capitalism's death agony upon the backs of the toilers. The Fourth International demands *employment* and *decent living conditions* for all.

Neither monetary inflation nor stabilization can serve as slogans for the proletariat because these are but two ends of the same stick. Against a bounding rise in prices, which with the approach of war will assume an ever more unbridled character, one can fight only under the slogan of a *sliding scale of wages*. This means that collective agreements should assure an automatic rise in wages in relation to the increase in prices of consumer goods.

Under the menace of its own disintegration, the proletariat cannot permit the transformation of an increasing section of the workers into chronically unemployed paupers, living off the slops of a crumbling society. *The right to employment* is the only serious right left to the worker in a society based upon exploitation. This right today is being shorn from him at every step. Against unemployment, "structural" as well as "conjunctural," the time is ripe to advance along with the slogan of public works, the slogan of a *sliding scale of working hours*. Trade unions and other mass organizations should bind the workers and the unemployed together in the solidarity of mutual responsibility. On this basis, all the work on hand would then be divided among all existing workers in accordance with how the extent of the working week is defined. The average wage of every worker remains the same as it was under the old working week. Wages, under a strictly guaranteed *minimum*, would follow the movement of prices. It is impossible to accept any other program for the present catastrophic period.

Property owners and their lawyers will prove the "unrealizability" of these demands. Smaller, especially ruined capitalists, in addition will refer to their account ledgers. The workers categorically denounce such conclusions and references. The question is not one of a "normal" collision between opposed material interests. The question is one of guarding the proletariat from decay, demoralization and ruin. The question is one of life or death of the only creative and progressive class, and by that token of the future of mankind. If capitalism is incapable of satisfying the demands, inevitably arising from the calamities generated by itself, then let it perish. "Realizability" or "unrealizability" are in the given instance a question of the relationship of forces, which can be decided only by the struggle. By means of this struggle, no matter what its immediate practical successes may be, the workers will best come to understand the necessity of liquidating capitalist slavery.

Trade Unions in the Transitional Epoch

In the struggle for partial and transitional demands, the workers, now more than ever before, need mass organizations; principally, trade unions. The powerful growth of trade unionism in France and the United States is the best refutation to the preachments of those ultra-left doctrinaires, who have been teaching that trade unions have "outlived their usefulness."

The Bolshevik-Leninist stands in the front-line trenches of all kinds of struggles, even when they involve only the most modest material interests or democratic rights of the working class. He takes active part in mass trade union[s] for the purpose of strengthening them and raising their spirit of militancy. He fights uncompromisingly against any attempt to subordinate the unions to the bourgeois state and bind the proletariat to "compulsory arbitration" and every other form of police guardianship—not only fascist but also "democratic." Only on the basis of such work within the trade unions is successful struggle possible against the reformists, including those of the Stalinist bureaucracy. Sectarian attempts to build or preserve small "revolutionary" unions, as a second edition of the party, signify in actuality the renouncing of the struggle for leadership of the working class. It is necessary to establish this firm rule: self-isolation of the capitulationist variety from mass trade unions, which is tantamount to a betrayal of the revolution, is incompatible with adherence to the Fourth International.

* * *

At the same time, the Fourth International resolutely rejects and condemns trade union fetishism, equally characteristic of trade unionists and syndicalists.

(a) Trade unions do not offer, and in line with their task, composition, and manner of recruiting membership, cannot offer a finished revolutionary program; in consequence, they cannot replace the *party*. The building of national revolutionary parties as sections of the Fourth International is the central task of the transitional epoch.

(b) Trade unions, even the most powerful, embrace no more than 20 to 25 per cent of the working class, and at that, predominantly the more skilled and better paid layers. The more oppressed majority of the working class is drawn only episodically into the struggle, during a period of exceptional upsurges in the labor movement. During such moments it is necessary to create organizations, *ad hoc*, embracing the whole fighting mass: strike committees, factory committees, and finally, Soviets.

(c) As organizations expressive of the top layers of the proletariat, trade unions, as witnessed by all past historical experience, including the fresh experience of the anarcho-syndicalist unions in Spain, developed powerful tendencies toward compromise with the bourgeois-democratic regime. In periods of acute class struggle, the leading functionaries of the trade unions aim to become masters of the mass movement in order to render it harmless. This is already occurring during the period of simple strikes; especially in the case of the mass sit-down strikes which shake the principle of bourgeois property. In time of war or revolution, when the bourgeoisie is plunged into exceptional difficulties, trade union leaders usually become bourgeois ministers.

Therefore, the sections of the Fourth International should always strive not only to renew the top leadership of the trade unions, boldly and resolutely in critical moments, advancing new militant leaders in place of routine functionaries and careerists; but also to create in all possible instances independent militant organizations corresponding more closely to the problems of mass struggle [in] bourgeois society; not stopping, if necessary, even in the face of a direct break with the conservative apparatus of the trade unions. If it be criminal to turn one's back to mass organizations for the sake of fostering sectarian fictions, it is no less so to passively tolerate subordination of the revolutionary mass movement to the control of openly reactionary or disguised conservative ("progressive") bureaucratic cliques. Trade unions are not ends in themselves; they are but means along the road to proletarian revolution.

Factory Committees

During a transitional epoch, the workers' movement does not have a systematic and well-balanced but a feverish and explosive character. Slogans as well as organizational forms should be subordinated to the indices of the movement. On guard against routine handling of a situation as against a plague, the leadership should respond sensitively to the initiative of the masses. Sit-down strikes, the latest phenomenon of this kind of initiative, go beyond the limits of "normal" capitalist procedure. Independently of the demands of the strikers, the temporary seizure of factories deals a blow to the idol, capitalist property. Every sit-down strike poses in a practical manner the question of who is boss of the factory: the capitalist or the workers?

If the sit-down strike raises this question episodically, the *factory committee* gives it organized expression. Elected by all the factory employees, the factory committee immediately creates a counterweight to the will of the administration.

To the reformist criticism of bosses of the so-called "economic royalist" type like Ford in contra-distinction to "good," "democratic" exploiters, we counterpose the slogan of factory committees as centers of struggle against both the first and the second.

Trade union bureaucrats, in accordance with their general conduct, will resist the creation of factory committees as they resist every bold step taken along the road of mobilizing the masses.

However, the wider the sweep of the movement, the easier will it be to break this resistance. Where the closed shop has already been instituted in "peaceful" times, the committee will formally coincide with the usual organ of the trade union, but will renew its personnel and widen its functions. The prime significance of the committee, however, lies in the fact that it becomes the militant staff for such working class layers as the trade union is usually incapable of moving to action. It is precisely from these more oppressed layers that the most self-sacrificing battalions of the revolution will come.

From the moment that the committee makes its appearance, a factual dual power is established in the factory. By its very essence, it represents the transitional state because it includes in itself two irreconcilable regimes: the capitalist and the proletaria[n]. The fundamental significance of factory committees is precisely contained in the fact that they open the doors if not to a direct revolutionary, then to a pre-revolutionary period—between the bourgeois and the proletarian regimes. That the propagation of the factory committee idea is neither premature nor artificial is amply attested to by the waves of sit-down strikes spreading through several countries. New waves of this type will be inevitable in the immediate future. It is necessary to begin a campaign in favor of factory committees in time in order not to be caught unawares.

"Business Secrets" and Workers' Control of Industry

Liberal capitalism, based upon competition and free trade, has completely receded into the past. Its successor, monopolistic capitalism not only does not mitigate the anarchy of the market but on the contrary imparts to it a particularly convulsive character. The necessity of "controlling" [the] economy, of placing state "guidance" over industry and of "planning" is today recognized—at least in words—by almost all current bourgeois and petty bourgeois tendencies, from fascist to social-democratic. With the fascists, it is mainly a question of "planned" plundering of the people for military purposes. The social-democrats prepare to drain the ocean of anarchy with spoonfuls of bureaucratic "planning." Engineers and professors write articles about "technocracy."[10] In their cowardly experiments in "regulation," democratic governments run head[long] into the invincible sabotage of big capital.

The actual relationship existing between the exploiters and the democratic "controllers" is best characterized by the fact that the gentlemen "reformers" stop short in pious trepidation before the threshold of the trusts and their business "secrets." Here the principle of "non-interference" with business dominates. The accounts kept between the individual capitalist and society remains the secret of the capitalist: they are not the concern of society. The motivation offered for the principle of business "secrets" is ostensibly, as

10 "**Technocracy**" was a petty-bourgeois movement in the U.S. in the 1930s that claimed to know how to end the Depression by putting the economy, and particularly the financial system, under the direction of engineers and other technical experts.

in the epoch of liberal capitalism, that of free "competition." In reality, the trusts keep no secrets from one another. The business secrets of the present epoch are part of a persistent plot of monopoly capitalism against the interest of society. Projects for limiting the autocracy of "economic royalists" will continue to be pathetic farces as long as private owners of the social means of production can hide from producers and consumers the maChinations of exploitation, robbery, and fraud. The abolition of "business secrets" is the first step towards actual control of industry.

Workers no less than capitalists have the right to know the "secrets" of the factory, of the trust, of the whole branch of industry, of the national economy as a whole. First and foremost, banks, heavy industry and centralized transport should be placed under an observation glass.

The next tasks of workers' control should be to explain the debits and credits of society, beginning with individual business undertakings; to determine the actual share of the national income wolfed by the individual capitalist and by all the exploiters taken together; to expose the behind-the-scenes deals and swindles of banks and trusts; finally, to reveal to all members of society that unconscionable squandering of human labor which is the result of capitalist anarchy and naked pursuit of profits.

No office-holder of the bourgeois state is in a position to carry out this work, no matter with how great authority one would wish to endow him. All the world was witness to the impotence of President Roosevelt and Premier Blum against the plottings of the "60" or "200 families" of their respective nations. To break the resistance of the exploiters, the mass pressure of the proletariat is necessary. Only factory committees can bring about real control of production[,] calling in—as consultants but not as "technocrats"—specialists sincerely devoted to the people[:] accountants, statisticians, engineers, scientists, etc.

* * *

The struggle against unemployment is not to be considered without the [call] for a broad and bold organization of *public works*. But public works can have a continuous and progressive significance for society, as for the unemployed themselves, only when they are made part of a general plan, worked out to cover a considerable number of years. Within the framework of this plan, the workers would demand resumption, as public utilities, of work in private businesses closed as a result of the crisis. Workers' control in such cases would be replaced by direct workers' management.

The working out of even the most elementary economic plan—from the point of view of the exploited, not the exploiters—is impossible without workers' control, that is, without the penetration of the workers' eye into all open and concealed springs of capitalist economy. Committees representing individual business enterprises should meet at conferences to choose corresponding committees of trusts, whole branches of industry, economic regions and finally, of national industry as a whole. Thus, workers' control becomes a *school for planned economy*. On the basis of the experience of control, the proletariat will prepare itself for direct management of nationalized industry when the hour for that eventuality will strike.

To those capitalists, mainly of the lower and middle strata, who of their own accord sometimes offer to throw open their books to the workers—usually to demonstrate the necessity of lowering wages—the workers answer that they are not interested in the bookkeeping of individual bankrupts or semi-bankrupts but in the account ledgers of all exploiters as a whole. The workers cannot and do not wish to accommodate the level of their living conditions to the exigencies of individual capitalists, themselves victims of their own regime. The task is one of reorganizing the whole system of production and distribution on a more dignified and workable basis. If the abolition of business secrets be a necessary condition to workers' control, then control is the first step along the road to the socialist guidance of [the] economy.

Expropriation of Separate Groups of Capitalists

The socialist program of expropriation, i.e., of political overthrow of the bourgeoisie and liquidation of its economic domination, should in no case during the present transitional period hinder us from advancing, when the occasion warrants, the demand for the expropriation of several key branches of industry vital for national existence or of the most parasitic group of the bourgeoisie.

Thus, in answer to the pathetic jeremiads of the gentlemen-democrats anent[11] the dictatorship of the "60 Families" of the United States or the "200 Families" of France, we counterpose the demand for the expropriation of these 60 or 200 feudalistic capitalist overlords.

In precisely the same way we demand the expropriation of the corporations holding monopolies on war industries, railroads, the most important sources of raw materials, etc.

The difference between these demands and the muddleheaded reformist slogan of "nationalization" lies in the following: (1) we reject indemnification; (2) we warn the masses against demagogues of the People's Front who, giving lip-service to nationalization, remain in reality agents of capital; (3) we call upon the masses to rely only upon their own revolutionary strength; (4) we link up the question of expropriation with that of seizure of the power by the workers and farmers.

The necessity of advancing the slogan of expropriation in the course of daily *agitation* in partial form, and not only in our propaganda in its more comprehensive aspects, is dictated by the fact that different branches of industry are on different levels of development, occupy a different place in the life of society, and pass through different stages of the class struggle. Only a general revolutionary upsurge of the proletariat can place the complete ex-

11 "Anent" is a synonym for "about," or "concerning."

propriation of the bourgeoisie on the order of the day. The task of transitional demands is to prepare the proletariat to solve this problem.

Expropriation of the Private Banks and State-ization of the Credit System[12]

Imperialism means the domination of *finance capital.*[13] Side by side with the trusts and syndicates, and very frequently rising above them, the *banks* concentrate in their hands the actual command over the economy. In their structure the banks express in a concentrated form the entire structure of modern capital: they combine tendencies of *monopoly* with tendencies of *anarchy.* They organize the miracles of technology, giant enterprises, mighty trusts; and they also organize high prices, crises and unemployment. It is impossible to take a single serious step in the struggle against monopolistic despotism and capitalistic anarchy—which supplement one another in their work of destruction—if the commanding posts of banks are left in the hands of predatory capitalists. In order to create a unified system of investments and credits, along a rational plan corresponding to the interests of the entire people, it is necessary to merge all the banks into a single national institution. Only the expropriation of the private banks and the concentration of the entire credit system in the hands of the state will provide the latter with the necessary actual, i.e., material resources—and not merely paper and bureaucratic resources—for economic planning.

The expropriation of the banks in no case implies the expropriation of bank deposits. On the contrary, the single *state bank* will be able to create much more favorable conditions for the small depositors than could the private banks. In the same way, only the state bank can establish for farmers,

12 The entire section entitled "**Expropriation of the Private Banks and State-ization of the Credit System**" (which appeared in the Russian language draft of May/June 1938) was omitted in both the 22 October 1938 *Socialist Appeal* and the SWP's 1939 book, *The Founding Conference of the Fourth International.* It was also omitted in the 1939 special issue of the British *Workers' International News* which published the program.
In 1946, when the SWP published a slightly different version of the *Transitional Program* as the first in its "Pioneer Pocket Library" series, this section was included without explanation. A note in the front of the pamphlet stated only that the SWP was "reprinting" the text because the 1939 book was no longer available. In addition to the section on the banks, the 1946 edition includes a number of minor textual changes, none of apparent political significance. Subsequent editions published by the SWP's Pathfinder Press in 1970, 1973, and 1974 generally follow the 1946 text and contain this passage. We have taken this part of the text from the 1946 Pioneer Pocket edition.

13 "**Finance capital**" is a Marxist term introduced by Rudolf Hilferding in his 1910 book of the same name to describe the fusion of industrial capital with banking interests to create powerful and aggressive monopolies, which strive to control state policy as a means of increasing their economic domination. In *Imperialism, the Highest Stage of Capitalism*, Lenin cited the domination of finance capital in the economies of the advanced industrial nations as an important factor in the tendency toward inter-imperialist war. He also pointed to the predatory role of finance capital in the oppression and exploitation of the colonial and neo-colonial masses in Asia, Africa and Latin America.

tradesmen and small merchants conditions of favorable, that is, cheap credit. Even more important, however, is the circumstance that the entire economy—first and foremost large-scale industry and transport—directed by a single financial staff, will serve the vital interests of the workers and all other toilers.

However, *the state-ization of the banks* will produce these favorable results only if the state power itself passes completely from the hands of the exploiters into the hands of the toilers.

The Picket Line—Defense Groups—Workers' Militia—The Arming of the Proletariat

Sit-down strikes are a serious warning from the masses addressed not only to the bourgeoisie but also to the organizations of the workers, including the Fourth International. In 1919–1920, the Italian workers seized factories on their own initiative, thus signaling the news to their "leaders" of the coming of the social revolution. The "leaders" paid no heed to the signal. The victory of fascism was the result.

Sit-down strikes do not yet mean the seizure of factories in the Italian manner; but they are a decisive step toward such seizures. The present crisis can sharpen the class struggle to an extreme point and bring nearer the moment of denouement. But that does not mean that a revolutionary situation comes on at one stroke. Actually, its approach is signalized by a continuous series of convulsions. One of these is the wave of sit-down strikes. The problem of the sections of the Fourth International is to help the proletarian vanguard understand the general character and tempo of our epoch and to fructify in time the struggle of the masses with ever more resolute and militant organizational measures.

The sharpening of the proletariat's struggle means the sharpening of the methods of counter-attack on the part of capital. New waves of sit-down strikes can call forth and undoubtedly will call forth resolute countermeasures on the part of the bourgeoisie. Preparatory work is already being done by the confidential staffs of big trusts. Woe to the revolutionary organizations, woe to the proletariat if it is again caught unawares!

The bourgeoisie is nowhere satisfied with official police and army. In the United States, even during "peaceful" times, the bourgeoisie maintains militarized battalions of scabs and privately-armed thugs in factories. To this must now be added the various groups of American Nazis. The French bourgeoisie at the first approach of danger mobilized semi-legal and illegal fascist detachments, including such as are in the army. No sooner does the pressure of the English workers once again become stronger than immediately the fascist bands are doubled, trebled, increased tenfold to come out in bloody march against the workers. The bourgeoisie keeps itself most accurately informed about the fact that in the present epoch the class struggle irresistibly tends to transform itself into civil war. The examples of Italy, Germany, Austria, Spain[14] and other countries taught considerably more to the magnates and lackeys of capital than to the official leaders of the proletariat.

The politicians of the Second and Third Internationals, as well as the bureaucrats of the trade unions, consciously close their eyes to the bourgeoisie's private army; otherwise, they could not preserve their alliance with it for even twenty-four hours. The reformists systematically implant in the minds of the workers the notion that the sacredness of democracy is best guaranteed when the bourgeoisie is armed to the teeth and the workers are unarmed.

The duty of the Fourth International is to put an end to such slavish politics once and for all. The petty-bourgeois democrats—including social-democrats, Stalinists and anarchists—yell louder about the struggle against fascism the more cravenly they capitulate to it in actuality. Only armed workers' detachments, who feel the support of tens of millions of toilers behind them, can successfully prevail against the fascist bands. The struggle against fascism does not start in the liberal editorial office but in the factory—and ends in the street. Scabs and private gun-men in factory plants are the basic nuclei of the fascist army. *Strike pickets* are the basic nuclei of the proletarian army. This is our point of departure. In connection with every strike and street demonstration, it is imperative to propagate the necessity of creating *workers' groups for self-defense*. It is necessary to write this slogan into the program of the revolutionary wing of the trade unions. It is imperative everywhere possible, beginning with the youth groups, to organize groups for self-defense; to drill and acquaint them with the use of arms.

A new upsurge of the mass movement should serve not only to increase the number of these units but also to unite them according to neighborhoods, cities, regions. It is necessary to give organized expression to the valid hatred of the workers toward scabs and bands of gangsters and fascists. It is necessary to advance the slogan of a *workers' militia* as the one serious guarantee for the inviolability of workers' organizations, meetings, and press.

Only with the help of such systematic, persistent, indefatigable, courageous agitational and organizational work, always on the basis of the experience of the masses themselves, is it possible to root out from their consciousness the traditions of submissiveness and passivity; to train detachments of heroic fighters capable of setting an example to all toilers; to inflict a series of tactical defeats upon the armed thugs of counter-revolution; to raise the self-confidence of the exploited and oppressed; to compromise fascism in the eyes of the petty-bourgeois and pave the road for the conquest of power by the proletariat.

Engels defined the state as bodies of "armed men." *The arming of the proletariat* is an imperative concomitant element to its struggle for liberation.

14 In **Italy, Germany, Austria and Spain** in the 1920s and 30s, the working class had displayed a willingness to fight, but as a result of the confusion, stupidity, cowardice and/or betrayals of its leadership, the workers' organizations were crushed and Mussolini, Hitler and Franco triumphed.

When the proletariat wills it, it will find the road and the means to arming. In this field, also, the leadership falls naturally to the sections of the Fourth International.

The Alliance of the Workers and Farmers

The brother-in-arms and counterpart of the worker in the country is the agricultural laborer. They are two parts of one and the same class. Their interests are inseparable. The industrial workers' program of transitional demands, with changes here and there, is likewise the program of the agricultural proletariat.

The peasants (farmers) represent another class: they are the petty bourgeoisie of the village. The petty bourgeoisie is made up of various layers: from the semi-proletarian to the exploiter elements. In accordance with this, the political task of the industrial proletariat is to carry the class struggle into the country. Only thus will he be able to divide his allies and his enemies.

The peculiarities of national development of each country find their queerest expression in the status of farmers and to some extent of the urban petty bourgeoisie (artisans and shopkeepers). These classes, no matter how numerically strong they may be, essentially are representative survivals of pre-capitalist forms of production. The sections of the Fourth International should work out with all possible concreteness a program of transitional demands concerning the peasants (farmers) and urban petty-bourgeoisie and conformable to the conditions of each country. The advanced workers should learn to give clear and concrete answers to the questions put by their future allies.

While the farmer remains an "independent" petty producer, he is in need of cheap credit, of agricultural machines and fertilizer at prices he can afford to pay, favorable conditions of transport, and conscientious organization of the market for his agricultural products. But the banks, the trusts, the merchants rob the farmer from every side. Only the farmers themselves, with the help of the workers, can curb this robbery. *Committees elected by small farmers* should make their appearance on the national scene and jointly with workers' committees and committees of bank employees take into their hands control of transport, credit, and mercantile operations affecting agriculture.

By falsely citing the "excessive" demands of the workers, the big bourgeoisie skillfully transforms the question of *commodity prices* into a wedge to be driven between the workers and farmers and between the workers and the petty bourgeoisie of the cities. The peasant, artisan, small merchant, unlike the industrial worker, office and civil service employee, cannot demand a wage increase corresponding to the increase in prices. The official struggle of the government with high prices is only a deception of the masses. But the farmers, artisans, merchants, in their capacity of consumers, can step into the politics of price-fixing shoulder to shoulder with the workers. To the capitalist's lamentations about costs of production, of transport and trade, the consumers answer: "Show us your books; we demand control over the fixing of prices." The organs of this control should be the *committees on prices*, made up of delegates from the factories, trade unions, cooperatives, farmers' organizations, the "little man" of the city, house-wives, etc. By this means the workers will be able to prove to the farmers that the real reason for high prices is not high wages but the exorbitant profits of the capitalists and the overhead expenses of capitalist anarchy.

* * *

The program for the *nationalization of the land and collectivization of agriculture* should be so drawn that from its very basis it should exclude the possibility of expropriation of small farmers and their compulsory collectivization. The farmer will remain owner of his plot of land as long as he himself believes it possible or necessary. In order to rehabilitate the program of socialism in the eyes of the farmer, it is necessary to expose mercilessly the Stalinist methods of collectivization,[15] which are dictated not by the interests of the farmers or workers but by the interests of the bureaucracy.

The expropriation of the expropriators likewise does not signify forcible confiscation of the property of artisans and shopkeepers. On the contrary, workers' control of banks and trusts—even more, the nationalization of these concerns, can create for the urban petty bourgeoisie incomparably more favorable conditions of credit, purchase, and sale than is possible under the unchecked domination of the monopolies. Dependence upon private capital will be replaced by dependence upon the State, which will be the more attentive to the needs of its small co-workers and agents the stronger the toilers themselves will keep control of the State in their hands.

The practical participation of the exploited farmers in the control of different fields of [the] economy will allow them to decide for themselves whether or not it would be profitable for them to go over to collective working of the land—at what date and on what scale. Industrial workers should consider themselves duty-bound to show farmers every cooperation in traveling this road: through the trade unions, factory committees, and, most importantly, through a workers' and farmers' government.

The alliance proposed by the proletariat, not to the "middle classes" in general but to the exploited layers of the urban and rural petty-bourgeoisie, against all exploiters, including those of the "middle classes"—can be based not on compulsion but only on free consent, which should be consolidated in

15 In 1928 Stalin abruptly abandoned his previous conciliatory policy toward the rich peasants (kulaks) when a grain strike threatened the cities with starvation. The bureaucratic regime's attempt to "liquidate" the kulaks through the forcible **collectivization** of peasant landholdings resulted in a virtual civil war in the countryside. Millions of people died, both from repression and mass starvation, and Soviet agriculture was dealt a blow from which it never fully recovered.

a special "contract." This "contract" is the program of transitional demands voluntarily accepted by both sides.

The Struggle Against Imperialism and War

The whole world outlook, and consequently also the inner political life of individual countries, is overcast by the threat of world war. Already the imminent catastrophe sends violent ripples of apprehension through the very broadest masses of mankind.

The Second International repeats its infamous politics of 1914[16] with all the greater assurance since today it is the Comintern which plays first fiddle in chauvinism. As quickly as the danger of war assumed concrete outline, the Stalinists, outstripping the bourgeois and petty bourgeois pacifists by far, became blatant haranguers for so-called "national defense."[17] The revolutionary struggle against war thus rests fully on the shoulders of the Fourth International.

The Bolshevik-Leninist policy regarding this question, formulated in the thesis of the International Secretariat (*War and the Fourth International,* 1934) preserves all of its force today. In the next period a revolutionary party will depend for success primarily on its policy on the question of war. A correct policy is composed of two elements: an uncompromising attitude on imperialism and its wars and the ability to base one's program on the experience of the masses themselves.

The bourgeoisie and its agents use the war question, more than any other, to deceive the people by means of abstractions, general formulas, lame phraseology: "neutrality," "collective security," "arming for the defense of peace," "national defense," "struggle against fascism," and so on. All such formulas reduce themselves in the end to the fact that the war question, i.e., the fate of the people, is left in the hands of the imperialists, their governing staffs, their diplomacy, their generals, with all their intrigues and plots against the people.

The Fourth International rejects with abhorrence all such abstractions which play the same role in the democratic camp as in the fascist: "Honor," "blood," "race." But abhorrence is not enough. It is imperative to help the masses discern, by means of verifying criteria, slogans, and demands, the concrete essence of these fraudulent abstractions.

"Disarmament?"—But the entire question revolves around who will dis-

16 In **August 1914**, when World War I broke out, the leaders of the Second (Socialist) International abandoned all the Marxist internationalist principles they had long proclaimed in order to support the war efforts of their "own" capitalist governments. Unlike most parties in the combatant nations, the Bolsheviks stood hard against the tidal wave of national chauvinism that accompanied the outbreak of hostilities.

17 The following sentence, which was in the original Russian draft, does not appear in any of the SWP editions: "They make an exception only for the fascist countries, i.e., those in which they don't play any role."

arm whom. The only disarmament which can avert or end war is the disarmament of the bourgeoisie by the workers. But to disarm the bourgeoisie the workers must arm themselves.

"Neutrality?"—But the proletariat is nothing like neutral in the war between Japan and China, or a war between Germany and the U.S.S.R. "Then what is meant is the defense of China and the U.S.S.R.?" Of course! But not by the imperialists who will strangle both China and the U.S.S.R.

"Defense of the Fatherland?"—But by this abstraction, the bourgeoisie understands the defense of its profits and plunder. We stand ready to defend the fatherland from foreign capitalists, if we first bind our own (capitalists) hand and foot and hinder them from attacking foreign fatherlands; if the workers and the farmers of our country become its real masters; if the wealth of the country be transferred from the hands of a tiny minority to the hands of the people; if the army becomes a weapon of the exploited instead of the exploiters.

It is necessary to interpret these fundamental ideas by breaking them up into more concrete and partial ones, dependent upon the course of events and the orientation of the thought of the masses. In addition, it is necessary to differentiate strictly between the pacifism of the diplomat, professor, journalist and the pacifism of the carpenter, agricultural worker, and charwoman. In one case, pacifism is a screen for imperialism; in the other, it is the confused expression of distrust in imperialism. When the small farmer or worker speaks about the defense of the fatherland, he means defense of his home, his families and other similar families from invasion, bombs and poisonous gas. The capitalist and his journalist understand by the defense of the fatherland the seizure of colonies and markets, the predatory increase of the "national" share of world income. Bourgeois pacifism and patriotism are shot through with deceit. In the pacifism and even patriotism of the oppressed there are elements which reflect on the one hand a hatred of destructive war and on the other a clinging to what they believe to be their own good—elements which we must know how to seize upon in order to draw the requisite conclusions.[18]

Using these considerations as its point of departure, the Fourth International supports every, even if insufficient, demand, if it can draw the masses to a certain extent into active politics, awaken their criticism and strengthen their control over the maChinations of the bourgeoisie.

From this point of view, our American section, for example, critically supports the proposal for establishing a referendum on the question of declaring war. No democratic reform[,] it is understood, can by itself prevent the rulers from provoking war when they wish it. It is necessary to give frank warning of this. But notwithstanding the illusions of the masses in regard to the proposed referendum, their support of it reflects the distrust felt by workers and

18 In the 1938 Russian draft the following text is substituted for the last sentence in this paragraph: "In the pacifism and even patriotism of the oppressed there is a progressive kernel, which it is necessary to seize upon in order to draw the requisite conclusions. It is necessary to counterpose against each other these two aspects of pacifism and patriotism."

farmers for bourgeois government and congress. Without supporting and without sparing illusions, it is necessary to support with all possible strength the progressive distrust of the exploited toward the exploiters. The more widespread the movement for the referendum becomes, the sooner will the bourgeois pacifists move away from it; the more completely will the betrayers of the Comintern be compromised; the more acute will distrust of the imperialists become.

From this viewpoint, it is necessary to advance the demand: electoral rights for men and women beginning with the age of eighteen. Those who will be called upon to die for the fatherland tomorrow should have the right to vote today. The struggle against war must first of all begin with the *revolutionary mobilization of the youth*.

Light must be shed upon the problem of war from all angles, hinging upon the side from which it will confront the masses at a given moment.

War is a gigantic commercial enterprise, especially for the war industry. The "60 Families" are therefore first-line patriots and the chief provocateurs of war. *Workers' control of war industries* is the first step in the struggle against the "manufacturers" of war.

To the slogan of the reformists: *a tax on military profit,* we counterpose the slogans: *confiscation of military profit* and *expropriation of the traffickers in war industries*. Where military industry is "nationalized," as in France, the slogan of *workers' control* preserves its full strength. The proletariat has as little confidence in the government of the bourgeoisie as in [an] individual bourgeois.

Not one man and not one penny for the bourgeois government!

Not an armaments program but a program of useful public works!

Complete independence of workers' organizations from military-police control!

Once and for all we must tear from the hands of the greedy and merciless imperialist clique, scheming behind the backs of the people, the disposition of the people's fate.

In accordance with this we demand:

Complete abolition of secret diplomacy; all treaties and agreements to be made accessible to all workers and farmers;

Military training and arming of workers and farmers under direct control of workers' and farmers' committees;

Creation of military schools for the training of commanders among the toilers, chosen by workers' organizations;

Substitution for the standing army of a *people's militia*, indissolubly linked up with factories, mines, farms, etc.

* * *

Imperialist war is the continuation and sharpening of the predatory politics of the bourgeoisie. The struggle of the proletariat against war is the continuation and sharpening of its class struggle. The beginning of war alters the situation and partially the means of struggle between the classes, but not the aim and basic course.

The imperialist bourgeoisie dominates the world. In its basic character the approaching war will therefore be an imperialist war. The fundamental content of the politics of the international proletariat will consequently be a struggle against imperialism and its war. In this struggle the basic principle is: "the chief enemy is in *your own* country," or "the defeat of *your own* (imperialist) government is the lesser evil."

But not all countries of the world are imperialist countries. On the contrary the majority are victims of imperialism. Some of the colonial or semi-colonial countries will undoubtedly attempt to utilize the war in order to cast off the yoke of slavery. Their war will be not imperialist but liberating. It will be the duty of the international proletariat to aid the oppressed countries in war against oppressors. The same duty applies in regard to aiding the U.S.S.R., or whatever other workers' government might arise before the war or during the war. The defeat of *every* imperialist government in the struggle with the workers' state or with a colonial country is the lesser evil.

The workers of imperialist countries, however, cannot help an anti-imperialist country through their own government, no matter what might be the diplomatic and military relations between the two countries at a given moment. If the governments find themselves in temporary and, by very essence of the matter, unreliable alliance, then the proletariat of the imperialist country continues to remain in class opposition to its own government and supports the non-imperialist "ally" through *its own* methods, i.e., through the methods of the international class struggle (agitation not only against their perfidious allies but also in favor of a workers' state in a colonial country;[19] boycott, strikes, in one case; rejection of boycott and strikes in another case, etc.).

In supporting the colonial country or the U.S.S.R. in a war, the proletariat does not in the slightest degree solidarize either with the bourgeois government of the colonial country or with the Thermidorian bureaucracy[20] of the U.S.S.R. On the contrary it maintains full political independence from the one as from the other. Giving aid in a just and progressive war, the revolutionary proletariat wins the sympathy of the workers in the colonies and in the U.S.S.R., strengthens there the authority and influence of the Fourth International, and increases its ability to help overthrow the bourgeois government in the colonial country, the reactionary bureaucracy in the U.S.S.R.

* * *

19 The Russian draft reads: "agitation in favor of the workers' state and of the colonial country."

20 On **Thermidor** the Ninth, according to the French revolutionary calendar, the radical government of Maximilien Robespierre was overthrown by a more conservative faction among the Jacobins (France's bourgeois revolutionaries). Trotsky described the conservative bureaucracy headed by Stalin as "Thermidorian" because, while hostile to the internationalist tradition of Bolshevism, it continued to employ revolutionary phrases and opposed the restoration of the *ancien régime*.

At the beginning of the war the sections of the Fourth International will inevitably feel themselves isolated: every war takes the national masses unawares and impels them to the side of the government apparatus. The internationalists will have to swim against the stream. However, the devastation and misery brought about by the new war, which in the first months will far outstrip the bloody horrors of 1914–1918, will quickly prove sobering. The discontent of the masses and their revolt will grow by leaps and bounds. The sections of the Fourth International will be found at the head of the revolutionary tide. The program of transitional demands will gain burning actuality. The problem of the conquest of power by the proletariat will loom in full stature.

* * *

Before exhausting or drowning mankind in blood, capitalism befouls the world atmosphere with the poisonous vapors of national and race hatred. *anti-semitism* today is one of the more malignant convulsions of capitalism's death agony.

An uncompromising disclosure of the roots of race prejudices and all forms and shades of national arrogance and chauvinism, particularly anti-semitism, should become part of the daily work of all sections of the Fourth International, as the most important part of the struggle against imperialism and war. Our basic slogan remains: workers of the world unite!

Workers' and Farmers' Government

This formula, "Workers' and Farmers' Government," first appeared in the agitation of the Bolsheviks in 1917 and was definitely accepted after the October Insurrection. In the final instance it represented nothing more than the popular designation for the already established dictatorship of the proletariat. The significance of this designation comes mainly from the fact that it underscored the idea of an *alliance between the proletariat and the peasantry* lodged in the base of the Soviet power.

When the Comintern of the epigones tried to revive the formula buried by history of the "democratic dictatorship of the proletariat and peasantry," it gave to the formula of the "workers' and peasants' government" a completely different, purely "democratic," i.e., bourgeois content, *counterposing* it to the dictatorship of the proletariat. The Bolshevik-Leninists resolutely rejected the slogan of the "workers' and peasants' government" in the bourgeois-democratic version. They affirmed then and affirm now that when the party of the proletariat refuses to step beyond bourgeois-democratic limits, its alliance with the peasantry is simply turned into a support for capital, as was the case with the Mensheviks and the Social Revolutionaries in 1917,[21] with the

21 The **Mensheviks** constituted the reformist wing of the Russian Social Democratic Labor Party (RSDLP) which advocated a strategic alliance with the liberal capitalists. The term "Mensheviks" (which means "minorityites") originated in 1903 when the RSDLP split into two factions. The Bolsheviks (or "majorityites") constituted the RSDLP's revolutionary wing. The **Social**

Chinese Communist party in 1925–1927, and as is now the case with the "People's Front" in Spain, France and other countries.

From April to September, 1917, the Bolsheviks demanded that the S.R.'s and Mensheviks break with the liberal bourgeoisie and take power into their own hands. Under this provision the Bolshevik Party promised the Mensheviks and the S.R.'s, as the petty bourgeois representatives of the workers and peasants, its revolutionary aid against the bourgeoisie; categorically refusing, however, either to enter into the government of the Mensheviks and S.R.'s or to carry political responsibility for it. If the Mensheviks and the S.R.'s had actually broken with the Cadets (liberals) and with foreign imperialism, then the "workers' and peasants' government" created by them could only have hastened and facilitated the establishment of the dictatorship of the proletariat. But it was exactly because of this that the leadership of petty bourgeois democracy resisted with all possible strength the establishment of its own government. The experience of Russia demonstrated and the experience of Spain and France once again confirm that even under very favorable conditions the parties of petty bourgeois democracy (S.R.'s, Social-Democrats, Stalinists, anarchists) are incapable of creating a government of workers and peasants, that is, a government independent of the bourgeoisie.

Nevertheless, the demand of the Bolsheviks, addressed to the Mensheviks and the S.R.'s: "Break with the bourgeoisie, take the power into your own hands!" had for the masses tremendous educational significance. The obstinate unwillingness of the Mensheviks and S.R.'s to take power, so dramatically exposed during the July days,[22] definitely doomed them before mass opinion and prepared the victory of the Bolsheviks.

The central task of the Fourth International consists in freeing the proletariat from the old leadership, whose conservatism is in complete contradiction to the catastrophic eruptions of disintegrating capitalism and represents the chief obstacle to historical progress. The chief accusation which the Fourth International advances against the traditional organizations of the proletariat is the fact that they do not wish to tear themselves away from the political semi-corpse of the bourgeoisie. Under these conditions the demand,

Revolutionaries (SRs) originated in 1900 as an organization of populists committed to mobilizing the peasantry for revolutionary struggle against Czarism. Both the Mensheviks and the majority (Right) SRs opposed the October 1917 Revolution, and many ended up in the camp of counterrevolution. Most of those who defended the revolution joined the Bolsheviks. The Left SRs initially participated in a coalition government with the Bolsheviks, but within a year were actively engaged in attempts to overthrow the new regime.

22 The **"July Days"** refers to a series of mass armed demonstrations against Alexander Kerensky's coalition government conducted by workers and sailors in Petrograd (subsequently known as Leningrad, today St. Petersburg) in July 1917. The Mensheviks, SRs and other reformist socialists, along with the liberal bourgeoisie, were terrified by the militant sentiment of the protests. The Bolsheviks sympathized with the demonstrators, but sought to avoid an immediate confrontation with Kerensky's Provisional Government because the masses in the rest of Russia were not ready to support such an action by the Petrograd workers. Kerensky used the demonstrations as a pretext to illegalize the Bolsheviks and imprison many of their leaders, including Trotsky.

systematically addressed to the old leadership: "Break with the bourgeoisie, take the power!" is an extremely important weapon for exposing the treacherous character of the parties and organizations of the Second, Third and Amsterdam Internationals.[23] The slogan, "Workers' and Farmers' Governments," is thus acceptable to us only in the sense that it had in 1917 with the Bolsheviks, i.e., as an anti-bourgeois and anti-capitalist slogan, but in no case in that "democratic" sense which later the epigones gave it, transforming it from a bridge to socialist revolution into the chief barrier upon its path.

Of all the parties and organizations which base themselves on the workers and peasants and speak in their name, we demand that they break politically from the bourgeoisie and enter upon the road of struggle for the workers' and farmers' government. On this road we promise them full support against capitalist reaction. At the same time, we indefatigably develop agitation around those transitional demands which should in our opinion form the program of the "Workers' and Farmers' Government."

Is the creation of such a government by the traditional workers' organizations possible? Past experience shows, as has already been stated, that this is to say the least highly improbable. However, one cannot categorically deny in advance the theoretical possibility that, under the influence of completely exceptional circumstances (war, defeat, financial crash, mass revolutionary pressure, etc.) the petty bourgeois parties, including the Stalinists may go further than they themselves wish along the road to a break with the bourgeoisie. In any case one thing is not to be doubted: even if this highly improbabl[e] variant somewhere at some time becomes a reality and the "Workers' and Farmers' Government," in the above mentioned sense, is established in fact, it would represent merely a short episode on the road to the actual dictatorship of the proletariat.

However, there is no need to indulge in guess-work. The agitation around the slogan of a workers-farmers government preserves under all conditions a tremendous educational value. And not accidentally. This generalized slogan proceeds entirely along the line of the political development of our epoch (the bankruptcy and decomposition of the old bourgeois parties, the downfall of democracy, the growth of fascism, the accelerated drive of the workers toward more active and aggressive politics). Each of the transitional demands should, therefore, lead to one and the same political conclusion: the workers need to break with all traditional parties of the bourgeoisie in order, jointly with the farmers, to establish their own power.

It is impossible in advance to foresee what will be the concrete stages of the revolutionary mobilization of the masses. The sections of the Fourth International should critically orient themselves at each new stage and advance such slogans as will aid the striving of the workers for independent pol-

23 The **Amsterdam International**, or International Federation of Trade Unions, was the body representing trade unions aligned with the Second International during the 1920s and 30s.

itics, deepen the class character of these politics, destroy reformist and pacifist illusions, strengthen the connection of the vanguard with the masses, and prepare the revolutionary conquest of power.

Soviets

Factory committees, as already stated, are elements of dual power inside the factory. Consequently, their existence is possible only under condition of increasing pressure by the masses. This is likewise true of special mass groupings for the struggle *against war*, of the *committee on prices* and all other new centers of the movement, the very appearance of which bears witness to the fact that the class struggle has overflowed the limits of the traditional organizations of the proletariat.

These new organs and centers, however, will soon begin to feel their lack of cohesion and their insufficiency. Not one of the transitional demands can be fully met under the conditions of preserving the bourgeois regime. At the same time, the deepening of the social crisis will increase not only the sufferings of the masses but also their impatience, persistence, and pressure. Ever new layers of the oppressed will raise up their heads and come forward with their demands. Millions of toil-worn "little men," to whom the reformist leaders never gave a thought, will begin to pound insistently on the doors of workers' organizations. The unemployed will join the movement. The agricultural workers, the ruined and semi-ruined farmers, the oppressed of the cities, the women-workers, housewives, proletarianized layers of the intelligentsia—all of these will seek unity and leadership.

How are the different demands and forms of struggle to be harmonized, even if only within the limits of one city? History has already answered this question: through *soviets*. These will unite the representatives of all the fighting groups. For this purpose, no one has yet proposed a different form of organization; indeed, it would hardly be possible to think up a better one. Soviets are not limited to an *a priori* party program. They throw open their doors to all the exploited. Through these doors pass representatives of all strata, drawn into the general current of the struggle. The organization, broadening out together with the movement, is renewed again and again in its womb. All political currents of the proletariat can struggle for leadership of the soviets on the basis of the widest democracy. The slogan of *soviets*, therefore, crowns the program of transitional demands.

Soviets can arise only at the time when the mass movement enters into an openly revolutionary stage. From the first moment of their appearance, the soviets, acting as a pivot around which millions of toilers are united in their struggle against the exploiters[,] become competitors and opponents of local authorities and then of the central government. If the factory committee creates a dual power in the factory, then the soviets initiate a period of dual power in the country.

Dual power in its turn is the culminating point of the transitional period. Two regimes, the bourgeois and the proletarian are irreconcilably opposed to each other. Conflict between them is inevitable. The fate of society depends on the outcome. Should the revolution be defeated—the fascist dictatorship of the bourgeoisie will follow. In case of victory—the power of the soviets, that is, the dictatorship of the proletariat and the socialist reconstruction of society, will arise.

Backward Countries and the Program of Transitional Demands

Colonial and semi-colonial countries are backward countries by their very essence. But backward countries are part of a world dominated by imperialism. Their development, therefore, has a *combined* character: the most primitive economic forms are combined with the last word in capitalist technique and culture. In like manner are defined the political strivings of the proletariat of backward countries: the struggle for the most elementary achievements of national independence and bourgeois democracy is combined with the socialist struggle against world imperialism. Democratic slogans, transitional demands and the problems of the socialist revolution are not divided into separate historical epochs in this struggle, but stem directly from one another. The Chinese proletariat had barely begun to organize trade unions before it had to provide for soviets. In this sense, the present program is completely applicable to colonial and semi-colonial countries, at least to those where the proletariat has become capable of carrying on independent politics.

The central task of the colonial and semi-colonial countries is the *agrarian revolution*, i.e., liquidation of feudal heritages, and *national independence*, i.e., the overthrow of the imperialist yoke. Both tasks are closely linked with one another.

It is impossible merely to reject the democratic program: it is imperative that in the struggle the masses outgrow it. The slogan for a National (or Constituent) Assembly preserves its full force for such countries as China or India. This slogan must be indissolubly tied up with the problem of national liberation and agrarian reform. As a primary step, the workers must be armed with this democratic program. Only they will be able to summon and unite the farmers. On the basis of the revolutionary democratic program, it is necessary to oppose the workers to the "national" bourgeoisie. Then at a certain stage in the mobilization of the masses under the slogans of revolutionary democracy, soviets can and should arise. Their historical role in each given period, particularly their relation to the National Assembly, will be determined by the political level of the proletariat, the bond between them and the peasantry and the character of the proletarian party policies. Sooner or later, the soviets should overthrow bourgeois democracy. Only they are capable of bringing the democratic revolution to a conclusion and likewise opening an era of socialist revolution.

The relative weight of the individual democratic and transitional demands in the proletariat's struggle, their mutual ties and their order of presentation, is determined by the peculiarities and specific conditions of each backward country and to a considerable extent—by the *degree* of its backwardness. Nevertheless, the general trend of revolutionary development in all backward countries can be determined by the formula of the *permanent revolution*[24] in the sense definitely imparted to it by the three revolutions in Russia (1905, February 1917, October 1917).

The Comintern has provided backward countries with a classic example of how it is possible to ruin a powerful and promising revolution. During the stormy mass upsurge in China in 1925–27,[25] the Comintern failed to advance the slogan for a National Assembly, and at the same time, forbade the creation of soviets. (The bourgeois party, the Kuomintang, was to replace, according to Stalin's plan, both the National Assembly and soviets.) After the masses had been smashed by the Kuomintang, the Comintern organized a caricature of a soviet in Canton. Following the inevitable collapse of the Canton uprising, the Comintern took the road of guerrilla warfare and peasant soviets with complete passivity on the part of the industrial proletariat. Landing thus in a blind alley, the Comintern took advantage of the Sino-Japanese war to liquidate "Soviet China" with a stroke of the pen, subordinating not only the peasant "Red Army" but also the so-called "Communist" Party to the identical Kuomintang, i.e., the bourgeoisie.

The betrayal of the international proletarian revolution by the Comintern for the sake of friendship with the "democratic" slave masters, could not but help it betray simultaneously also the struggle for the liberation of the colo-

24 "**The formula of permanent revolution**" refers to the theory of revolutionary development initially put forward by Trotsky and Parvus (Alexander Helphand) in 1904–06. This theory postulated that the democratic achievements of the classical bourgeois revolutions (England in the 17th century, France in the 18th) could only be fulfilled in Russia through a seizure of state power by the proletariat, supported by the peasantry.

This proved an accurate projection of the course of the Russian Revolution. In what Lenin called the "dress rehearsal" of 1905, the rising of workers and peasants against the Czarist regime was opposed by the liberal bourgeoisie who favored a gradualist course of autocratic self-reform. After the overthrow of the Czar in February 1917, the bourgeois Provisional Government, headed by Alexander Kerensky, was chiefly concerned with maintaining "order" (i.e., protecting the interests of the landlords, bankers and foreign investors) at the expense of the workers and peasants. The workers' state created by the October Revolution was left to undertake both the democratic tasks (land to the tiller, freedom for oppressed nationalities, etc.) and the socialist tasks (expropriation of key industries, beginning of economic planning, etc.).

25 In China during 1925–27, a massive wave of worker-peasant rebellions broke out against the corrupt and despotic warlords and their imperialist sponsors. China was at the brink of a social revolution, but the Chinese Communist Party (CCP), under strict instructions from Moscow, acted as the loyal left wing of the bourgeois-nationalist Kuomintang (KMT) and systematically sought to moderate the demands and actions of the workers and peasants. In early 1926, the KMT was enrolled in the Comintern as an associate party. Stalin insisted that the KMT "bloc of four classes" (national bourgeoisie, urban petty bourgeoisie, peasants and workers) represented an "anti-imperialist" force whose unity must be safeguarded. The leadership of the CCP, and the Trotskyist Left Opposition, strongly objected to this policy but to no avail. In 1927 Chiang Kai-shek launched a bloody coup against the left and brutally massacred tens of thousands of CCP cadre and supporters.

nial masses, and, indeed, with even greater cynicism than practiced by the Second International before it. One of the tasks of People's Front and "national defense" politics is to turn hundreds of millions of the colonial population into cannon fodder for "democratic" imperialism. The banner on which is emblazoned the struggle for the liberation of the colonial and semi-colonial peoples, i.e., a good half of mankind, has definitely passed into the hands of the Fourth International.

The Program of Transitional Demands in Fascist Countries

It is a far cry today from the time when the strategists of the Comintern announced the victory of Hitler as being merely a step toward the victory of Thaelmann.[26] Thaelmann has been in Hitler's prisons now for more than five years. Mussolini has held Italy enchained by fascism for more than sixteen years. Throughout this time, the parties of the Second and Third Internationals have been impotent not only to conduct a mass movement but even to create a serious illegal organization, even to some extent comparable to the Russian revolutionary parties during the epoch of Czarism.

Not the least reason exists for explaining these failures by reference to the power of fascist ideology. (Essentially, Mussolini never advanced any sort of ideology.) Hitler's "ideology" never seriously gripped the workers. Those layers of the population which at one time were intoxicated with fascism, i.e., chiefly the middle classes, have had enough time in which to sober up. The fact that a somewhat perceptible opposition is limited to Protestant and Catholic church circles is not explained by the might of the semi-delirious and semi-charlatan theories of "race" and "blood," but by the terrific collapse of the ideologies of democracy, social-democracy and the Comintern.

The collapse of the Paris Commune[27] paralyzed the French workers for nearly eight years. After the defeat of the 1905 Russian revolution, the toiling masses remained in a stupor for almost as long a period. But in both instances the phenomenon was only one of physical defeat, conditioned by the relationship of forces. In Russia, in addition, it concerned an almost virgin proletariat. The Bolshevik fraction had at that time not celebrated even its third birthday. It is completely otherwise in Germany where the leadership came

26 **Ernst Thaelmann** was installed, with Moscow's support, as the chairman of the German Communist Party (KPD) in 1925. He remained its central leader through the fatal years of Hitler's rise to power. He loyally implemented Stalin's suicidal policies of denouncing the Social Democratic Party as "social fascist" and refused to participate in united-front actions against the Nazis. The criminal sectarian passivity of the KPD (captured by the formula "After Hitler—Us") was an important factor in the Nazi victory. A few weeks after Hitler took power in January 1933, Thaelmann was captured and sent to jail. In August 1944 he was executed in the Buchenwald concentration camp.

27 In the aftermath of the Franco-Prussian War, in March 1871, the Parisian masses rebelled against Adolphe Thiers' reactionary bourgeois government and created the **Paris Commune**, the first workers' government in history. The Commune lasted for little more than two months, before being bloodily suppressed by Thiers' forces which murdered tens of thousands of Communards. Karl Marx drew the lessons of the experience of the Commune in his 1871 pamphlet entitled "The Civil War in France."

from powerful parties, one of which had existed for seventy years, the other—almost fifteen. Both these parties, with millions of voters behind them, were morally paralyzed before the battle and capitulated without a battle. (History has recorded no parallel catastrophe. The German proletariat was not smashed by the enemy in battle.) It was crushed by the cowardice, baseness, [and] perfidy of its own parties. Small wonder then that it has lost faith in everything in which it had been accustomed to believe for almost three generations. Hitler's victory in turn strengthened Mussolini.

The protracted failure of revolutionary work in Spain[28] or Germany is but the reward for the criminal politics of the Social-Democracy and the Comintern. Illegal work needs not only the sympathy of the masses but the conscious enthusiasm of its advanced strata. But can enthusiasm possibly be expected for historically bankrupt organizations? The majority of those who come forth as emigre leaders are either demoralized to the very marrow of their bones, agents of the Kremlin and the G.P.U.,[29] or social-[d]emocratic ex-ministers, who dream that the workers by some sort of miracle will return them to their lost posts. Is it possible to imagine even for a minute these gentlemen in the role of future leaders of the "anti-fascist" revolution?

And events on the world arena—the smashing of the Austrian workers, the defeat of the Spanish revolution, the degeneration of the Soviet State—could not give aid to a revolutionary upsurge in Italy and Germany. Since for political information the German and Italian workers depend in great measure upon the radio, it is possible to say with assurance that the Moscow radio station, combining Thermidorian lies with stupidity and insolence, has become the most powerful factor in the demoralization of the workers in the totalitarian states. In this respect, as in others[,] Stalin acts merely as Goebbels' assistant.

At the same time, the class antagonisms which brought about the victory of fascism, continuing their work under fascism, too, are gradually undermining it. The masses are more dissatisfied than ever. Hundreds and thousands of self-sacrificing workers, in spite of everything, continue to carry on revolutionary mole-work. A new generation, which has not directly experienced the shattering of old traditions and high hopes, has come to the fore. Irresistibly, the molecular preparation of the proletarian revolution proceeds beneath the heavy totalitarian tombstone. But for concealed energy to flare into open revolt, it is necessary that the vanguard of the proletariat find new perspectives, a new program and a new unblemished banner.

Herein, lies the chief handicap. It is extremely difficult for workers in fascist countries to make a choice of a new program. A program is verified by experience. And it is precisely experience in mass movements which is lacking in countries of totalitarian despotism. It is very likely that a genuine proletarian success in one of the "democratic" countries will be necessary to give impetus to the revolutionary movement on fascist territory. A similar effect is

28 The Russian draft reads "Italy" instead of "Spain."
29 The GPU (State Political Administration) was the name of Stalin's secret police.

possible by means of a financial or military catastrophe. At present, it is imperative that primarily propagandistic, preparatory work be carried on[,] which will yield large scale results only in the future. One thing can be stated with conviction even at this point: once it breaks through, the revolutionary wave in fascist countries will immediately be a grandiose sweep and under no circumstances will stop short at the experiment of resuscitating some sort of Weimar[30] corpse.

It is from this point onward that an uncompromising divergence begins between the Fourth International and the old parties, which outlive their bankruptcy. The emigre "People's Front" is the most malignant and perfidious variety of all possible People's Fronts. Essentially, it signifies the impotent longing for a coalition with a non-existent liberal bourgeoisie. Had it met with success, it would simply have prepared a series of new defeats of the Spanish type for the proletariat. A merciless exposure of the theory and practice of the "People's Front" is therefore the first condition for a revolutionary struggle against fascism.

Of course, this does not mean that the Fourth International rejects democratic slogans as a means of mobilizing the masses against fascism.[31] On the contrary, such slogans at certain moments can play a serious role. But the formulas of democracy (freedom of press, the right to unionize, etc.) mean for us only incidental or episodic slogans in the independent movement of the proletariat and not a democratic noose fastened to the neck of the proletariat by the bourgeoisie's agents (Spain!). As soon as the movement assumes something of a mass character, the democratic slogans will be intertwined with the transitional ones; factory committees, it may be supposed, will appear before the old routinists rush from their chancelleries to organize trade unions; soviets will cover Germany before a new Constitutional Assembly will gather in Weimar. The same will be true of Italy and the rest of the totalitarian and semi-totalitarian countries.

Fascism plunged these countries into political barbarism. But it did not change their social structure. Fascism is a tool in the hands of finance capital and not of feudal landowners. A revolutionary program should base itself on the dialectics of the class struggle, obligatory also to fascist countries, and not on the psychology of terrified bankrupts. The Fourth International rejects with disgust the ways of political masquerade which impelled the Stalinists, the former heroes of the "Third Period,"[32] to appear in turn behind the masks

30 Germany's **Weimar Republic** was established in 1919 after the abdication of Kaiser Wilhelm II. It was the product of an aborted proletarian revolution that succeeded in overthrowing the absolutism of the Hohenzollerns (Germany's royal dynasty) but, through the intervention of the social democrats, left capitalist property intact. Throughout its existence, which ended with the Nazi takeover in 1933, the Weimar Republic was wracked by extreme social, economic and political instability.

31 The last part of the sentence ("as a means of mobilizing the masses against fascism") did not appear in the 1938 Russian draft.

32 In 1928 the Stalinized Comintern proclaimed that post-World War I capitalism had entered its third and final phase, and that the outbreak of socialist revolution was imminent. From 1928 (until the theory of the **"Third Period"** was finally abandoned in 1934) the Comintern instructed

of Catholics, Protestants, Jews, German nationalists, liberals—only in order to hide their own unattractive face. The Fourth International always and everywhere appears under its own banner. It proposes its own program openly to the proletariat in fascist countries. The advanced workers of all the world are already firmly convinced that the overthrow of Mussolini, Hitler and their agents and imitators will occur only under the leadership of the Fourth International.

The U.S.S.R. and Problems of the Transitional Epoch[33]

The Soviet Union emerged from the October Revolution as a workers' state. State ownership of the means of production, a necessary prerequisite to socialist development, opened up the possibility of rapid growth of the productive forces. But the apparatus of the workers' state underwent a complete degeneration at the same time; it was transformed from a weapon of the working class into a weapon of bureaucratic violence against the working class and more and more a weapon for the sabotage of the country's economy. The bureaucratization of a backward and isolated workers' state and the transformation of the bureaucracy into an all-powerful privileged caste is the most convincing refutation—not only theoretically but this time practically—of the theory of socialism in one country.

The U.S.S.R. thus embodies terrific contradictions. But it still remains a *degenerated workers' state*. Such is the social diagnosis. The political prognosis has an alternative character: either the bureaucracy, becoming ever more the organ of the world bourgeoisie in the workers' state, will overthrow the new forms of property and plunge the country back to capitalism; or the working class will crush the bureaucracy and open the way to socialism.

To the sections of the Fourth International, the Moscow Moscow Trials came not as a surprise and not as a result of the personal madness of the Kremlin dictator, but as the legitimate off-spring of the Thermidor. They grew out of the unbearable conflicts within the Soviet bureaucracy itself, which, in turn, mirror the contradictions between the bureaucracy and the people, as well as the deepening antagonisms among the "people" themselves. The bloody "fantastic" nature of the Moscow Trials gives the measure of the intensity of the contradictions and by the same token predicts the approach of the denouement.

The public utterances of former foreign representatives of the Kremlin, who refused to return to Moscow, irrefutably confirm in their own way that all shades of political thought are to be found among the bureaucracy: from

its sections to launch "red" unions alongside existing ones, and to refuse joint actions with Social Democrats or any other elements of the workers' movement, all of which were denounced as "social fascists." The Third-Period tactics of the Communists in Germany helped pave the way for the uncontested victory of the Nazis.

33 In the Russian draft this subhead reads: "The situation of the USSR and the tasks of the transitional epoch."

genuine Bolshevism (Ignace Reiss) to complete fascism (F. Butenko).[34] The revolutionary elements within the bureaucracy, only a small minority, reflect, passively it is true, the socialist interests of the proletariat. The fascist, counter-revolutionary elements, growing uninterruptedly, express with ever greater consistency the interests of world imperialism. These candidates for the role of *compradores* consider, not without reason, that the new ruling layer can insure their positions of privilege only through rejection of nationalization, collectivization and monopoly of foreign trade in the name of the assimilation of "Western civilization," i.e., capitalism. Between these two poles, there are intermediate, diffused Menshevik-S.R.-liberal tendencies which gravitate toward bourgeois democracy.

Within the very ranks of that so-called "classless" society, there unquestionably exist groupings exactly similar to those in the bureaucracy, only less sharply expressed and in inverse proportions: conscious capitalist tendencies distinguish mainly the prosperous part of the kolkhozes[35] and are characteristic of only a small minority of the population. But this layer provides itself with a wide base for petty bourgeois tendencies of accumulating personal wealth at the expense of general poverty, and are consciously encouraged by the bureaucracy.

Atop this system of mounting antagonisms, trespassing ever more on the social equilibrium, the Thermidorian oligarchy, today reduced mainly to Stalin's Bonapartist clique,[36] hangs on by terroristic methods. The latest judicial frame-ups were aimed as a blow *against the left*. This is true also of the mopping up of the leaders of the Right Opposition, because the right group of the old Bolshevik Party, seen from the viewpoint of the bureaucracy's interests and tendencies, represented a *left* danger. The fact that the Bonapartist clique, likewise in fear of its own right allies of the type of Butenko, is forced in the interests of self-preservation to execute the generation of Old Bolsheviks almost to a man, offers indisputable testimony of the vitality of revolutionary traditions among the masses as well as of their growing discontent.

Petty-bourgeois democrats of the West, having but yesterday assayed the Moscow Moscow Trials as unalloyed gold, today repeat insistently that there

34 **Ignace Reiss** was an important Soviet intelligence operative in Western Europe, who declared for Trotsky and the Fourth International in July 1937. Six weeks later he was murdered by Stalinist agents in Switzerland. In 1969 his widow, Elisabeth Poretsky, published an account of his life entitled *Our Own People*.

Fyodor Butenko was a young Soviet diplomat posted in Rumania who, in early 1938, defected to Mussolini's Italy where he issued a statement described by Trotsky as "semi-fascist" in character.

35 **Kolkhoze** is the Russian term for "collective farm."

36 **Bonapartism** is a term used to describe dictatorial regimes in which the state apparatus appears to operate independently of the ruling class because, "the warring classes balance each other so nearly that the state power, as ostensible mediator, acquires, for the moment, a certain degree of independence of both", (Frederick Engels, *Origin of the Family, Private Property and the State*). Trotsky's views on Stalin's Bonapartism and the relationship between the "dictatorship of the bureaucracy" and the "dictatorship of the proletariat" are put forward in "The Workers' State, Thermidor and Bonapartism" (1 February 1935).

is "neither Trotskyism nor Trotskyists within the U.S.S.R." They fail to explain, however, why all the purges are conducted under the banner of a struggle with precisely this danger. If we are to examine "Trotskyism" as a finished program, and, even more to the point, as an organization, then unquestionably "Trotskyism" is extremely weak in the U.S.S.R. However, its indestructible force stems from the fact that it expresses not only revolutionary tradition but also today's actual opposition of the Russian working class. The social hatred stored up by the workers against the bureaucracy—this is precisely what from the viewpoint of the Kremlin clique constitutes "Trotskyism." It fears with a deathly and thoroughly well-grounded fear the bond between the deep but inarticulate indignation of the workers and the organization of the Fourth International.

The execution of the generation of Old Bolsheviks and of the revolutionary representatives of the middle and young generations has yet more swung the political pendulum to the side of the right, the bourgeois wing of the bureaucracy and its allies throughout the land. From them, i.e., from the right, we can expect ever more determined attempts in the next period to revise the socialist character of the U.S.S.R. and bring it closer in pattern to "Western civilization" in its fascist form.

From this perspective, impelling concreteness is imparted to the question of the "defense of the U.S.S.R." If tomorrow the bourgeois-fascist grouping, the "fraction of Butenko," so to speak, should attempt the conquest of power, the "fraction of Reiss" inevitably would align itself on the opposite side of the barricades. Although it would find itself temporarily the ally of Stalin, it would nevertheless defend not the Bonapartist clique but the social base of the U.S.S.R., i.e., the property wrenched away from the capitalists and transformed into State property. Should the "fraction of Butenko" prove to be in alliance with Hitler, then the "fraction of Reiss" would defend the U.S.S.R. from military intervention, inside the country as well as on the world arena. Any other course would be a betrayal.

Although it is thus impermissible to deny in advance the possibility, in strictly defined instances, of a "united front" with the Thermidorian section of the bureaucracy against open attack by capitalist counter-revolution, the chief political task in the U.S.S.R. still remains the *overthrow of this same Thermidorian bureaucracy*. Each day added to its domination helps rot the foundations of the socialist elements of [the] economy and increases the chances for capitalist restoration. It is in precisely this direction that the Comintern moves as the agent and accomplice of the Stalinist clique in strangling the Spanish revolution and demoralizing the international proletariat.

As in fascist countries, the chief strength of the bureaucracy lies not in itself but in the disillusionment of the masses, in their lack of a new perspective. As in fascist countries, from which Stalin's *political* apparatus does not differ save in more unbridled rough-shoddedness, only preparatory propagandistic work is possible today in the U.S.S.R. As in fascist countries, the impetus to the Soviet workers' revolutionary upsurge will probably be given by events outside the country. The struggle against the Comintern on the world arena is the most important part today of the struggle against the Stalinist dictatorship. There are many signs that the Comintern's downfall, because it does not have a *direct* base in the G.P.U., will precede the downfall of the Bonapartist clique and the entire Thermidorian bureaucracy in general.

* * *

A fresh upsurge of the revolution in the U.S.S.R. will undoubtedly begin under the banner of the struggle against *social inequality* and *political oppression*. Down with the privileges of the bureaucracy! Down with Stakhanovism![37] Down with the Soviet aristocracy and its ranks and orders! Greater equality of wages for all forms of labor!

The struggle for the freedom of the trade unions and the factory committees, for the right of assembly and freedom of the press will unfold in the struggle for the regeneration and development of *Soviet democracy*.

The bureaucracy replaced the soviets as class organs with the fiction of universal electoral rights—in the style of Hitler-Goebbels. It is necessary to return to the soviets not only their free democratic form but also their class content. As once the bourgeoisie and kulaks were not permitted to enter the soviets, so now *it is necessary to drive the bureaucracy and the new aristocracy out of the soviets*. In the soviets there is room only for representatives of the workers, rank and file kolkhozists, peasants and Red Army men.

Democratization of the soviets is impossible without *legalization of soviet parties*. The workers and peasants themselves by their own free vote will indicate what parties they recognize as soviet parties.

A revision of *planned economy* from top to bottom in the interests of producers and consumers! Factory committees should be returned the right to control production. A democratically organized consumers' cooperative should control the quality and price of products.

Reorganization of the *kolkhozes* in accordance with the will and in the interests of the workers there engaged!

The reactionary *international policy* of the bureaucracy should be replaced by the policy of proletarian internationalism. The complete diplomatic correspondence of the Kremlin to be published. *Down with secret diplomacy!*

All political Moscow Trials, staged by the Thermidorian bureaucracy, to be reviewed in the light of complete publicity and controversial openness and integrity.[38] Only the victorious revolutionary uprising of the oppressed masses can revive the Soviet regime and guarantee its further development toward

37 **Stakhanovism** was a speed-up movement introduced by the Stalinist bureaucracy in 1935, named after Alexi Stakhanov, a "model" coal miner. Selected workers, in optimal circumstances (sometimes including assistants), achieved exceptional results which were used to set new (higher) production norms.

38 The Russian draft includes the following: "The organizers of the forgeries must bear the punishment they deserve. It is impossible to put this program into practice without overthrowing the bureaucracy, which maintains itself through violence and forgery."

socialism. There is but one party capable of leading the Soviet masses to insurrection—the party of the Fourth International!

Down with the bureaucratic gang of Cain-Stalin!
Long live Soviet Democracy!
Long live the international socialist revolution!

Against Opportunism and Unprincipled Revisionism

The politics of Leon Blum's party in France demonstrate anew that reformists are incapable of learning anything from even the most tragic lessons of history. French Social-Democracy slavishly copies the politics of German Social-Democracy and goes to meet the same end. Within a few decades the Second International intertwined itself with the bourgeois democratic regime, became, in fact, a part of it, and is rotting away together with it.

The Third International has taken to the road of reformism at a time when the crisis of capitalism definitely placed the proletarian revolution on the order of the day. The Comintern's policy in Spain and China today—the policy of cringing before the "democratic" and "national" bourgeoisie—demonstrates that the Comintern is likewise incapable of learning anything further or of changing. The bureaucracy which became a reactionary force in the U.S.S.R. cannot play a revolutionary role on the world arena.

Anarcho-syndicalism in general has passed through the same kind of evolution. In France, the syndicalist bureaucracy of Leon Jouhaux[39] has long since become a bourgeois agency in the working class. In Spain, anarcho-syndicalism shook off its ostensible revolutionism and became the fifth wheel in the chariot of bourgeois democracy.

Intermediate centrist organizations centered about the London Bureau,[40] represent merely "left" appendages of Social Democracy or of the Comintern. They have displayed a complete inability to make head or tail of the political situation and draw revolutionary conclusions from it. Their highest point

39 **Leon Jouhaux**, general secretary of the French CGT (General Confederation of Labor), supported French imperialism in both world wars. After World War II, he led the anti-communist split from the CGT that produced *Force Ouvrière*.

40 The **London Bureau** originated in 1932 as the International Labor Community (IAG), an international confederation of left social democrats. In 1935 it was renamed the "International Bureau of Revolutionary Socialist Parties." In 1938 it included the Spanish POUM (Workers Party of Marxist Unification), the German SAP (Socialist Workers Party), the British ILP (Independent Labour Party), Jay Lovestone's American Independent Labor League, Heinrich Brandler's German KPO (Communist Party Opposition) and Marceau Pivert's French PSOP (Workers and Peasants Socialist Party). The "revolutionary socialists" of the London Bureau opposed the creation of the Fourth International, and aspired to little more than pressuring the social democracy and the Stalinists.

The London Bureau was a typically "centrist" formation: dismissive of the "sectarianism" of the Fourth International, it combined sometimes leftish criticisms with a refusal to clearly break from the fundamental conceptions of reformism. As Trotsky observed in his March 1934 article "Centrism and the Fourth International":

> "A centrist occupies a position between an opportunist and a Marxist somewhat analogous to that which a petty bourgeois occupies between a capitalist and a proletarian: he kowtows before the first and has contempt for the second."

was the Spanish P.O.U.M.,[41] which under revolutionary conditions proved completely incapable of following a revolutionary line.

* * *

The tragic defeats suffered by the world proletariat over a long period of years doomed the official organizations to yet greater conservatism and simultaneously sent disillusioned petty bourgeois "revolutionists" in pursuit of "new ways."[42] As always during epochs of reaction and decay, quacks and charlatans appear on all sides, desirous of revising the whole course of revolutionary thought. Instead of learning from the past, they "reject" it. Some discover the inconsistency of Marxism, others announce the downfall of Bolshevism. There are those who put responsibility upon revolutionary doctrine for the mistakes and crimes of those who betrayed it; others who curse the medicine because it does not guarantee an instantaneous and miraculous cure. The more daring promise to discover a panacea and, in anticipation, recommend the halting of the class struggle. A good many prophets of "new morals" are preparing to regenerate the labor movement with the help of ethical homeopathy. The majority of these apostles have succeeded in becoming themselves moral invalids before arriving on the field of battle. Thus, under the aspect of "new ways[,]" old recipes, long since buried in the archives of pre-Marxian socialism, are offered to the proletariat.

The Fourth International declares uncompromising war on the bureaucracies of the Second, Third, Amsterdam and Anarcho-Syndicalist Internationals,[43] as on their centrist satellites; on reformism without reforms; democracy in alliance with the G.P.U.; pacifism without peace; anarchism in the service of the bourgeoisie; on "revolutionists" who live in deathly fear of revolution. All of these organizations are not pledges for the future but decayed survivals of the past. The epoch of wars and revolutions will raze them to the ground.

The Fourth International does not search after and does not invent panaceas. It takes its stand completely on Marxism as the only revolutionary doctrine that enables one to understand reality; unearth the cause behind the defeats and consciously prepare for victory. The Fourth International continues the tradition of Bolshevism which first showed the proletariat how to conquer power. The Fourth International sweeps away the quacks, charlatans

41 The **POUM** (Workers Party of Marxist Unification) was founded in Spain in 1935 as a fusion between the Communist Left (former Spanish Trotskyists led by Andres Nin) and the Workers' and Peasants' Bloc led by Joaquin Maurin. Trotsky bitterly opposed this unification, as the politics of the Maurin group were much closer to Nicolai Bukharin's Right Opposition than to the Left Opposition. During the Spanish Civil War, the centrist POUM, which began by half-heartedly criticizing the class-collaborationist popular front, ended up joining it. This did not prevent the Stalinists from subsequently smashing the POUM and murdering Nin.

42 Here, and at the end of the paragraph, "new ways" appeared as "new words" in the Russian draft.

43 The **Anarcho-Syndicalist International** (also known as the International Workingmen's Association) was an organization of anarcho-syndicalist trade unions. Founded in Berlin in 1922, its most important member was the Spanish CNT, but it also had sizeable affiliates in Argentina, Germany, Italy and Portugal.

and unsolicited teachers of morals. In a society based upon exploitation, the highest moral is that of the social revolution. All methods are good which raise the class consciousness of the workers, their trust in their own forces, their readiness for self-sacrifice in the struggle. The impermissible methods are those which implant fear and submissiveness in the oppressed before their oppressors, which crush the spirit of protest and indignation or substitute for the will of the masses the will of the leaders; for conviction—compulsion; for an analysis of reality—demagogy and frame-up. That is why Social Democracy, prostituting Marxism, and Stalinism—the antithesis of Bolshevism—are both mortal enemies of the proletarian revolution and its morals.

To face reality squarely; not to seek the line of least resistance; to call things by their right names; to speak the truth to the masses—no matter how bitter it may be; not to fear obstacles; to be true in little things as in big ones; to base one's program on the logic of the class struggle;[44] to be bold when the hour for action arrives—these are the rules of the Fourth International. It has shown that it could swim against the stream. The approaching historical wave will raise it on its crest.

Against Sectarianism

Under the influence of the betrayal by the historic organizations of the proletariat, certain sectarian moods and groupings of various kinds arise or are regenerated at the periphery of the Fourth International. At their base lies a refusal to struggle for partial and transitional demands, i.e., for the elementary interests and needs of the working masses, as they are today. Preparing for the revolution means to the sectarians the convincing of themselves of the superiority of socialism. They propose turning their backs to the "old" trade unions, i.e., to tens of millions of organized workers, as if the masses could somehow live outside of the conditions of the actual class struggle! They remain indifferent to the inner struggle within reformist organizations—as if one could win the masses without intervening in their daily strife! They refuse to draw a distinction between bourgeois democracy and fascism—as if the masses could help but feel the difference on every hand!

Sectarians are capable of differentiating between but two colors: red and black. So as not to tempt themselves, they simplify reality. They refuse to draw a distinction between the fighting camps in Spain for the reason that both camps have a bourgeois character. For the same reason they consider it necessary to preserve "neutrality" in the war between Japan and China.[45] They deny the principled difference between the U.S.S.R. and the imperialist countries, and because of the reactionary policies of the Soviet bureaucracy

44 The Russian draft reads, "to base oneself on the logic of the class struggle."

45 The **war between Japan and China** began in September 1931 when Japanese troops invaded Manchuria in north-eastern China, and established a puppet state there. Japan's imperialist aggression against China continued throughout the 1930s and during World War II. It was marked by brutal massacres of civilians, the most infamous of which was the "Rape of Nanking" in 1937, in which some 300,000 people were murdered.

they reject defense of the new forms of property created by the October Revolution against the onslaughts of imperialism. Incapable of finding access to the masses, they therefore zealously accuse the masses of inability to raise themselves to revolutionary ideas.

These sterile politicians generally have no need of a bridge in the form of transitional demands because they do not intend to cross over to the other shore. They simply dawdle in one place, satisfying themselves with a repetition of the self-same meager abstractions. Political events are for them an occasion for comment but not for action. Since sectarians, as in general every kind of blunderer and miracle-man, are toppled by reality at each step, they live in a state of perpetual exasperation, complaining about the "regime" and "the methods" and ceaselessly wallowing in small intrigues. In their own circles they customarily carry on a regime of despotism. The political prostration of sectarianism serves to complement shadow-like the prostration of opportunism, revealing no revolutionary vistas. In practical politics, sectarians unite with opportunists, particularly with centrists, every time in the struggle against Marxism.

Most of the sectarian groups and cliques, nourished on accidental crumbs from the table of the Fourth International, lead an "independent" organizational existence, with great pretensions but without the least chance for success. Bolshevik-Leninists, without waste of time, calmly leave these groups to their own fate. However, sectarian tendencies are to be found also in our own ranks and display a ruinous influence on the work of the individual sections. It is impossible to make any further compromise with them even for a single day. A correct policy regarding trade unions is a basic condition for adherence to the Fourth International. He who does not seek and does not find the road to the masses is not a fighter but a dead weight to the party. A program is formulated not for the editorial board or for the leaders of discussion clubs but for the revolutionary action of millions. The cleansing of the ranks of the Fourth International of sectarianism and incurable sectarians is a primary condition for revolutionary success.

The Road to the Woman-Worker—The Road to the Youth[46]

The defeat of the Spanish revolution, engineered by its "leaders;" the shameful bankruptcy of the People's Front in France and the exposure of the Moscow juridical swindles—these three facts in their aggregate deal an irreparable blow to the Comintern and, incidentally, grave wounds to its allies: the Social-Democrats and Anarcho-Syndicalists. This does not mean, of course, that the members of these organizations will immediately turn to the Fourth International. The older generation, having suffered terrible defeats, will leave the movement in significant numbers. In addition, the Fourth Interna-

46 In both the 1938 and 1939 SWP versions this subhead reads: "The Road to the Woman-Worker—The Road to the Youth," but in the 1946 and subsequent editions (and the Russian draft) it reads: "Open the Road to the Woman-Worker! Open the Road to the Youth!"

tional is certainly not striving to become an asylum for revolutionary invalids, disillusioned bureaucrats and careerists. On the contrary, against a possible influx into our party of petty bourgeois elements, now reigning in the apparatus of the old organizations, strict preventive measures are necessary: a prolonged probationary period for those candidates who are not workers, especially former party bureaucrats; prevention from holding any responsible post for the first three years, etc. There is not and there will not be any place for careerism, the ulcer of the old Internationals, in the Fourth International. Only those who wish to live for the movement, and not at the expense of the movement, will find access to us. The revolutionary workers should feel themselves to be the masters. The doors of our organization are wide open to them.

Of course, even among the workers who had at one time risen to the first ranks, there are not a few tired and disillusioned ones. They will remain, at least for the next period, as by-standers. When a program or an organization wears out, the generation which carried it on its shoulders wears out with it. The movement is revitalized by the youth who are free of responsibility for the past. The Fourth International pays particular attention to the young generation of the proletariat. All of its policies strive to inspire the youth with belief in its own strength and in the future. Only the fresh enthusiasm and aggressive spirit of the youth can guarantee the preliminary successes in the struggle; only these successes can return the best elements of the older generation to the road of revolution. Thus it was, thus it will be.

Opportunist organizations by their very nature concentrate their chief attention on the top layers of the working class and therefore ignore both the youth and the woman-worker. The decay of capitalism, however, deals its heaviest blows to the woman as a wage-earner and as a housewife. The sections of the Fourth International should seek bases of support among the most exploited layers of the working class; consequently, among the women-workers. Here they will find inexhaustible stores of devotion, selflessness and readiness to sacrifice.

Down with the bureaucracy and careerism! Open the road to the youth! Turn to the woman-worker! These slogans are emblazoned on the banner of the Fourth International. *Under the banner of the Fourth International!*

Sceptics ask: but has the moment for the creation of the Fourth International[47] yet arrived? It is impossible, they say, to create an International "artificially;" it can only arise out of great events, etc., etc. All of these objections merely show that the sceptics are not good for the building of a new International. They are good for scarcely anything at all.

The Fourth International has already arisen out of great events: the greatest defeats of the proletariat in history. The cause for these defeats is to be found in the degeneration and perfidy of the old leadership. The class strug-

47 Instead of "the Fourth International," the Russian draft reads "a new international."

gle does not tolerate an interruption. The Third International, following the Second, is dead for purposes of revolution. Long live the Fourth International!

But has the time yet arrived to proclaim its creation?...the sceptics are not quieted down. The Fourth International, we answer, has no need of being "proclaimed." It exists and it fights. Is it weak? Yes, its ranks are not numerous because it is still young. They are as yet chiefly cadres. But these cadres are pledges for the future. Outside of these cadres there does not exist a single revolutionary current on this planet really meriting the name. If our International be still weak in numbers, it is strong in doctrine, program, tradition, in the incomparable tempering of its cadres. Who does not perceive this today, let him in the meantime stand aside. Tomorrow it will become more evident.

The Fourth International, already today, is deservedly hated by the Stalinists, [s]ocial-democrats, bourgeois liberals and fascists. There is not and there cannot be a place for it in any of the People's Fronts. It uncompromisingly gives battle to all political groupings tied to the apron-strings of the bourgeoisie. Its task—the abolition of capitalism's domination. Its aim—socialism. Its method—the proletarian revolution.

Without inner democracy—no revolutionary education. Without discipline—no revolutionary action. The inner structure of the Fourth International is based on the principles of *democratic centralism*; full freedom in discussion, complete unity in action.

The present crisis in human culture is the crisis in the proletarian leadership. The advanced workers, united in the Fourth International, show their class the way of exit out of the crisis. They offer a program based on international experience in the struggle of the proletariat and of all the oppressed of the world[48] for liberation. They offer a spotless banner.

Workers—men and women—of all countries, place yourselves under the banner of the Fourth International. It is the banner of your approaching victory!

48 The Russian draft substitutes "in general" for "of the world."

Part Two

Revolutionary Work in the American Labor Movement: 1920s–1950s

Program for Power: Early Communist Work in the Trade Unions

By Chris Knox. Reprinted from Workers Vanguard *No. 22, 8 June 1973*

Opportunists denounce the Spartacist League as "sectarian" for our insistence that only a full transitional program can properly orient the struggle in the trade unions against the union bureaucracy and against capitalism. In its 16 April *Bulletin*, for instance, the pseudo-Trotskyist Workers League denounces Spartacist in a frenzied front page editorial:

> "Spartacist says essentially the following about the struggle in auto. Wages, line speed, job security, grievances, and the right to strike are all trade union demands. But Marxists, at least according to Spartacist, are for revolution *as opposed to* winning these 'reformist' demands. Spartacist therefore concludes that the basic demand that must be made is: 'Communism!' Nothing less will satisfy these ferocious blabber mouths." [emphasis ours]

This gross distortion of our position appeared as part of a defense of the auto program of the Trade Union Alliance for a Labor Party (TUALP), the latest organizational embodiment of the WL's program for the unions. This auto program consists solely of points on wages, job security, speedup, grievances, workers rights, overtime, pensions, health, safety and vacations. It thus totally omits not only the labor party (!), but any reference to racial or sexual discrimination, economic protectionism, war, or the question of power (the slogans of workers control and a workers government), all of which directly affect the unions in the epoch of imperialism. The WL defense rests its case with the assertion that "simple trade union demands" are "profoundly revolutionary".

The Workers League is merely one example—and certainly not the most organizationally significant example—of the pervasive opportunism of the U.S. left today, which passively caves in to trade-union economism and workerism, i.e., the worship of the present level of the class struggle.

The Trotskyist "Transitional Program," adopted in 1938 at the founding conference of the Fourth International, was presented by Trotsky as a program for the trade unions. It was designed to provide not "opposition" to reform demands, as the WL alleges, but a *bridge* between the day-to-day trade-union struggles and the revolutionary goals of the proletariat. The program included demands for a sliding scale of wages and hours to combat unemployment; for factory committees, workers control and expropriation of industry and banks; for struggle against discrimination against minorities and against imperialist war; and, most importantly, for a clear expression of the goal of working-class power: for soviets and a workers government.

Apologists for Reformism

Like the WL, the International Socialists claim to agree with the Transitional Program, but find the SL "sectarian" and "revolutionary posturers" for applying it to the present-day situation in the unions. The WL justifies its position that trade-union demands are "revolutionary" on the grounds of the intensity of the capitalist crisis, which it claims makes even minimal demands impossible to attain under capitalism. The IS, in contrast, defends its accommodation to economism on the grounds that the crisis isn't intense *enough*: when the class struggle is at a higher level, "then" the full Transitional Program will be "relevant." By these two mutually exclusive rationales, both groups arrive at the same position of rejection of the Transitional Program in practice! They are joined in this conclusion by the other ostensibly "Trotskyist" tendencies, each travelling its own variation on these two paths: the minuscule Spark group, the Class Struggle League and, of course, the Socialist Workers Party. The SWP, in its total abandonment of its Trotskyist heritage, has developed particularly odious "transitional" bridges to feminism, black nationalism, youth culture, etc., while ignoring, for the most part, work in the trade unions (or conducting it on the most minimal basis, avoiding all opposition to the trade-union bureaucracy).

The abandonment of the Transitional Program in practice is nothing more nor less than a return to the flawed conceptions which preceded both the Fourth and Third Internationals, i.e., to the old social-democratic conception of "minimum" and "maximum" program: the first for day-to-day issues, the second for Sunday speech-making about "socialism." The social-democratic trade-union bureaucracy opposed any intrusion of the "maximum" program into the "real" work of the party. It is thus quite natural that for these supposed "Trotskyists" of today, the Transitional Program has taken on the character of a "maximum" program, the intrusion of which into their "real" practice would upset the opportunism which is possible only on the basis of their minimum program.

Having thus come together in opposition to the Transitional Program in practice, it is equally natural that the ostensible "Trotskyists" find themselves rubbing shoulders with the Maoists and Stalinists of all varieties, particularly the Communist Party, which long ago abandoned the program of Lenin and Trotsky for a return to a reformist practice totally consistent with its overall strategy of forming broad blocs between the labor movement and the liberal bourgeoisie (the "popular front"). Thus the United National Caucus in the auto union, a trade-unionist, bureaucratic-careerist group, is a typical catchall supported by the CP, IS and CSL particularly. Even the frenzied National Caucus of Labor Committees, which claims to reject trade unionism altogether, can be found in UNC meetings alongside CP supporters pushing the same pop frontist, liberal politics with a different organizational format. That the WL politically belongs in the UNC is clear not only from its auto program, but from its absurdly sectarian reason for avoiding endorsement: that the UNC doesn't fight hard enough for wages!

International Communist Strategy

The Spartacist League alone stands not only on the Transitional Program as formulated by Trotsky, but on its antecedents as developed by the first four congresses of the Communist International (CI) and carried out (not without errors) by CI sections during its revolutionary period through 1923. The trade-union work of the Workers (Communist) Party of the U.S., particularly through its trade-union arm, the Trade Union Educational League (TUEL), provides an example of communist work in the unions with tremendous relevance for today.

At once the reformists of all varieties will exclaim, "But that was a different period, one in which revolution was seen as the order of the day by masses of workers!" The period was indeed different, but the tasks of the communists in the trade unions were not so different as the opportunists rush to assume. The Third Congress of the CI directed that:

> "In the United States of North America..., the communists are confronted with the first and simplest task of creating a communist nucleus and connecting it with the working masses."
>
> —"Thesis on Tactics," *Theses and Resolutions adopted at the Third World Congress of the Communist International*, June 22–July 12, 1921

While the level of strike activity and general class consciousness was higher, the vanguard party in the U.S. was still a very small force facing a reactionary bureaucracy in the trade unions which it had to expose and replace in order to gain the confidence and leadership of the workers.

This situation was typical throughout the CI, despite the fact that most of the European parties were much larger than the American section and therefore in a better position to gain hegemony of class leadership. Through lack of preparation, and without an experienced cadre and leadership, the Communist Parties were unable to take advantage of the massive post-war revolutionary wave, which peaked during 1919–1920 in Europe and America. Lenin wrote *"Left-wing" Communism, An Infantile Disorder* in 1920 precisely to combat tendencies which saw the revolution as inevitable and opposed work in the unions or for partial demands as "opportunist." The Second and Third Congresses of the CI (1920 and 1921) fought for the utilization of all arenas and all methods of struggle in order to deepen connections with the masses and combat the false leaders of the workers. By the Fourth Congress (1922) Lenin and Trotsky were continuing this effort with a proposal for the tactic of united fronts with Social Democrats and others in order to demonstrate to the workers that only the Communists were for a genuine class front against the bourgeoisie on the basis of consistent struggle for all the workers' interests, including immediate interests. Lenin and Trotsky were prepared to force a split with all those "ultra-leftists" who still considered such a course opportunist.

The work of the TUEL in the 1922–23 period was an expression in the U.S. of the "united front" tactics Lenin and Trotsky were urging throughout the CI. These tactics were seen as necessary precisely because the revolutionary wave had *ebbed*, and the Communist Parties were not in a position to exercise leadership of the working class immediately. The trade-union work of the Workers (Communist) Party was undertaken on the basis of the defeat in factional struggle of the ultra-leftists who urged "dual unionism" i.e., opposition to any work in the dominant, reactionary American Federation of Labor (AFL)—and underground work on principle, thereby avoiding all contact with partial demands and the mass movement itself. (The ultra-leftists had been largely responsible for the failure to seize the opportunities of 1919–1920.)

Origins of the TUEL

The TUEL was not simply a creation of the W(C)P, but was taken over by it in 1922 as the result of a fusion with William Z. Foster's group of Chicago-based trade-union militants. While the bulk of the left in the preceding epoch had been ardently dual unionist, Foster had become convinced that this strategy was sterile and in effect surrendered the fight for leadership of the organized workers to their reactionary, craft leaderships. But Foster bent the stick too far the other way, and was willing to surrender his political program in order to remain in a position to apply pressure to the Gompers bureaucracy to support his organizing drives. Thus in 1919, when called before a Senate investigating committee looking into the steel strike Foster was organizing, Foster dropped his entire political program, ardently avowing his patriotism and his selling of Liberty Bonds during the war.

From Foster's side, the fusion with the W(C)P was based on his agreement with Lenin's "boring from within" tactic, an explicit reversal for the U.S. Communists. Foster continued to lead the TUEL and became the head of the party's trade-union work. Thus if anything, one would expect to find in the TUEL of this period not sectarian errors, but opportunist ones, whether because of Foster's trade-unionist predilections or an over-zealous application of the CI's united-front line.

In general we find neither, however, though the W(C)P did make errors which affected its trade-union work. Under the leadership of the Party, the TUEL was re-founded in 1922 squarely on the basis of the program of the CI. Despite its emphasis on the "turn to the masses" and willingness to struggle for partial demands, the CI's program was clearly conceived of as *transitional*:

> *"The alternative offered by the Communist International in place of the minimum program of the reformists and centrists is: the struggle for the concrete need of the proletariat and demands, which, in their application, undermine the power of the bourgeoisie, organize the proletariat, for the transition to the proletarian dictatorship, even if the latter have not yet grasped the meaning of such proletarian dictatorship....*
>
> "In formulating their partial demands, the Communist Parties must take heed that these demands, based on the deeply rooted needs of the masses, are such as will organize the masses and not merely lead them into struggle. All concrete watchwords, originating in the economic needs of the workers, must be assimilated to the struggle for the control of production, which must not assume the form of a bureaucratic organization of social economy under capitalism, but of an organization fighting against capitalism through workers committees as well as through revolutionary trade unions." [emphasis in original]
>
> —"Thesis on Tactics"

The TUEL, while it conducted mass campaigns and made united-front alliances with sections of the trade-union bureaucracy around key individual issues, such as amalgamation of the craft unions into mass industrial unions, for recognition of Soviet Russia and for a labor party, *began* with its full program and propagandized for it throughout all its work.

In addition, unlike almost every trade-union caucus today—and certainly all those supported by the opportunist "Trotskyists" and other "revolutionaries"—the TUEL had a *political* conception of membership. In order to join, one had to have general agreement with the basic program, which was described and summarized in eight points in Foster's *Bankruptcy of the American Labor Movement* (*Labor Herald* Library, 1922). The first point was "abolish capitalism, for a workers republic":

> "The Trade Union Educational League proposes to develop the trade unions from their present antiquated and stagnant condition into modern, powerful labor organizations, capable of waging successful warfare against capital.... Instead of advocating the prevailing shameful and demoralizing nonsense about harmonizing the interests of capital and labor, it is firing the workers' imagination and releasing their wonderful idealism and energy by propagating the inspiring goal of abolition of capitalism and the establishment of a workers republic."

This was intended to be a transitional formulation for "dictatorship of the proletariat," in exactly the same way as Trotsky's call for a "Workers and Farmers Government" in the 1938 program. Throughout the program of the CI and its sections in this period, the concept of transitional demands is manifest: obviously they were not a later "invention" of Trotsky!

The second point in the TUEL program was, "Repudiate class collaborationism, for a class struggle policy." This was a general demand designed to sum up the entire alternate perspective to be presented to the reactionary AFL bureaucracy.

The third point was for affiliation of the unions to the Red International of Labor Unions (RILU), which was the international trade-union arm of the CI. Founded in 1922, the RILU provided an organizing pole for oppositionists in the established unions and for the many unions, often led by revolutionary syndicalists attracted to the banner of the Russian Revolution, which had been ruthlessly expelled from the established federations by Social Democrats and reformists.

The fourth point was "Support the Russian Revolution." The revolution, of course, had split the workers movement of the entire world between those who wanted to make revolution in their own countries and those who did not. Beyond this, however, the demand had specific connotations in campaigns conducted by the TUEL for aid to alleviate the famine, diplomatic recognition, etc.

Fifth was the demand for industrial unionism, which was the key trade-union issue, since the vast bulk of the industrial workers, including a disproportionately large section of the non-English-speaking immigrants, was unorganized. This demand counterposed masses of workers to the conservative, craft-based bureaucracy.

Sixth was "Combat dual unionism," which the TUEL was constantly forced to raise against the influence of other radicals, such as the Wobblies (IWW), who urged the abandonment of the struggle and set up dual unions every time the bureaucracy succeeded in a new outrage. The TUEL advocated an orientation toward work in the established unions even on the part of expelled locals or sections, with affiliation to RILU as a long-range alternative. The TUEL and RILU's call for trade-union unity, however, was never the "unity" of capitulation! RILU/TUEL insisted that expelled union bodies seek readmittance, but only on the basis of their freedom to continue propagandizing for class-struggle policies. (This contrasts sharply with the trade-union reformism of the Workers League, which advocated reunification of the breakaway Social Services Employees Union [SSEU] in New York with its AFL-CIO parent on the *bureaucracy's* sellout terms.)

Seventh was a demand for a shop delegate system. Shop floor representation was generally lacking in unions at the time. Finally, the eighth point was for independent working-class political action. This rapidly transformed itself into the demand for a labor party, which was then distorted by the W(C)P leadership into the campaign for the Farmer-Labor Party.

Blocs Based on Program

Thus the TUEL began with membership based on its full program, which was raised in all the unions in which it did work through its members and the monthly organ, Labor Herald. In addition, together with the W(C)P operating in its own name, the TUEL conducted broad campaigns around key demands such as recognition, amalgamation and a labor party, in which it entered united-front alliances with sections of the trade-union bureaucracy such as the Fitzpatrick/Nockels/Brown leadership of the Chicago Federation of Labor

(CFL). The issues on which the TUEL made united-front alliances were key parts of the TUEL program around which masses of workers could be mobilized in opposition to the bulk of the bureaucracy. With the exception of the bloc with Fitzpatrick's Farmer-Labor Party, they were not political compromises, but points on which sections of the bureaucracy were forced to come over to the Communists, which tended to build Communist leadership of the mass movement. Thus after a year of working on the amalgamation campaign (which Foster had gotten approved by the CFL without even bothering to consult Fitzpatrick beforehand), the W(C)P's forces dramatically outnumbered Fitzpatrick's at the 1923 Chicago convention of the Farmer-Labor Party. Furthermore, the issues on which the Communists made blocs tended to reinforce each other, creating a vast political gulf between the party's allies and the rest of the trade-union bureaucracy. Thus Fitzpatrick, who supported recognition, amalgamation and a labor party, was cut off financially by the AFL bureaucracy and denounced as a Communist "dupe" by Gompers.

One serious criticism modifies this perspective, however. Despite the W(C)P's initial call for a labor party as a "class party" with "the abolition of wage slavery, the establishment of a workers republic and a collectivist system of production" (*For a Labor Party*, a statement by the Workers Party, October 1922), as its goals, the Pepper/Lovestone leadership failed to carry out this line consistently: the Farmer-Labor campaign into which they took the party was flawed. Besides approaching the program of the proposed party as though it has to be reformist, thereby capitulating in advance to the trade-union bureaucracy (see *WV* No. 13, November 1972), they failed to recognize the contradiction of the F-LP as a hopeless attempt to combine in one party the class interests of two classes: the working class and a section of the petty bourgeoisie. This error was compounded later, after the split with Fitzpatrick at the 1923 convention, into further errors, for which the CI had to call Pepper/Lovestone to task. Instead of simply entering Fitzpatrick's F-LP, the Communists should have held out the single-class party issue as their condition for support, while continuing to bloc with Fitzpatrick on other issues.

In addition, other, less serious criticisms can be made of the party and its trade-union work during this period, but they do not change our overall assessment of the work in 1922–23 as exemplary. If the TUEL had succeeded in taking over the AFL on the basis of its program and united-front alliances, the AFL would have been in the hands of revolutionary leadership. Further political struggle and clarification—even splits—would no doubt have been necessary, but only to prevent political retreat, not to establish the basic revolutionary beachhead.

Union Elections

Foster's chief strategy for union elections was to make blocs with trade-union allies rather than simply running TUEL candidates. But support was generally made on the basis of the TUEL program. Thus Ross Knudsen, backed by TUEL for president of the Machinists union in 1922, won 30% of the votes on the basis of supporting RILU, industrial unionism and the call for a workers republic. The TUEL did not support intra-bureaucratic rivalries or careerists limiting their programs to "better" unionism. It blocked with and gave critical support to other elements only on the basis of qualitative *political* counterposition to the pro-capitalist bureaucracy as such.

The test of a correct united front or bloc is that the issues upon which it is based would have to be *abandoned* before any reintegration into the mainstream of the trade-union bureaucracy is possible. All bureaucrats, at all times, are for "trade-union democracy," but when Fitzpatrick split with the Communists in 1923, in order to go back to Gompers, he had to *reverse* himself on everything he had been saying previously, opposing amalgamation, Soviet recognition and independent working-class politics. This he did with a vengeance throughout the labor movement, becoming a virulent anti-communist and aid to Gompers' reactionary drive.

This drive gained momentum as prosperity and relative capitalist stabilization set in after 1923. The break with Fitzpatrick left the Communists without substantial allies in the labor movement. The TUEL had grown explosively, as had the W(C)P, especially during 1922, but the ranks lacked an experienced cadre to hold them together, and the party, having let the earlier wave of mass upsurge pass it by, was not firmly rooted in the workers movement. The TUEL was branded a "dual union" and virtually driven underground by the end of 1924 through a wave of expulsions of its militants from the unions.

Stalinism Perverts the TUEL

In 1923, with the illness of Lenin and the defeat of the abortive revolution in Germany, a triumvirate of Kamenev, Zinoviev and Stalin took political control in the Soviet Union and began to twist the CI into an agent of the foreign policy of the new Soviet bureaucracy. This turned the trade-union work of the Communist Parties, as it did all other political questions, into footballs for unprincipled factional warfare in which *renunciation* of previously-held views became the standard for acceptance by the international leadership. Thus the Passaic strike of 1926, which was led by Communists, was at first backed by the Ruthenberg leadership of the party as a factional ploy directed against Foster and the TUEL, but it was dropped later by all factions when a shift in the line of the CI to the right (Stalin's first move against the "left" leaning Zinoviev) indicated a revival of work through the TUEL rather than directly by the Communist Party.

The TUEL was continued by the CP until 1928 (when it was transformed into a "third period" dual-unionist organization). During the late 1920's, the program of the TUEL degenerated, under the influence of the new leadership of the CI, into one which turned the united-front *tactic* into a *strategy*. As dictated by an Executive Committee of the CI (ECCI) resolution on the American question in 1927, the TUEL program was to consist of five watered down points: organize the unorganized, for trade-union democracy, amalgamation, a labor party and "an aggressive struggle against the capitalists." The resolution called, in effect, for bringing "all progressives willing to fight against the policies of the reactionaries" into the TUEL. The dividing line between the TUEL member and the temporary ally was completely obliterated.

In order to cover up this obliteration and firm up the Stalinist conception of the left-center coalition as a permanent strategy, Foster purposefully blurred the original distinction in his later writings (Foster, *American Trade Unionism*, 1947). In order to do this, he relied on his earlier references to the TUEL as a united front (one of which was quoted, unfortunately without comment, in *WV* No. 18, April 1973). The TUEL had not *been*, in fact, a united front, but a membership organization of Communist trade unionists and others designed to bring the Communist program into the trade unions. It *carried out* united-front alliances with other elements. As such it was politically identical to trade-union caucuses supported by the Spartacist League today, though organizationally pan-union instead of limited to a particular union.

A united front, on the other hand, is a bloc on the basis of the immediate interests of the workers, designed to unite the working class as a whole against the capitalists. While the united front can take many forms (a temporary alliance, a trade union, or, at the highest stage, a soviet), in no case is it the same as, or a substitute for, the intervention of the vanguard party with its program into the workers movement. This is precisely the distinction that Foster and the Stalinist Communist Party blurred over. Foster tried to give the impression that the entire program of the TUEL had always been to bloc with "progressives" around the demands of the big campaigns, and equated the functioning of the W(C)P and TUEL in the 1922–24 period with the functioning of his earlier independent group of trade-union militants:

> "The organized forces behind this big TUEL movement [1922 campaigns] took the form of a broad united front of left wingers and progressives. The Communist Party and the TUEL were the driving left-wing forces, while the progressives, chiefly the Fitzpatrick-Nockels Farmer-Labor Party group, co-operated sympathetically. It was essentially a continuation and growth of the combination that had carried through the packinghouse and steel campaigns."
>
> —*From Bryan to Stalin*, 1936

Thus Foster's conclusion was that there was no difference between a bloc which dropped the political program in order to appease the most reactionary elements and a bloc based on a section of the program of the CI, while the full program was simultaneously carried into the unions by the TUEL itself throughout the duration of the bloc. What this meant for CP trade-union work after the Stalinist degeneration was obvious: get the best bloc you can, but bloc at any price.

For a Political Alternative

The CP's turn to dual unionism in 1928 was a betrayal which not only pulled the rug out completely from under the bulk of its trade-union work at the time, but also helped ensure that reactionary reformists—such as John L. Lewis of the UMW—would retain leadership of the labor movement through the period of organization of the mass of unskilled workers. Foster fully endorsed not only this turn but every subsequent betrayal of the CP, including the World War II no-strike pledge.

When Lewis and others organized the CIO—precisely to prevent the rise of revolutionary leadership!—an important change took place in the manner of capitalist rule and labor discipline. Strikes which earlier would have been met with police, troops, shootings and jailings were now dealt with through the mediation of the trade-union bureaucracy, which guaranteed labor discipline in return for periodic favors.

The CIO drive took trade unionism to its limits in its ability to solve outstanding social questions such as unemployment and made the need for a working-class *political* perspective more obviously necessary. The CIO bureaucrats and their CP allies therefore had the task of heading off and tying to the bourgeoisie the incipient political motion of the workers, which arose at this time chiefly in the form of a movement for a labor party. This they did through passing off a class-collaborationist bloc with the liberal bourgeoisie (the "popular front") as a "working-class" strategy. The bureaucracy's task of betrayal was completed through the subordination of the unions to the imperialist Second World War in exchange for increased recognition by the companies and the government.

Since the basic trade-union tasks were thus accomplished under reformist leadership, the main organizational task of the revolutionists in the trade unions changed from that of providing revolutionary leadership in trade-union struggles—as the Trotskyists had exemplified in the Minneapolis strikes of 1934—to that of providing a *political* alternative to the reformist bureaucracy. This was recognized by Trotsky in his codification of the Transitional Program in 1938.

If this was true in the late 1930's, now more than ever the character of the period requires a full political program in the trade unions. The important difference from earlier periods is not the subjective factors such as lower consciousness—the fruits of past defeats and betrayals—but the *objective* condition that trade unionism *must* be either the direct tool of capitalist imperialism in its new drive to discipline the work force for international competition and new wars, or the revolutionary instrument of the international proletariat. There can be no middle road between these alternatives, as Trotsky insisted in "Trade Unions in the Epoch of Imperialist Decay" (1940).

The line is drawn ever more sharply: individual unions are less and less able to cope with the problems that confront them (inflation, layoffs, national and international corporate migration, etc.), all of which are determined by the global relationship of class forces and inter-imperialist rivalries. Yet precisely because of this contradiction union leaderships are more and more dependent on outside political forces. For any trade-union leader or would be leader who bases himself on anything less than the program and struggle of the international proletariat, there is very quickly no alternative other than reliance on a section of the liberal bourgeoisie.

The only alternative to the capitulation to imperialism which this necessarily entails is the viewpoint of the international proletariat, and this is expressed only by the Transitional Program and the effort to rebuild the Trotskyist world vanguard party. Thus only a leadership based on the full Transitional Program can be fully prepared to meet all questions and turn the unions from the disciplinary agents of an ever predatory imperialism into true weapons of the working class in its international struggle against capitalism.

Trotskyist Work in the Trade Unions, Part 1

By Chris Knox. Reprinted from Workers Vanguard *No. 25, 20 July 1973*

The Trotskyist movement has a proud tradition of struggle for the principles of Leninism, under difficult conditions and against heavy odds. In the United States, the core of the leadership which built the original Trotskyist organization (Communist League of America 1928–34) kept up the struggle for over three decades, before the vicissitudes of the Cold War anti-communist witch-hunt finally caught up with them and caused their political degeneration and departure from Bolshevism in the early 1960's. The Spartacist League was born in the fight against the degeneration of the Trotskyist movement—in the Socialist Workers Party—and claims the tradition as its own.

This tradition includes the struggle of the Left Opposition against the bureaucratic degeneration of the USSR, the campaign for a workers united front against fascism in Germany, and the battle to build a new, Fourth International to provide an alternative proletarian leadership to the bankrupt Social Democrats and Stalinists.

As in the course of every preceding phase of the struggle for revolutionary socialism, however, it was inevitable that the Trotskyists would make mistakes. Correction of earlier mistakes, while in no way repudiating the earlier struggles and tradition, has been integral to the growth and political and theoretical armament of the movement. If one holds the early Lenin, for instance, up to the mirror of the whole body of Leninism—which incorporates the experience of the Russian Revolution and struggle to build the Communist International—one finds many errors and shortcomings. As James P. Cannon, communist leader and pioneer American Trotskyist, put it, discussing the development of the democratic-centralist vanguard party conception in 1944:

> "If our party stands today on far higher ground [than] that occupied by the amorphous rebel workers' movement prior to the First World War—and that is indubitably the case—it is not due solely to the superiority of our program, but also to the consistent application in practice of the principles and methods of Bolshevik organization. The experience of a quarter of a century has convinced us over and over again that this is the right way, the only way, to build a revolutionary party....
>
> "In politics nothing is more stupid, more infantile than to retrace ground that had already been covered, to go back and start all over again as if nothing had happened and nothing has been learned."
>
> —*Letters from Prison*

Just as Lenin had early shortcomings which reflected the social-democratic movement he was struggling to transcend, so the American

Trotskyists made mistakes which reflected, in part, the arena of the degenerating Communist Party from which they emerged, and in part the national political environment in which they functioned. The history of Trotskyist work in the trade unions in the U.S. was in the main exemplary and includes such high points as the Minneapolis Teamster strike of 1934, which was a model of mass mobilization as well as the first instance of organizing of trucking on the lines of industrial unionism; and the SWP's struggles against the no-strike pledge and the War Labor Board in World War II. However, it also reveals consistent errors which must be studied and corrected by revolutionists today if the movement is to be armed against new dangers. While this history has yet to be fully researched and recorded, its main outlines can be critically examined

CP Degeneration in the Twenties

Cannon, Shachtman, Abern and the other founders of American Trotskyism were recruited to Trotsky's Opposition suddenly, in 1928, after the issue of "Trotskyism" was considered closed in the American CP, and without having undergone the experience of a conscious struggle against the Stalinist degeneration of the party in the twenties. This degeneration had hopelessly corrupted the bulk of the leadership and cadre of the CP and demoralized, tamed or driven away most of the members.

The leadership of the party was firmly in the hands of Jay Lovestone, a hated, distrusted and cynical factionalist, who controlled the party through organizational manipulation and unprincipled political adaptationism. Identified with the Bukharinite right wing internationally, the Lovestone clique was steering the party in the direction of unbridled opportunism based on pessimism. In the trade unions, Lovestone's policy was to rely heavily on maneuvers at the top in the trade-union bureaucracy, coupled with political overtures to liberals in the form of pacifism, etc. Given the sharp decline of the AFL, this policy meant concentration on the privileged skilled trades, the small minority of the workers who were organized, and virtually no orientation to the masses of unskilled workers.

In the Stalinized Communist International (CI) of the late twenties, leadership of the national sections depended on being able to sense the winds of political change in Moscow and change one's line in time. The rampant factionalism, soon to be replaced by monolithism, had become completely unprincipled. Thus while Lovestone's right-wing opportunism fit his natural predilections and organizational methods, his faction was no more or less identified with any particular political program than was that of his chief opponent, William Z. Foster. Both sought power through adapting to the Comintern breezes, which had been blowing distinctly to the right since 1926, when Stalin blocked with Bukharin against Trotsky, Zinoviev and the ultra-lefts.

Cannon, although he too was influenced by the degeneration of the Communist International, as early as 1925 formed a third faction, the purpose of which was to fight for the liquidation of the programless factions and the building of a collective leadership. It was a somewhat demoralized Cannon who reluctantly attended the Sixth Congress of the CI in 1928, at which he accidently discovered a copy of Trotsky's critique of the draft program, and became convinced of Trotsky's analysis of the degeneration of the International as based on the interests of the national-bureaucratic elite in the USSR.

'The Right Danger in the American Party'

At the time of the Sixth CI Congress Cannon had formed a bloc (a temporary alliance, not a fusion of groups) with Foster's group on the basis of the document, "The Right Danger in the American Party." This document, like the bloc that produced it, was contradictory: it was both a principled condemnation of the gross opportunist errors of Lovestone, and a platform for an unprincipled attempt by the Fosterites to get control of the CP on the basis of what they sensed was a new left turn in the making in the Comintern.

Stalin was indeed preparing a new left turn, though he was not ready to break openly with Bukharin at the time of the Sixth Congress. As usual, the turn was forced on Stalin by circumstances which grew out of the previous line. In addition, the turn of 1928 was a plot to outflank the Left Opposition: first to expel Trotsky, then to appear to adopt his slogans. Many members of the opposition fell into the trap and capitulated to Stalin.

"The Right Danger," later reprinted in the Trotskyists' paper, the *Militant*, on which the Trotskyists continued to stand after their expulsion, reflected the signals being sent out from Moscow before the Sixth Congress, indicating the approach of the new "Third Period" turn. It attempted to use against Lovestone letters from the CI complaining about this and that, and pressure from the Red International of Labor Unions (RILU-CI trade-union arm) for more work to organize the unorganized into new unions. While correctly attacking the grossly opportunist and capitulatory blocs of Lovestone with various elements of the trade-union bureaucracy, the document tended to slip into the fallacious third period "united front from below" conception:

> "The C.I. line against the United Front from the top with reactionary trade union, liberal and S.P. leaders, and for united front with the workers against them, applies with special emphasis in America."
>
> —*Militant*, 15 December 1928

While the "Right Danger" thus contained some errors reflecting the developing new Stalinist zigzag (and was furthermore limited solely to the consideration of American questions), it was in the main correct. It was principled, from Cannon's point of view, on the need to form new unions in places where the AFL was decrepit or non-existent. While Foster was the extreme AFL-fetishist, the partisan of "boring from within," Cannon had broken with

Foster in 1926 over the Passaic strike, which he felt was an example in which a new union should have been formed under Communist leadership.

After their summary expulsion from the CP, which occurred on the basis of their views alone as soon as they solidarized with Trotsky, the Trotskyists attempted to make the most of Stalin's adoption of their slogans and continued to expose Lovestone, who was belatedly jumping on the third period bandwagon. The Trotskyists claimed Moscow's new slogans, "Against the Kulak! Against the Nepmen! Against the Bureaucrats!" as their own and took credit for the pressure leading to the CP's formation of new unions in mining, textiles and needle trades. These were the areas which the Trotskyists had felt were most ripe for the open formation of new unions, in conjunction with continued oppositional work in what was left of the old AFL unions. Initial Trotskyist trade-union work centered on these unions, particularly mining in southern Illinois.

This position for new unions in areas abandoned and betrayed by the AFL bureaucrats was soon to be distorted by the Stalinists into a position of dual unions *on principle,* and opposition to work in the old unions. As consistently presented by the Trotskyist Opposition (both before and after it became "Trotskyist"), however, the "new unions" line conformed to both the objective situation and the CP's ability to intervene in the situation. The AFL unions had been on a rampage of class collaborationism, destruction of militancy and expulsion of "reds" throughout most of the twenties. The thrust of this reactionary drive by the bureaucracy was explicitly against the organization of the masses of unskilled workers into industrial unions, which alone could overcome craft myopia and accomplish the organization of the bulk of the working class. The result was that the AFL unions not only refused to organize new workers, but they shrank drastically, driving away new workers and anyone who wanted to organize them in the process. By the end of the twenties, the crisis of proletarian leadership took the form of the lack of leadership to organize the unorganized.

The duty of revolutionary leadership was, in fact, to fill this gap, and smash the AFL bureaucracy in the process. This condition continued into the thirties, until finally a section of the AFL bureaucracy moved to organize the mass production industries precisely out of fear that if the AFL leadership didn't do it, the reds would. This resulted in the setting up of the CIO which, while it entailed a bitter rivalry with the old AFL leadership, was primarily a matter of the formation of new unions for the unorganized industries rather than a case of rivals directly competing for the same workers with the old unions.

The Trotskyists proceeded from the concrete situation in each case, and advocated new unions only where the struggle to take over the old unions had clearly exhausted itself against the stone wall of bureaucratism. Mining was such a case. The rank and file in areas such as southern Illinois were so disgusted with the betrayals and utter disregard for democracy of the Lewis machine that the basis for a new union really displacing the old shell existed. Opposition leaders in the CP before 1928 had to fight Lovestone policies which were a capitulation not only to the slow moving "progressives" (Brophy, Hapgood, etc.) but to the Lewis machine itself! The formation of the National Miners Union (NMU) by the CP, in conjunction with anti-Lewis leaders, came too late and was further sabotaged by other CP errors of an adventurist character. Rank-and-file pressure caused the progressives to try again in 1932, however, and the CP went along reluctantly with setting up the Progressive Miners of America.[1]

Despite the objective conditions favoring new unions, the CP's third period red unions were a disastrous betrayal. They were disasters because of the manner in which the CP attempted to form them: too late at first, in the case of mining and needle trades, but then increasingly too precipitously, without preparation. Strikes were called in the same manner, as an adventure on the part of a small handful, rather than on the basis of conscious preparation of the mass of the workers. Furthermore, the CP's policy was a betrayal, because it made a principle for the whole movement out of what should have been merely a tactic for particular circumstances. While the CP claimed throughout to be for continued opposition inside the old unions, the core of third period sectarianism made this impossible. The AFL leadership, as well as the Socialist Party, Trotskyists, Musteites, and all other tendencies, were denounced as "social-fascists" and otherwise not part of the workers movement in any sense. This made the united front, in which communists bloc with non-communist working-class leaders in order to expose them and advance the struggle at the same time—an essential part of communist work in the trade unions—impossible. While destroying its handful of new unions through sectarianism and adventurism, the Stalinists thus abandoned and sabotaged work in the old unions, which left the reactionary bureaucrats in control. This not only delayed the final introduction of industrial unions on a mass scale, but ensured that when such unions were formed, reactionaries would lead them.

From the moment at which the "new unions" position of the CP began to mushroom into the full-scale sectarianism of the third period, the Trotskyists fought to expose these errors and warn of the dangers. With tremendous prescience, they warned:

> "The new 'theories' are attempting to rationalize the AFL out of existence as a federation of unions and abstractly preclude the possibility of its future expansion and growth in an organizational sense....
>
> "The abandonment of ... struggle [in the AFL] now taking place under the cover of high-sounding 'radicalism' will only prevent the crystallization of an insurgent movement within the old unions and free the hands of the bureaucrats for more effective sabotage of the new unions, for these two processes

1 The following correction appeared in the 3 August 1973 *Workers Vanguard*:
"Part I of this series indicated that the Stalinists went along reluctantly with setting up the Progressive Miners of America. Actually, they only entered it later, after the final abandonment of the 'Third Period.'"

> are bound together. The result will be to strengthen the effectiveness of the AFL bureaucracy as a part of the capitalist war machine."
>
> —"Platform of the Communist Opposition," *Militant*, 15 February 1929

Trotskyist opposition to the sectarianism and adventurism of the third period, like the opposition to Lovestone's opportunism, was consciously linked to Cannon's earlier positions in the CP. As such, it carried forth certain errors which contributed to the mistakes of the later work of the Trotskyists in the trade unions.

In addition to condemning Lovestone's opportunism in the late twenties, the opposition groups (Foster and Cannon) condemned as sectarian his tendency to work exclusively through party fractions in the trade unions rather than building sections of the Trade Union Educational League (TUEL), the party's trade-union organization. This tendency on the part of the Lovestone group dated back to the 1924–25 left turn in the CI. In the U.S., the Ruthenberg/Lovestone faction (Ruthenberg died in 1927) used this turn for factional advantage against Foster, by substituting direct party work in the unions for building the TUEL, which was Foster's main organizational base. While Cannon had always been for a flexible policy on work in the unions, including building new unions when called for, he was also against the "narrow" conception of the TUEL, which was developed at this time, in which the latter was closely identified with the party. Instead, he was for broad united-front blocs, while maintaining the independence and freedom to criticize of the party:

> "In 1925 the present Opposition conducted a struggle against the narrowing of the TUEL into a purely Communist body with a Communist program and for broadening it into a united front organization. This was one of the most progressive struggles in the history of the party."
>
> —"Platform of the Opposition"

The "Platform" of 1929 then goes on to condemn both the abandonment of united-front tactics with the onset of the third period and earlier failures of both a left and right character: failure to build broad united-front movements where possible and failure to struggle for a leading role of the party within such blocs and movements (including warning that "progressive" bloc partners will betray, etc.).

The error which was buried in this polemic was that the TUEL was designed precisely to be the vehicle to bring the main outlines of the Communist program directly into the unions. It was a membership organization based on a program, not a bloc or united front. It *carried out* united fronts with other forces. Since these other forces, and much of the TUEL membership itself, had melted away or been driven out of the unions by 1924, the *increased* identification between the TUEL and the Communist Party engineered by Ruthenberg/Lovestone seemed to Cannon to be a sectarian error: rather, the party should be using the TUEL to seek new allies. Yet Cannon advocated the same watering down of the TUEL's political nature as did the degenerating Comintern in the late twenties. This watering down gave rise to a policy of blocs as a permanent strategy (the "left-center coalition") from 1927 on (see *WV* No. 22, 8 June 1973).

Cannon's position on trade-union work, then, called for principled united fronts and blocs around the immediate burning issues, together with vigorous party-building and maintenance of the party as an independent force, free to criticize its bloc partners, and always striving to play a leading role. Rather than being confused on the nature of the united front, which he was not, Cannon simply dismissed the TUEL, or the need for anything like the TUEL, as anything other than a vehicle for such blocs or united fronts. This left him with no conception of an organized pole for the recruitment of militants to the full party program for the trade unions, i.e., what the TUEL had been during its period of greatest success (and before the Stalinist degeneration of the CI set in). It is not surprising, then, that the Trotskyists never attempted to create anything like the TUEL, such as caucuses based on the Trotskyist Transitional Program, in the course of their trade-union work. What caucuses they did create had the character of temporary blocs, usually based on immediate, trade-union issues. This meant that the party itself, able to function openly only outside the unions, was the only organized pole for recruitment to the full program.

That the problems with this approach didn't become manifest until much later, after the rise of the CIO, was due primarily to the nature of the period, which called above all for a united front for the organization of the unorganized into industrial unions. This called for capable revolutionary trade-union organizing, which the Trotskyists, particularly the experienced militants of Minneapolis and Cannon himself, were prepared to conduct. This perspective led the Trotskyists into some of the Stalinist dual unions, the progressives' PMA, and leadership of the historic Minneapolis truck drivers' strikes of 1934.

The Minneapolis strikes stand to this day as a model of revolutionary trade-union organizing. Together with the San Francisco and Toledo general strikes of the same year, the Minneapolis strikes were an important precursor to the organization of all mass production workers along industrial lines.

Trotskyist Work in the Trade Unions, Part 2: Minneapolis 1934—General Strike!

By Chris Knox. Reprinted from Workers Vanguard *No. 26, 3 August 1973*

Throughout the 1930's the American Trotskyists had to work under an overwhelming organizational disadvantage compared to the Stalinists. Expelled in the late 1920's from a Communist Party which had already undergone years of political degeneration, the Trotskyist forces at first numbered no more than 100 as opposed to the CP's 7,000. Furthermore, after Stalin's abrupt shift into the "Third Period" in 1929, many elements in the CP who had been sympathetic to Trotsky were superficially impressed by the new ultra-leftism and apparent adoption of some of the slogans of the Left Opposition and were induced to remain in the CP. The main initial source of Trotskyist recruitment was thus frozen off.

Despite the extreme sectarianism of the "Third Period," the CP reversed its decline and began to grow again during the early years of the Depression. CP-initiated unemployed leagues held militant demonstrations and attracted new forces. Despite the radical disproportion of forces, however, the CP could not tolerate the political threat represented by Trotsky's analysis and program. It immediately set out to destroy the American Trotskyists through physical gangsterism and cowardly exclusionism within the workers movement. Trotskyist meetings around the country were attacked by thugs and sometimes broken up.

> "In those dog days of the movement we were shut off from all contact.... Whenever we tried to get into a workers organization we would be expelled as counter-revolutionary Trotskyists. We tried to send delegations to unemployed meetings. Our credentials would be rejected on the grounds that we were enemies of the working class. We were utterly isolated, forced in upon ourselves."
>
> —James P. Cannon, *History of American Trotskyism*

Under such circumstances, the Trotskyists did little mass work. Their first duty was to save as many of the vanguard cadre as possible for the program of the revolution. A premature turn to mass work would have in fact meant meaningless, sterile isolation—an abandonment of the Trotskyist program. Opportunities for intervention such as the Progressive Miners of America in 1932 were the exception rather than the rule.

The victory of fascism in Germany in 1933 was a monumental defeat which went unopposed by the Communist International and caused only isolated defections in its ranks. The Left Opposition concluded that the Third International had definitively gone over to support of the bourgeois order, and pronounced it dead as a potentially revolutionary force. Instead of continuing to act as a bureaucratically-expelled faction of the CI, the Trotskyists announced their intention to build a new party and a new international. This coincided with a slight economic upturn which renewed confidence among employed workers and stimulated a dramatic upturn in the class struggle. Strikes increased, and the Trotskyists fought hard to break out of their isolation. They published special editions of the *Militant* for big events such as the Paterson silk strike, sent their leaders on tours, and even managed to speak at some of the larger unemployed conferences, despite continued hooliganism by the CP.

Into the AFL

The Depression heightened the crisis of proletarian leadership caused by the refusal of the bureaucratic, craft leadership of the American Federation of Labor to organize the unorganized in the 1920's. While millions were thrown out of work and millions more forced to accept wage cuts, the AFL continued its class-collaborationist, do-nothing policy, showing no more concern over the unemployment question than the capitalist government itself. After the 1929 stock market crash, AFL-head William Green had even offered the bosses a no-strike pledge, if only they would stop wage cuts (which, of course, they did not, prompting only more inaction by Green)! Most union leaders simply counseled passive acceptance of rampant wage-slashing by the bosses while the AFL campaigned against government unemployment insurance. John L. Lewis of the Mineworkers toured the country putting down strikes against wage cuts. By 1933, AFL membership, continuing its decline, hit a low of slightly over two million, which was about half what it had been in 1920.

The Rooseveltian "New Deal" economic program (under the National Industrial Recovery Act of 1933—NRA) was designed to improve business by encouraging "rationalization" (promoting government-backed trustification) and raise public confidence in the system through a massive propaganda campaign. However, the strike wave beginning in early 1933 included a high proportion of unorganized industrial workers, which caused Roosevelt to cave into pressure from the AFL to include a "right to organize" clause (section 7-A of NRA). Actually representing no change in the realm of legal rights, the vague clause had the effect of both promoting company unions and building the authority of the AFL unions: in either case, it was designed to provide the bosses with an agency to contain the upsurge.

While the bosses busily set up company unions to control the workers, the AFL unions also began to expand—despite the fact that many of these unions had previously been reduced to discredited shells—because the AFL appeared to be the agency through which the benefits of the "New Deal" would filter down. The Trotskyists immediately recognized the vital implications of this trend for revolutionary work in the class struggle. "We must march with this instinctive movement and influence it from within," wrote Cannon in the *Militant* (2 September 1933).

The Stalinists, meanwhile, were still maintaining their ruinous "Third Period" policy of creating dual "red" unions everywhere. The supposition had been that the unorganized masses would be organized directly by the CP, over the heads of the AFL. A mere trifle had been lacking for the realization of this plan—the mass movement. Despite some party growth, sectarian isolation of the Communists had been the general result. The established unions were showing some new life, but the Stalinists had destroyed the basis for intervention with their absurd characterization of the AFL as "social fascist" and ordered their people out. The pure sectarianism of their line is illustrated by the fact that where real, industrial unions existed independently from the AFL, but not under Stalinist control—such as the Progressive Miners in the Southern Illinois coal fields and the Amalgamated Food Workers in New York City—the Stalinists maintained their paper "unions" anyway, "independent"of the independents!

The Trotskyist position was in no way a change in basic policy, despite the fact that they had earlier urged the formation of new unions, independent of the AFL, in some areas. The Trotskyists carried forth the Leninist policy of seeking to reach the masses as long as they remained in the reactionary unions, without placing any confidence in the reactionary bureaucracy. The surge into the AFL was a dramatic confirmation of Lenin's policy, and condemnation of Stalinist ultra-leftism, but, as Cannon continued:

> "By this we do not at all commit ourselves to the fetishistic belief in the possibility of transforming the AF of L into a fighting instrument of the workers. We do not expect Green and Co. to organize the masses of unskilled workers.... The resurgent struggles of the masses ... will probably break out of the formal bounds of the AF of L and seek expression in a new trade union movement."
>
> —*Militant,* 2 September 1933

The course of the upsurge confirmed the Trotskyists' analysis. Massive strikes occurred, but the establishment of new mass unions along industrial lines was thwarted in strike after strike by AFL leaders. The craven betrayal of the nation-wide textile workers' strike in 1934, for instance, confirmed the South as an open-shop haven, which condition persists to this day.

In the entire period, there were only three real victories, all led by revolutionists or professed revolutionists: Stalinists led the San Francisco waterfront strike; the Musteite American Workers Party, later to fuse with the Trotskyists, led the Toledo Auto-Lite strike; and Trotskyists led the Minneapolis truck drivers' strikes. These strikes were successful because they established powerful new unions along industrial lines which spread throughout whole industries and regions. The organization of the bulk of the proletariat under revolutionary leadership, finally displacing the reactionary AFL leaders, clearly loomed. To head off this threat, a section of the AFL leaders later formed the CIO.

Hotel Strike Debacle: a Test of Principle

The turn to mass work did not change the sharp limitations on the Trotskyists' forces. They could only intervene directly in those unions in which they already had supporters. One such place was the Hotel and Restaurant section of the Amalgamated Food Workers of New York, an independent union, which began an organizing drive and called a general strike of hotel workers in early 1934, before the Minneapolis strikes. One Trotskyist particularly, B. J. Field, was propelled into the strike leadership, and the Trotskyists launched vigorously into the struggle. Putting the *Militant* on a special, three-times-a-week basis, they called on the Stalinists to merge their small "red" union into the AFW, urged a united-front policy aimed at the AFL, warned the workers against reliance on Roosevelt's "New Deal," and singled out recognition of the union as the key goal.

In the middle of the strike, however, Field began to pull away from the Trotskyists' Communist League (CLA) and showed signs of opportunism. He collaborated too closely with trade-union bureaucrats and government mediators, caved in to red-baiting launched by the bosses, and ignored his party comrades. As Cannon put it, "He disregarded the fraction of his own party in the union—which is always the sign of a man who has lost his head" *(History of American Trotskyism)*. With the national spotlight on the "Trotskyist" strike, the CLA expelled Field and denounced his turn to "respectability" in the middle of the struggle. While opportunists howled, the Trotskyists had demonstrated the strength of their principles to serious observers: no matter how temporarily important, mass leaders were always to be subordinated to the general will of the party and its guiding principles.

If the hotel strike had been a disappointment, the Trotskyists soon had another chance to demonstrate that they could lead mass struggle. In the Minneapolis Communist League of about 40 members and sympathizers, they had a core of experienced trade unionists from the CP—with backgrounds stretching back into the pre-CP left wing of the Socialist Party and Wobblies (IWW)—headed by Ray Dunne and Carl Skoglund. Both had been delegates to the Central Labor Union (local AFL council), and had been expelled from their unions in the red purges of the 1920's. In the CP, Dunne had been aligned with the Cannon group while Skoglund had been closer to Foster, but both (along with two of Dunne's three brothers) were summarily expelled simply for questioning the expulsion of the leading Trotskyists. Subsequently they did pioneer work organizing the CLA in Minneapolis, and by the turn to mass work in 1933, they were ready to begin a campaign to organize an industrial truck drivers' union which they had planned before their expulsion from the CP in 1928.

Three Strikes That Transformed the Northwest

They began by recognizing that even though the AFL had failed to win a strike in Minneapolis in decades (the city was a notorious citadel of the open shop), it was necessary to work through the established unions. Orienting toward General Drivers' Local 574, they made a bloc with a minority of the Local exec board, headed by President Bill Brown, which was willing to aid them in a militant organizing drive. Purposefully avoiding an immediate confrontation with the rest of the local bureaucracy, they planned to flood the local with newly-organized workers, cutting across craft divisions, and conduct a strike for recognition of the union by the trucking industry on an industrial basis. The question of leadership would be resolved in the process, through the test of the class struggle.

Since Dunne and Skoglund were working in the coal yards at the time, they began with a coal yard drivers' strike in February 1934, picking the middle of winter, when it would be most effective. Through meticulous attention to detail and advance planning, they took the bosses by surprise, shutting the yards down completely and involving masses of workers in picketing. The strike won union recognition in three days.

This increased their base and authority within the union and laid the groundwork for a general strike of drivers and warehousemen throughout Minneapolis in May, which was equally well prepared, also took the bosses by surprise, and won fairly quickly. The Trotskyists insisted on the inclusion of the warehousemen ("inside workers"), since this made the union truly industrial in nature, including everyone in the companies concerned except office workers.

The bosses retaliated and provoked a third strike in July which lasted over a month. International Brotherhood of Teamsters' President Daniel Tobin, an arch-reactionary craft unionist, aided the bosses by starting a red-baiting campaign against the strike leadership. Despite the imposition of martial law by Farmer-Labor Governor Olson and the virtual exhaustion of the strikers in a war of attrition, the third strike solidly established the union and the legitimacy of the strike leadership. The bosses didn't dare try again to smash the former, and Tobin, though he kept trying, couldn't drive out the latter. It took a full scale war-crisis and government prosecution for "communism" to drive the Trotskyists from the leadership in the Minneapolis Teamsters in the 1940's. Before then, Minneapolis had become a highly-organized union town, and the Teamsters had spread throughout the Northwest. Farrell

Dobbs' campaign to organize the over-the-road drivers provided the basis for transforming the Teamsters into an industrial union.

Strong Words From the Fourth Marx Brother

The Stalinists immediately attempted to discredit the Trotskyists' role in the Minneapolis strikes. William F. Dunne, an old friend of Cannon and the one Dunne brother who had become a Stalinist, was selected by the Browder leadership of the CP to prove his loyalty by doing the "job" on the Trotskyists, including his brothers. This he did with a vengeance, even going to the point of likening his three brothers in Minneapolis to "the three Marx Bros." His articles reflected the ultra-left phase the Stalinists were only beginning to abandon. Calling the Trotskyists "a group of strikebreakers in the service of the bourgeoisie and the labor aristocracy," Dunne characterized the Minneapolis settlements as betrayals caused by cowardice, subservience to local AFL bureaucrats and Olson, and general covering up for the "fascist" "New Deal" on the part of the Trotskyists. Dunne claimed that the Trotskyists prevented the development of a full general strike, purposefully holding back the revolutionary thrust of the masses.

In following up these criticisms on the scene, the local Stalinists were severely handicapped by their total lack of any supporters directly involved in the strike, despite the fact that District 9 of the CP, covering Minneapolis, had been the third largest in the Party in 1928. The CP had completely isolated itself from the mass movement. As it attempted to present inflammatory criticism from the outside, the Trotskyists had to oppose physical assaults by angry workers on CP supporters on more than one occasion. Despite the fact that the union had an elected rank-and-file strike committee of 100, the Stalinists demanded "rank and file control" of the strike, and representation for their paper organizations on the strike committee. Only a short time later, when the CP dropped its characterization of the "New Deal" as fascist in favor of a popular-front alliance with Roosevelt and union bureaucrats, the Minneapolis CP lined up with the reactionary Tobin as the latter attempted to smash Local 574 by setting up a paper rival, "Local 500," and launching gangland thug attacks on 574 members.

NCLC Echoes 'Third Period'

The CP's "Third Period" criticisms were echoed recently, with a distinctly Marcusite crackpot twist, by the National Caucus of Labor Committees (NCLC) in its review of Dobbs' *Teamster Rebellion* (*New Solidarity*, 31 July–4 August 1972). "Dobbs sees only the military aspects of the strikes," says the NCLC:

> "... He fails to understand that it was the role of outside forces supporting the Teamsters which was decisive—the embryonic never-realized United Front....

> "The failure of the Trotskyists to adequately conceptualize the process of organizing the class-for-itself led them to constantly blunt the revolutionary dynamic of the situation."

These proponents of substitutionalism through fraudulent "united fronts" criticize the SWP for being bogged down in "militant trade unionism," to the point that they "aborted" the "development of a genuine mass strike movement." Magically, the incorporation of "outsiders" (who? the CP's paper unemployed organizations? farmers?) in the strike leadership on an equal basis with union members would have changed all this. The NCLC claims that the American Trotskyists ignored the "class-for-itself" model provided by Trotsky in his writings on the German crisis, citing (incredibly!) Trotsky's "What Next?" (1932).

Hardly intending to renounce the qualitatively leading role of the employed proletariat as does the Labor Committee, Trotsky (who never used the "class-for-itself" hocus-pocus schematisms of the NCLC) pointed out in "What Next?" that simple trade union strikes could accomplish nothing in the presence of mass unemployment unless the workers addressed themselves to this question, "drawing the unemployed into the struggle hand in hand with the employed." But the American Trotskyists understood this very well. They raised the question of unemployment in the *Militant*, fought for a shorter work week, and counterposed the united-front tactic to the CP's sectarianism in the unemployed movement. In Minneapolis, before the strikes, Trotskyist intervention to this effect in an unemployed conference was followed by a CP walkout.

Furthermore, the Minneapolis strikes were one of the most dramatic examples of broad-based organizing in American history. The leadership took meticulous care at all stages of the struggle to keep tabs on and mobilize support from other unions as well as women, petty bourgeois, professionals, farmers. The unemployed got particular attention. The Trotskyists successfully drew them into the strike struggle and attempted to organize them and support their struggles for better benefits and against grievances. After the strikes, a special unemployed organization, affiliated to the union, was constituted, and part of the leadership assigned to help run it. Relief benefits in Minneapolis were soon the best in the country, and the chances of unemployed workers being mobilized to scab on strikes were slim.

The strike leaders had a good sense of the mood of the workers and the relationship of class forces. If there were some aspects in which they erred slightly on the side of tactical conservatism, this was certainly not a major characteristic of their leadership. Far from "holding back" the struggle or consciousness of the workers, they advanced both to an entirely new level. Shachtman and Cannon came to Minneapolis to help put out a daily strike bulletin, the *Organizer*, which explained everything in terms of the basic conflict between worker and capitalist. Settlement terms were never overrated, but recognized clearly as temporary stopping points, involving necessary compromises, in the ongoing class struggle. Propaganda struggles were waged against backward attitudes, e.g., male chauvinism. The following point, written by Cannon, appeared in the *Organizer* for 18 August:

> "We see the issue between capital and labor as an unceasing struggle between the class of exploited workers and the class of exploiting parasites. It is all a war. What decides in this war, as in all others, is power. The exploiters are organized to grind us down into the dust. We must organize our class to fight back. *And the women are half of the working class.* Their interests are the same as ours and they are ready to fight for them. Therefore: organize them to take part in the class battle. This is the idea behind the wonderful organization of the Ladies Auxiliary, and its effective cooperation with the union in the struggle.
>
> "Of course, Local 574 cannot claim to be the pioneer in grasping this idea and carrying it into practice. There have been numerous examples of attempts along this line ... one that did much to inspire us—belongs to the Progressive Miners of Illinois." [emphasis in original]
>
> —*Notebook of an Agitator*

The General Strike Question

At the end of the May strike, the CP claimed that the Trotskyists reneged on their call for a city-wide general strike by accepting a settlement, thereby holding back the struggle. What the Stalinists ignored was that the main goal of the struggle up to that point—recognition of the union—was achieved. To press forward arbitrarily would have left the objectives unclear and been an adventurous risk of everything that had been gained. The Stalinists wanted a general strike against Olson. But in their ultra-left haste to denounce the Farmer-Labor governor as a "fascist," they forgot one small detail: the workers, who had voted him into power, had the illusion that he was on their side. Furthermore, he controlled the bulk of the AFL leadership through F-LP affiliation. An adventurous move at the wrong time could have isolated 574 and led to its destruction. As Trotsky pointed out in "What Next?" (merely one of many, many points the NCLC forgot to read):

> "Even though Rosa Luxemburg overestimated the *independent* importance of the general strike in the question of power, she understood quite well that a general strike could not be declared arbitrarily, that it must be prepared for by the whole preceding course of the workers' movement, by the policies of the party and the trade unions." [emphasis in original]

The Trotskyists worked to expose Olson's real role, but they knew it would take events in the class struggle to do it. When Olson moved in troops in July, the workers thought he was protecting their interests and began cooperating with the troops. The leadership knew better, and at the risk of some initial unpopularity, the *Organizer* worked to expel these illusions. This was necessarily a slow process of education, but Olson himself speeded it up considerably by raiding the union headquarters and throwing the strike leaders in the stockade. The *Organizer* could then call for a "general protest strike" without the fear of isolation of the leadership at the hands of Olson and his

AFL friends. The mere call for a general strike was sufficient to get the headquarters back and the leaders out of jail.

The worst the Trotskyists can be accused of with regard to Olson in the strike events is lack of prior warning as to the role he would play, i.e., an over-adaptation at first to the backward consciousness of the workers. In their organizing drive before the May strike, the leadership built a mass meeting at which they demanded that Olson address the workers. This was correct, but building the meeting without simultaneous warnings as to Olson's real nature as the head of a section of the capitalist state was an opportunist tactical error.

> "The organizing committee also started a pressure campaign to line up Governor Olson as a speaker at the meeting. This was done for two reasons: advance publicity listing the governor as a speaker would help in getting a big turnout for the meeting; and if Olson addressed the workers, he would have to go on record in support of the union campaign."
> —Farrell Dobbs, *Teamster Rebellion*

Thus the organizers used Olson's name without, at the same time, attempting to expose him as a faker; thereby they helped create some of the illusions that plagued them. This error flowed in part from a theoretical misunderstanding of the Farmer-Labor Party—a bloc of two classes—as a working-class party (this will be taken up further in Part 3). That this error was subordinate within the general thrust of the Trotskyists' practice is indicated by the fact that they didn't hesitate to attack Olson in the heat of the crisis, even though it went against the stream to do so.

Hardly "holding back" the struggle, the leadership held out to the point of exhaustion of the ranks. At the end, the strike had become a war of attrition, and there was a small but dangerous back-to-work trickle. Nevertheless, the main objectives were won. As Cannon pointed out to the Stalinists after the May strike, these "quack doctors whose patients always die," (referring to the record of disastrous, Stalinist-led ultra-left "strikes") could not point to a single example of newly-organized workers having achieved so much (*Militant*, 16 June 1934).

The Toledo Auto-Lite strike, which peaked after the May strike in Minneapolis, is held up as an "alternative" to Minneapolis by the NCLC on the absurd grounds that the revolutionary leaders were the heads of unemployed leagues, and had to be brought in from "outside" (*New Solidarity*, 16–20 October 1972). In fact, the only difference this made was that the Minneapolis strikes had better and more conscious advance planning, and afterwards the leadership, having worked inside the union from the beginning, was in a better position to thoroughly displace the craft-minded reactionaries. Both strikes used essentially the same revolutionary methods of mass struggle and achieved similar goals. The same can be said of the San Francisco waterfront strike, in which the Stalinists were involved. This strike was successful because the Stalinists opportunistically worked with leaders like Bridges who were *inside* the AFL longshoremen's union, which was technically "social-fascist" at the time! The Stalinists did have a dual union on the scene, but it was essentially a useless hindrance and a potentially dangerous divisive factor. When the police raided it along with the Wobblies, arresting hundreds, the workers on strike were not moved to defend it as their own.

Workers Party Formed, NCLC Notwithstanding

The NCLC complains that the Trotskyists spent too much time being militant trade unionists and thus failed to build "a significant revolutionary force in the Thirties." Holding up ex-preacher Muste's American Workers Party as conscious followers of Trotsky's German writings, the NCLC "forgets" that shortly after the Minneapolis and Toledo strikes, the AWP and the CLA *fused* to form the Workers Party! This fusion came about because the Trotskyists correctly saw the AWP as a leftward-moving centrist force and aggressively approached it, seeking to separate the sound, proletarian elements from the rootless petty-bourgeois dilettantes and other Marcus-like garbage which the AWP had picked up in its long history of unpolitical unemployed work. It was the American Trotskyists that supplied the better Musteites with a program, not the other way around. The work of the two groups in similar strikes hastened this process. Afterwards, the fused organization worked jointly to consolidate the earlier Toledo victory in the Chevrolet transmission strike in Toledo in 1935, which they almost succeeded in spreading throughout the GM empire. (This was the first successful GM strike, and was a vital precursor to the later organization of auto.)

The period of the 1933–1934 upsurge required exactly the kind of trade-union tactics Cannon advocated: a broad but principled united-front bloc around the key burning issues. In 1934, organization of the unorganized was such an issue. It clearly separated those willing to follow revolutionary leadership from the vast bulk of the trade-union bureaucracy of the time, and the Trotskyists were correct to bloc on this issue and struggle to lead successful organizing campaigns. Precisely this kind of activity in Minneapolis, Toledo and San Francisco threatened to solve the crisis of leadership in favor of the revolutionists, but the Trotskyists were too small to carry it through. The betrayals of the much larger Communist Party were responsible for the fact that when industrial workers were fully organized, reactionaries controlled their unions. The later blocs of the Stalinists with these CIO reactionaries—for the popular front with Roosevelt—has nothing at all in common with the Trotskyist united front in Minneapolis to achieve union recognition.

The Trotskyists' mistake (besides the theoretical misconception on the nature of the F-LP two-class party) was that they lacked different tactical weapons in their arsenal for different conditions and periods. An independent, Trotskyist-led caucus, expressing a full program of transitional demands for the unions, wasn't so important in 1934 as later, since in 1934 the Trotskyists were in a position to implement their most important demands in practice (although consciousness of the need for political caucuses might have gone hand-in-hand with greater consciousness of the need to make political warnings and criticisms in advance of the crisis, as in the case of Olson at the mass meeting). Later, however, when they weren't in a position to provide direct leadership of the class, the Trotskyists showed inflexibility. They never betrayed the workers as did the Stalinists, but they did miss opportunities and commit some opportunist errors through a policy of blocking too frequently and almost always working through united fronts many of which lacked the clarity of the blocs to organize the unorganized of 1934. Instead of emphasizing their program, they used organizational weakness as an excuse to over-concentrate on alliances around minimum demands.

Trotskyist Work in the Trade Unions, Part 3: The Primacy of Politics

By Chris Knox. Reprinted from Workers Vanguard *No. 27, 31 August 1973*

After the formation of the Workers Party (WP) through the fusion of the Musteite American Workers Party with the Trotskyist Communist League of America (CLA) in 1934, the Trotskyists' organizational course took them into the leftward-moving Socialist Party in 1936. After winning a sizeable section of the SP youth they then split off from the Social Democrats to found the Socialist Workers Party (SWP) in 1938. During this period of upsurge, the Trotskyists grew and continued to do trade-union work and other mass work, giving the lie to Stalinist assertions that the Minneapolis strikes of 1934 were the only mass work the Trotskyists ever did. The Trotskyists led mass unemployed leagues, conducted mass defense work and worked in the unions in mining, textiles, auto, food workers, maritime, steel and teamsters, among others. Less spectacular than the Minneapolis strikes perhaps, nevertheless this work was of lasting importance and vital to the building of the revolutionary vanguard in the U.S.

The Trotskyists' policy of broad united fronts continued to play a vital and useful role as long as the bulk of the reactionary AFL bureaucracy fought the establishment of industrial unions. The Workers Party declared its main goal to be the formation of a "national progressive movement" for militant industrial unionism (*New Militant*, 19 January 1935), and the Trotskyists hoped, with good reason, to win the leadership of important sections of the working class by being the most consistent fighters for this minimum but key immediate need of the working class. At the same time they did not hide their socialist politics, in contrast to the Stalinists who attempted to masquerade as simple pro-Roosevelt militants. As much as possible, the Trotskyists operated as open revolutionists. Gerry Allard, CLA member and a leader of the Progressive Miners of America in southern Illinois, addressed the miners about an approaching strike in the following terms:

> "Being a Marxist, a revolutionist, it is my opinion that we should militarize the strike, revamp the Women's Auxiliary along the original lines, augment our forces by seeking the organizational support of the powerful unemployed movement in Illinois, seek allies in the rank and file of the United Mine Workers of America, and go forward once again with the same determination that built this union. This is the road of struggle ...."
>
> —*New Militant*, 30 March 1935

Allard went on to appeal to the miners to see their struggle in the broadest possible context, as the impetus for the organization of auto, steel, rubber, etc.

Toledo, 1935: Conflagration in Auto

Following up on the work of the Musteites in the great Auto-Lite strike of 1934, the Workers Party played a key role in a strike at the Toledo Chevrolet transmission plant in 1935, being instrumental in getting GM workers in Cincinnati, Cleveland, Norwood and Atlanta to strike simultaneously. Two Trotskyists, Cochran and Beck, leaders of the Workers Party and Spartacus Youth respectively, were arrested while picketing the Flint, Michigan headquarters of Chevrolet in an attempt to spread the strike into the auto capital (*New Militant,* 11 May 1935).

The spreading of this strike throughout the GM empire was prevented only by the relative organizational weakness of the Trotskyists and the diligent, strike-breaking efforts of the AFL's appointed head of the auto union, Francis Dillon. Dillon personally headed off a sympathy strike of Buick workers in Detroit and sabotaged the strike at its base in Toledo by threatening to withdraw the local's charter and splitting the strike leadership at the key point. GM agreed to a wage increase and published a stipulation that it would meet with the union leadership, but because of Dillon's treachery there was no signed contract. The workers went back solidly organized and undefeated, however, since the company had the militant 1934 strike in mind and had made no attempt to operate the plant with scabs. It was the first GM strike the company had failed to smash, and was an inspiration for the later auto sit-down strikes which built the UAW and established the CIO.

After the strike, the Workers Party published a critical assessment of the strike leadership of which it had been a part, denouncing sloppiness, lack of attention to details (such as not calling sufficient strike committee meetings) and the "fundamental error" of allowing the daily strike paper, *Strike Truth,* to be suppressed (*New Militant*, 18 May 1935). This performance was in sharp contrast to the Minneapolis truckers' strikes the year previous, in which meticulous attention to tactical and organizational details and the hard-hitting regular strike daily had been instrumental in achieving the ultimate victory of the strike. At the same time the Trotskyists were able to recruit the most conscious workers to their organization, with the Minneapolis branch of the CLA increasing from 40 to 100 members and close sympathizers during 1934 alone. Many years later, Cannon analyzed the main weakness of the work in Toledo as the failure to consolidate lasting organizational gains. He blamed this on Muste, who was a "good mass worker" but "tended to adapt himself" to the mass movement too much for a Leninist, at the expense of developing firm nuclei "on a programmatic basis for permanent functioning" (*History of American Trotskyism*).

First Auto Union Caucus Formed

The Workers Party was still working under the disadvantage in Toledo that the revolutionary leadership of the 1934 strike had been brought in from outside the union, thereby lacking sufficiently deep roots to hold the militants together against Dillon's maneuvering in 1935. Today the Marcusite National Caucus of Labor Committees, a group which has not the faintest idea of what it means to organize the working class, lauds precisely this weakness as the hallmark of revolutionary strategy. Their hero Muste soon thereafter abandoned the WP to return to the church. The deficiencies of the Trotskyists' trade-union tactics were not to be found in "overrating the unions" as the NCLC crackpots would have us believe, but in the failure to organize firm class-struggle nuclei "on a programmatic basis for permanent functioning" *within the unions*. The struggles in Toledo gave birth to the first auto union caucus, the Progressives of UAW Local 18384, but its program was limited to the militant unionism of the broad united fronts the Trotskyists advocated: for industrial unions, reliance on the power of the ranks as opposed to arbitration or government boards, etc. As such, it had the episodic character of a united front and lacked the clear revolutionary political distinctiveness which became crucial after the establishment of industrial unions under reformist leadership in the late 1930's.

Another point made by Cannon in drawing the balance sheet of the Workers Party period should be made elementary reading for the Labor Committee, which fetishizes unemployed organizing. The mass unemployed organizations inherited by the Trotskyists in their fusion with the Musteites were highly unstable:

> "We reached thousands of workers through these unemployed organizations. But further experience also taught us an instructive lesson in the field of mass work too. Unemployed organizations can be built and expanded rapidly and it is quite possible for one to get illusory ideas of their stability and revolutionary potentialities. At the very best they are loose and easily scattered formations; they slip through your fingers like sand. The minute the average unemployed worker gets a job, he wants to forget the unemployed organization...."
>
> —*History of American Trotskyism*

The Making of the Modern Teamsters Union

The most lasting achievement of Trotskyist trade-union work in the 1930's was the transformation of the Teamsters from a localized, federated craft union into a large industrial union. In the 1930's, while long-distance trucking was becoming more and more important, the Teamsters union was still limited to local drivers, divided by crafts (ice drivers, milk drivers, etc.)

and dependent on local conditions. Based in their stronghold in Minneapolis, the Trotskyists spread industrial unionism throughout the Northwest through the Teamsters. An 11-state campaign led by Farrell Dobbs to organize over-the-road drivers included conquest of the all-important hub of Chicago and established the principle of the uniform area-wide contract. The campaign's achievements were solidified through a major strike struggle centered in Omaha, Nebraska in 1938, which was won through the same skillful organization that had succeeded in Minneapolis. As in Minneapolis, the building of the party went hand-in-hand with the strike, resulting in an SWP branch in Omaha.

Especially in the mid-1930's, the mass work of the Trotskyists was far-reaching and significant out of proportion to their size. Yet the Trotskyists knew they were not yet a real party and could not become a party leading significant sections of the masses in struggle until the centrist and reformist forces blocking the path were removed. It was for this reason that the Trotskyists entered the SP in 1936: the SP was large, included a rapidly-growing left wing (particularly in the youth) and was attracting militant workers who could be won to Trotskyism. The Trotskyists had to defeat sectarians in their own ranks, led by Oehler, who assumed that the party could be built directly, through the orientation of a propaganda group to the masses. The Cannon-led majority of the WP hardly ignored mass work. It was, in fact, an important part of the entry maneuver. While in the Socialist Party the Trotskyists established new trade-union fractions, notably in maritime (principally the Sailors Union of the Pacific) and auto, meanwhile considerably embarrassing the reformist SP leaders by their class-struggle policies. When they emerged from the SP more than doubled in size in 1938, the Trotskyists, though still small, were in a better position than ever to conduct work in the unions.

CIO Victories Pose Question of Politics

The rise of the CIO through the massive struggles of 1936–37 transformed the labor movement and altered the terms of class struggle in favor of the workers. The organized workers were in a better position to resist the onslaughts of capitalism; however, the new unions were controlled by a bureaucratic layer which shared the pro-capitalist, class-collaborationist politics of the old AFL bureaucracy. Having reluctantly presided over the militant struggles which established the CIO, these new bureaucrats desired nothing more than to establish "normal" trade-union relations with the capitalists, gain influence in capitalist politics, etc. As inter-imperialist war drew closer, the ruling class was gradually forced to temporarily lay aside its attempt to destroy the unions and accept the coalition which the bureaucracy readily offered. Thus the trade-union bureaucracy was qualitatively expanded and consolidated as the chief agency for disciplining the work force, replacing for the most part the Pinkertons and bloody strike-breaking as the principal means of capitalist rule in the hitherto unorganized mass production industries. This process was completed during the Second World War, when the ruling class allowed the completion of union organizing in key areas in exchange for full partnership of the trade-union bureaucracy in the imperialist war effort (the no-strike pledge, endorsement of the anti-labor wage controls, strike-breaking, etc.).

Besides displacing organization of the unorganized as the key immediate issue, this transformation placed the question of politics in the foreground. The industrial unions had been built, but they alone were clearly insufficient to deal with the outstanding social questions—unemployment, war, etc.—which determined the conditions under which they struggled. With the renewal of depression conditions in mid-1937–38, accompanied by increased employer resistance to union demands, opposition to Roosevelt burgeoned and mass sentiment for a labor party developed, expressed through such agencies as Labor's Non-Partisan Political League (LNPL), the CIO political arm and the Farmer-Labor Party of Minnesota. In order to head off this movement, the bureaucracy invented the myth of Roosevelt as a "friend of labor" and used the Stalinist Communist Party, closely integrated into the CIO bureaucracy, to pass off this warmed-over Gompers policy as a "working-class" strategy—the popular front. The CP unceremoniously dropped its earlier calls for a labor party.

The Trotskyist Transitional Program

The primary task of revolutionists in the labor movement had shifted, therefore, from leading the struggle for industrial unions to providing a political pole of opposition to the class-collaborationist bureaucracy. The Transitional Program ("Death Agony of Capitalism and the Tasks of the Fourth International"), adopted by the SWP in 1938, was written by Trotsky largely to provide the basis for such a struggle. It contained demands designed to meet the immediate felt needs and problems of the workers (wages, unemployment, working conditions, approaching war and fascism) with alternatives leading directly to a struggle against the capitalist system itself: a sliding scale of wages and hours, workers control of industry, expropriation of industry without compensation, workers militias, etc. Most importantly, the program proposed transitional organizational forms and measures designed to advance the workers' ability to struggle for these demands and to provide the basis for the overthrow of capitalism: factory committees, soviets, arming of the proletariat and workers and farmers government (as a popular designation of the dictatorship of the proletariat).

Also in 1938, Trotsky urged his American followers to enter formations such as the LNPL and fight for a labor party based on the trade unions, armed with the Transitional Program as the political alternative to the class collaborationism of the Stalinists and trade-union bureaucrats. This reversed the Trotskyists' earlier position of opposing the call for a labor party on the grounds that the utterly reactionary character of the Gompersite labor bureaucracy could allow the organizing of mass industrial unions directly under the leadership of the revolutionary party. This would have effectively bypassed the need for the transitional demand of a labor party. With the organization of the CIO on the basis of militant trade-union reformism, the balance of power between the revolutionaries and the labor bureaucrats was shifted in favor of the latter. But as the strike struggles achieved the original goal of union organization, and as Roosevelt's policies led to economic downturn, the newly organized and highly combative rank and file of the CIO unions began to come into direct political conflict with their pro-Roosevelt leaders. The call for a labor party became a crucial programmatic weapon to mobilize a class-struggle opposition to the Lewis bureaucracy.

Though politically armed to meet the new situation, the American Trotskyists nevertheless failed to find a consistent form of expression for their program within the unions. While they propagandized for the Transitional Program in their press and conducted campaigns for specific demands such as workers defense guards, labor party, struggle against approaching war, etc., their day-to-day trade-union work continued on the old basis of united fronts around immediate issues. As the organization of the unions proceeded and the opposition of the bureaucracy to organizing industrial unions receded, this united-front policy turned into a bloc around simple trade-union militancy with whole sections of the non-Stalinist, "progressive" trade-union bureaucracy. Criticism of these bureaucrats tended to take the form of pushing for consistent trade-union militancy rather than building a revolutionary political alternative, so that when the "progressive" bureaucracy lined up with Roosevelt for war in 1940, an embarrassing lack of political distinction between the Trotskyists in the trade unions and these "progressives" was revealed.

The course of events in the Northwest Teamsters was a graphic example. For two years after the 1934 strikes in Minneapolis, the Tobin leadership of the Teamsters International continued to try to smash the Trotskyist leadership of Local 574, using red-baiting, gangsters and a rival local. Then a subtle shift began to occur. As the Trotskyists spread out, building support for the campaign to organize the over-the-road drivers, more and more bureaucrats became won over, including the key leader in Chicago, whose adherence went a long way toward ensuring the success of the campaign. Finally, by the time of the 1938 Omaha strike, Tobin himself began actively cooperating, even supporting the organizing drive against his old allies who still sought to preserve the local power of the Joint Councils at the expense of modernization, and appointing Farrell Dobbs International Organizer.

The 1936–37 strike struggles had finally rendered pure craft unionism obsolete even within the AFL, and old-line craft unionists began to tail the CIO both in order to enhance their organizational power and because the bourgeoisie itself was less resistant and more willing to accept organization of the workers in exchange for the use of the bureaucracy as its labor lieutenant.

Throughout the entire area of Dobbs' 11-state campaign, the only serious challenge mounted by the bosses was in Omaha.

The united front to organize the over-the-road drivers was not wrong, but the Trotskyists lacked the means to distinguish themselves politically from the bureaucracy. This could have been done through a caucus based on the Transitional Program. The *Northwest Organizer* was founded in 1935 as the organ of a pan-union caucus formation, the Northwest Labor Unity Conference, but the NLUC's program was limited to militant, class-struggle union organizing, under the slogan, "All workers into the unions and all unions into the struggle." Eventually the *Northwest Organizer* became the organ of the Minneapolis Teamsters Joint Council and the NLUC lapsed, since its oppositional role was liquidated. When Tobin began to line up behind the war effort, the Trotskyists in Minneapolis opposed the war and won over the Central Labor Union, but they lacked the basis for a factional struggle in the union as a whole that a political caucus orientation might have provided. Dobbs simply submitted his resignation as organizer in 1940, without waging a political fight. A few years later, Tobin finally was able to crush the Trotskyist leadership in Minneapolis, with the aid of the government's first Smith Act anti-communist trial of the leading militants.

The Two-Class Party

The bloc with "progressive" trade unionists was reflected politically in the Trotskyists' orientation to the Minnesota Farmer-Labor Party, with which most of the local trade unions were affiliated. Left-leaning FLP supporters were an important component of the Trotskyists' united front. In 1929, the excellent document, *Platform of the Communist Opposition*, had pointed out:

> "The organization of two classes in one party, a Farmer-Labor Party, must be rejected in principle in favor of the separate organization of the workers, and the formation of a political alliance with the poor farmers under the leadership of the former. The opportunist errors of the [Communist] Party comrades in the Farmer-Labor Party of Minnesota and other states [in 1924] flowed inevitably from and were secondary to the basically false policy of a two-class party, in which the farmer and worker are ostensibly on an 'equal basis,' but where in reality the petty-bourgeois ideology of the former actually dominates."
>
> —*Militant*, 15 February 1929

Written by the American Trotskyists, this statement thus carried forth in hard political terms the criticisms made by Trotsky of the Pepper leadership of the CP in 1924. Pepper had blithely made a fundamental revision of Marxism in order to tail the radical farmers of the FLP into the third capitalist party movement of LaFollette. The Minneapolis Trotskyists, however, failed to implement this policy in their orientation to the FLP. In 1935 they critically supported the FLP candidate for mayor of Minneapolis (despite the current

Workers Party position against labor party formations), and in 1938 they supported FLP Governor Benson in the primaries as well as in the general election, without in either case mentioning the need for the "separate organization of the workers." The SWP's September 1938 program for the FLP endorses the adherence of both mass workers' and mass farmers' organizations to the FLP and complains only of the inordinate power of the ward clubs, through which the Stalinists eventually wielded the dominant influence in the FLP. This necessarily blurred the SWP's campaign for a working-class labor party based on the Transitional Program, since in their program for the FLP they were forced to emphasize demands for the petty-bourgeois farmers (loans, easing tax burdens, etc.) which watered down the working-class content of their program and was the inevitable result of the petty-bourgeois nature of the FLP as a two-class party. While not politically fatal in itself, this lack of clarity was a reflection of an accommodationist bloc with the left wing of the trade-union bureaucracy.

Furthermore, the Trotskyists compounded their inflexible united-front trade-union tactics with an overreaction to Stalinism. The 1938 SWP trade-union resolution stated categorically:

> "While always expanding our program independently and maintaining our right of criticism, our Party in a certain sense supports the 'lesser evil' within the unions. The Stalinists are the main enemy.... We unite with all serious elements to exclude the Stalinists from control of the unions."
>
> —*Socialist Appeal*, 26 November 1938

The Stalinist CP, many times larger than the Trotskyists, was indeed a key political enemy in the unions. Having shifted to the right from a destructive policy of self-isolation during the "Third Period" (1929–35), the CP had become intimate advisers to the CIO bureaucracy and hard right-wingers in the unions, doing whatever possible to crush and expel the Trotskyists. Its main aim was to preserve links to the liberals and the collaboration of the labor movement with Roosevelt and U.S. imperialism. The CP participated directly in the bourgeoisie's attempt to militarize the labor movement for the war. Thus in maritime, while the CP and its allies were busy weakening the 1936 West Coast longshore strike, wrecking the militant Maritime Federation of the Pacific and giving back-handed support to the government's effort to break the seamen's union hiring halls through the Copeland Act, the Trotskyists made a correct united front bloc with the militant but "anti-political" Lundberg leadership of the SUP [Sailors Union of the Pacific].

Nevertheless, the determination of the SWP to unite with the politically undefined "all *serious* elements" against the Stalinists in all cases reflected trade-union adaptationism. The SWP's reasoning was that, unlike standard trade-union reformists, the Stalinists were the agency of an alien force outside the unions—the bureaucratic ruling elite of the Soviet Union—and therefore willing to destroy the unions to achieve their ends. This was an implicit "third campist" denial of Stalinism as a tendency within the labor movement. That the Trotskyists never drew this logical conclusion from their position and pulled back from it later did not prevent them from falling into errors as a result of it even while the CP was at its worst during the popular front period (1935–39).

The worst such error was the SWP's "auto crisis" which peaked in January 1939. The UAW was a key battleground between Trotskyists, Stalinists and social democrats in the CIO. Wielding power with a bureaucratic heavy hand, UAW President Homer Martin, a left-leaning trade-union reformist, went so far in his battle against the Stalinists that he eventually lost all authority. To the left of the Stalinists on some issues, he was at base reactionary and made a concerted effort to smash wildcat strikes. The SWP, however, extended critical support to Martin to stop the Stalinists. The crisis came while Cannon was in Europe following the founding conference of the Fourth International in Fall 1938. The SWP Political Committee was being run by Shachtman and Burnham, who were soon to draw the full conclusions from their Stalinophobia and lead a faction out of the SWP (in 1940) denying that the Soviet Union was any kind of workers state and refusing to defend it, and likewise denying that the Stalinists were a tendency within the workers movement. With their own measure of bureaucratic highhandedness, Shachtman and Burnham tried to ram a pro-Martin policy down the throats of the auto fraction in 1938 just as Martin was leading a rump convention of the UAW out of the CIO, back into the AFL and eventually to oblivion. The bulk of the auto union dumped Martin and held its own pro-CIO convention. The SWP had to do an abrupt and embarrassing about-face entailing two issues of *Socialist Appeal* which contradicted each other, for which Shachtman and Burnham refused to acknowledge responsibility.

During the Hitler-Stalin Pact period (1939–41), the beginning of World War II, a general reversal of positions took place. Reflecting Stalin's deal with Hitler and turn away from the earlier alliance with France, Britain and the U.S., the CP conducted a grudging but definite turn to the left, denouncing the "imperialist" war, alienating its liberal allies and reinvigorating its working class base. The "progressive" trade unionists with whom the Trotskyists had been blocking on trade-union issues meanwhile became central in the pro-war, patriotic lineup. As a result of this switch, in discussions between the SWP leadership and Trotsky in Mexico in 1940, all the inadequacies of the Trotskyists' trade-union work then became manifest (see "Discussions with Trotsky," in his *Writings, 1939–40*). "The Stalinists are the problem," pointed out Cannon: "By their change in line they dealt a heavy blow. We were forging ahead when they made the switch, paralysing our work." Despite this damaging admission, the SWP leaders were opposed to a policy of maneuver to take advantage of the new situation. Trotsky proposed critical support to the CP candidates in the 1940 elections. He had to reiterate that this was theoretically possible, since the Stalinists had made a sharp, though temporary, left turn and were just as much part of the labor movement as the equally reactionary forces in the unions with whom the Trotskyists had until then been blocking. The SWP leaders objected, saying that it would disrupt the work in the trade unions, in which what were admittedly blocs at the top with "progressives" had been necessary in order for a small force of revolutionists to come forward and begin political work in the unions. Criticizing his followers for lack of initiative, Trotsky went to the core of the problem:

> "I believe we have the critical point very clear. We are in a block with the so-called progressives—not only fakers but honest rank and file. Yes, they are honest and progressive but from time to time they vote for Roosevelt—once in four years. This is decisive. You propose a trade union policy, not a Bolshevik policy. Bolshevik policies begin outside the unions.... You are afraid to become compromised in the eyes of the Rooseveltian trade-unionists."

To the American leaders' protestations that their forces were too small to preserve an independent course, Trotsky said, "Our real role is that of third competitor," distinct from both Stalinists and "progressives," stating that his proposal for maneuver "presupposes that we are an independent party." Thus the discussions uncovered the fact that the Trotskyists' lack of an independent political pole *in the unions*, distinct from episodic blocs and united fronts around immediate issues, had compromised their general ability to maneuver and their independence as a party. They had become over-identified with their bloc partners.

In his report of these discussions to the party, Cannon agreed with most of Trotsky's points in some revealing passages, while continuing to oppose the proposal for critical support to the CP in the elections:

> "...our work in the trade unions up till now has been largely a day-to-day affair based upon the daily problems and has lacked a general political orientation and perspective. This has tended to blur the distinction between us and pure and simple trade unionists. In many cases, at times, they appeared to be one with us. It was fair weather and good fellows were together....
>
> "Then all of a sudden, this whole peaceful routine of the trade union movement is disrupted by overpowering issues of war, patriotism, the national elections, etc. And these trade unionists, who looked so good in ordinary times, are all turning up as patriots and Rooseveltians."
>
> —*Socialist Appeal,* 19 October 1940

Thus the primacy of politics in trade-union work had snuck up on the SWP and clubbed it over the head. The problem had not been caused by lack of a principled struggle for the program, nor primarily by blocs which were unprincipled in character. Criticism of bureaucratic allies in the public press had sometimes been weak, but the SWP had vigorously struggled in the public domain for its program, while raising key agitational demands in the unions. The main lack had been a consistent pole, in the unions, for the struggle for the Transitional Program and against the bureaucracy in all its manifestations, i.e., a struggle for *revolutionary* leadership *of* and *in* the unions. Instead of developing such caucus formations as the Progressives of the UAW and the Northwest Labor Unity Conference into political formations in opposition to the bureaucracy, as the early Communists' Trade Union Educational League had been, the Trotskyists allowed these formations to be limited politically to the character of united fronts: episodic alliances based on immediate issues. As such, not only did they not last, but the Trotskyists themselves, in the unions, became politically identified almost exclusively through these united fronts, rather than through the struggle to build the vanguard party.

Size was not a factor, since in some ways the problem was at its worst where the Trotskyists were strongest, in the Northwest Teamsters. Rather, the SWP demonstrated a lack of flexibility of tactics and an unwillingness to upset its policy of continual blocs with "progressive" trade unionists on day-to-day issues by a hard, political drive for power based on revolutionary answers to the larger issues. But the larger issues dominated the day-to-day issues, and as imperialist world war drew closer the Trotskyists had to pay the price of isolation for their earlier failure to appear as an independent force in the unions. Unfortunately, they were unable to absorb the lessons of this period sufficiently to prevent the repetition of these characteristic errors. The Trotskyists continued, especially after World War II, to rely on a policy of united fronts on trade-union issues, rather than the construction of political formations within the unions—caucuses—to mount a comprehensive fight for a full revolutionary program.

Trotskyist Work in the Trade Unions, Part 4: Stalinism and Social-Patriotism

By Chris Knox. Reprinted from Workers Vanguard *No. 28, 14 September 1973*

With the onset of World War II and the wave of jingoism which swept away their trade-unionist allies of the pre-war period, the Trotskyists were forced to retreat. They adopted a "policy of caution" in the unions, which meant virtual inaction, especially at first. Although the Socialist Workers Party (SWP) was driven from its main base in the Minneapolis Teamsters through a combination of government persecution and attack by the Teamsters bureaucracy and the Stalinists, in general the "policy of caution" had the desired effect of protecting the trade-union cadre from victimization.

However, the "policy of caution" had another side to it. With the rupture of their alliances with the "progressive" trade unionists, the Trotskyists had not dropped their reliance on blocs around immediate issues in the unions. They merely recognized that with both the Stalinists and "progressives" lined up for the war, Roosevelt and the no-strike pledge, there was no section of the trade-union bureaucracy with which they could make a principled bloc. Thus their inaction was in part a recognition that any action along the lines to which they were accustomed in the trade unions would be opportunist, i.e., would necessarily entail *unprincipled* blocs and alliances. Any action not involving blocs and alliances with some section of the trade-union bureaucracy was virtually inconceivable.

At first, the rupture of the earlier alliances and enforced inactivity had a healthy effect, exposing the limitations of such alliances and enforcing the recognition that in trade-union work as in all other spheres of party-building, only principled political agreement assures permanence:

> "There is only one thing that binds men together in times of great stress. That is agreement on great principles....
>
> "All those comrades who think we have something, big or little, in the trade union movement should get out a magnifying glass in the next period and look at what we really have. You will find that what we have is our party fractions and the circle of sympathizers around them. That is what you can rely on.... The rule will be that the general run of pure and simple trade unionists, the nonpolitical activists, the latent patriots—they will betray us at the most decisive moment. What we will have in the unions in the hour of test will be what we build in the form of firm fractions of convinced Bolsheviks."
>
> —James P. Cannon, "The Stalinists and the United Front,"
> *Socialist Appeal*, 19 October 1940

As the war dragged on, however, opportunities for activity mounted as the workers chafed under the restrictions imposed upon them by their leaders in the name of the imperialist conflict. Rank-and-file rebellion, in the form of unauthorized strikes, broke out in a mounting wave starting in 1942. These led to mounting opposition to the solid, pro-war bureaucratic phalanx. For the most part, the SWP went very slow on participation in these struggles. It wasn't until 1945 that a formal change of policy was made, although exceptions to the rule began earlier.

While seeking to preserve their precious trade-union cadre through a policy of inaction within the unions, the Trotskyists concentrated on public propaganda and agitational campaigns aimed at the unions largely from the outside, through the party press. The campaign against the war centered largely on the defense case of the Minneapolis 18—the 18 Trotskyists and leaders of the Minneapolis Teamsters who were railroaded to jail under the Smith Act.

Minneapolis Defense Case

The 18 were the first victims of the Smith Act of 1940, which was the first law since the Alien and Sedition Act of 1798 to make the mere advocacy of views a crime. Initiated in 1941 directly by Roosevelt (ostensibly at the request of Teamsters President Tobin), the case was an important part of the drive by the bourgeoisie, working hand-in-hand with its agents, the labor bureaucrats, to "purify" and discipline the work force for subordination to the imperialist war. The legal persecution consummated Tobin's attempts to get rid of the Trotskyists in Minneapolis, which had coincided with the lining up of the bureaucracy for the war.

However, because of its clear and open contradiction with the stated principles of bourgeois democracy, and thus with the stated goals of the war, the Smith Act prosecution of the Trotskyists caused a rupture within the bureaucracy and became a point of opposition to the government throughout the labor movement. Publishing the testimony of the chief defendant, James P. Cannon, and the closing argument of the defense attorney, Albert Goldman, as pamphlets (*Socialism On Trial* and *In Defense of Socialism*), the SWP exploited the case heavily as a basic defense of socialist ideas and principled opposition to the imperialist war. Though they failed to prevent the destruction of the militant Minneapolis Teamsters local under the combined hammer blows of Tobin and Roosevelt, the Trotskyists' propaganda campaign around the case had a significant impact and aided party recruiting.

The vicious treachery of the Stalinists was underlined and exposed to many by their refusal to defend the Trotskyists against this persecution by the class enemy. Despite the fact that the CP was still opposed to the entry of the U.S. into the war at the time (during the Hitler-Stalin Pact period, 1939–41), it leapt at once onto the prosecutor's bandwagon.

> "The Communist Party has always exposed, fought against and today joins the fight to exterminate the Trotskyite Fifth Column from the life of our nation."
>
> —*Daily Worker,* 16 August 1941

More than any other force on the left, it was Stalinism, through such fundamental betrayals of class principles as this, which poisoned class consciousness and undermined the fighting ability of the proletariat. Later, during the cold-war witchhunt, when the CP was the victim of the same Smith Act and bureaucratic purge, the militant workers were so disgusted with its role that they were mobilized by anti-communist bureaucrats who smashed virtually every last vestige of class-conscious opposition in the labor movement. Despite its strong position within the CIO bureaucracy in 1941, the CP was unable to prevent the CIO and many of its affiliates from denouncing the Minneapolis prosecution; in 1949, however, the CP's betrayal of the Minneapolis defendants was held up to it by opportunists in the CIO as an excuse for not defending it against the witchhunt. The Trotskyists defended the CP in 1949, but the CP refused their help, wrecking its own defense committees in order to keep Trotskyists out.

Defense Policy Criticized

While the conduct of the Trotskyists' defense in the Minneapolis trial was a good *defensive* exposition of the ideas of socialism, it was clearly deficient in not taking an *offensive* thrust, in failing to turn the tables on the system and to put it on trial. The Spanish Trotskyist Grandizo Munis raised this criticism, among others, of the SWP leaders' defense policy. Although he failed to take sufficiently into account the need for defensive formulations to protect the party's legality, Munis correctly complained of a lack of political offensive in Cannon's testimony.

> "It was there, replying to the political accusations—struggle against the war, advocacy of violence, overthrow of the government by force—where it is necessary to have raised the tone and turned the tables, accuse the government and the bourgeoisie of a reactionary conspiracy; of permanent violence against the majority of the population, physical, economic, moral, educative violence; of launching the population into a slaughter also by means of violence in order to defend the Sixty Families."
>
> —"A Criticism of the Minneapolis Trial"

In his reply, Cannon correctly condemned Munis for demanding ultra-left adventurist "calls to action" instead of propaganda, but he failed to adequately answer the charge of political passivity and of a weak, defensive stance. His reply ("Political Principles and Propaganda Methods") overemphasized the need to patiently explain revolutionary politics to a backward working class, lacking in political consciousness. After the war, when the shackles of war discipline were removed from the working class, this error was inverted in an overemphasis of the momentary upsurge in class struggle.

Lewis and the Miners: 1943

Most of the opportunities for intervention in the unions during the war consisted in leading rank-and-file struggles against a monolithic, pro-war bureaucracy. The exception to this pattern was Lewis and the UMW. Having broken with Roosevelt before the war because of what he felt to be insufficient favors and attention, Lewis authorized miners' strikes in 1943 which broke the facade of the no-strike pledge. This galvanized the opposition of the rest of the bureaucracy, which feared a general outpouring of strike struggles. Not only the rabidly patriotic, pro-war CP, but other bureaucrats as well, heaped scorn on the miners, calling them "fascist."

While the SWP was correct in its orientation toward united-front support to Lewis against the government and the bulk of the trade-union bureaucracy, the tone of this support failed to take into account the fact that Lewis was a reformist trade unionist, completely pro-capitalist, who therefore *had* to betray the eager following he was gathering by authorizing strikes during the war. He did this, performing what was perhaps his greatest service for capitalism, by heading off the rising tide of sentiment for a labor party. Focusing opposition to Roosevelt on himself, Lewis misled and demoralized masses of workers throughout the country by advocating a vote for the Republican, Wendell Wilkie, in the 1944 elections. Instead of warning of Lewis' real role, the *Militant* appears not only supportive but genuinely uncritical during the 1943 strikes.

> "[Lewis] despite his inconsistencies and failure to draw the proper conclusions ... has emerged again as the outstanding leader of the union movement, towering above the Greens and Murray as though they were pygmies, and has rewon the support of the miners and the ranks of other unions."
> —*Militant*, 8 May 1943

Though written from the outside, and therefore unable to intervene directly, the articles on the 1943 miners' strikes by Art Preis nevertheless reveal an unwarranted infatuation with Lewis which was evoked by the SWP's overconcentration on blocs with left bureaucrats, to the detriment of the struggle for revolutionary leadership.

The struggle against the no-strike pledge reached its highest pitch in the United Auto Workers, which had a militant rank and file and a tradition of democratic intra-union struggle not because of the absence of bureaucracy, but because of the failure of any one bureaucratic tendency to dominate. Despite their fundamental agreement on the war and no-strike pledge, the counterposed tendencies continued to squabble among themselves as part of their endless competition for office. The wing around Reuther tried to appear to the left by opposing the excesses of the Stalinists such as the latter's proposal for a system of war-time incentive pay to induce speed-up, but in reality was no better on the basic issue of the war.

Auto Workers Fight the No-Strike Pledge

The struggle reached a peak at the 1944 UAW convention. Debate around the issue raged through five days of the convention. The highly political delegates were on their toes, ready for bureaucratic tricks. On the first day, they defeated by an overwhelming margin a proposal to elect new officers early in the convention and insisted that this be the last point: after positions on the issues were clear. The Reuther tendency dropped to its lowest authority during the war because of its role in saving the day for the no-strike pledge, through proposing that the pledge be retained until the issue could be decided by a membership referendum.

The convention was marked by the appearance of the Rank and File Caucus, an oppositional grouping organized primarily by local leaders in Detroit. It was based on four points: end the no-strike pledge, labor leaders off the government War Labor Board, for an independent labor party and smash the "Little Steel" formula (i.e., break the freeze on wage raises). This caucus was the best grouping of its kind to emerge during the war. A similar local leadership oppositional grouping in the rubber workers' union was criticized by the SWP for its contradictory position: while opposing the no-strike pledge and War Labor Board, it nevertheless favored the war itself (*Militant*, 26 August 1944).

The SWP's work around the UAW RFC was also a high point in Trotskyist trade-union work. Though representing only a partial break from trade-union reformism by secondary bureaucrats, the RFC was qualitatively to the left of the bureaucracy as a whole. Its program represented a break with the key points upon which the imperialist bourgeoisie relied in its dependence on the trade unions to keep the workers tied to the imperialist aims of the state. The SWP was correct to enter and build this caucus, since pursuance of its program was bound to enhance revolutionary leadership.

The SWP's support, however, was not ingratiating or uncritical as was its early support to Lewis. As the caucus was forming before the convention, the SWP spoke to it in the following terms, seeking to maximize political clarity:

> "This group, in the process of development and crystallization, is an extremely hopeful sign, although it still contains tendencies opposed to a fully-rounded, effective program and some who are still reluctant to sever completely their ties with all the present international leaders and power cliques.
>
> "There is a tendency which thinks that all the auto workers' problems will be solved simply by elimination of the no-strike pledge. They fail to take into

> account the fundamental problem: that the basic issues confronting the workers today can and will be solved, in the final analysis, only by political means."
>
> —*Militant*, 2 September 1944

The article went on to advocate a labor party based on the trade unions with a "fundamental program against the financial parasites and monopolists." The caucus adopted the demand for a labor party. It led the fight against the no-strike pledge at the convention and made an impressive showing, although it failed to secure a majority in a direct vote against the pledge.

Despite encouraging developments such as this, the SWP did not formalize a general return to activity in the unions until 1945, when it made a belated turn to a perspective of "organizing left-wing forces" around opposition to the no-strike pledge, War Labor Board, and for a labor party. In 1944, a small oppositional grouping was formed in the SWP by Goldman and Morrow based on Stalinophobia and a perspective of reunification with the Shachtmanite Workers Party, which had split off in 1940. On its way out of the SWP, this grouping was able to make factional hay out of the "policy of caution." Referring to the SWP's inactivity, a member of this faction asked pointedly, "When workers do move on a mass scale, why should they follow anyone who did not previously supply some type of leadership?" (A. Winters, "Review of Our Trade Union Policy," *Internal Bulletin* Vol. VI, No. 9, 1944).

Replying to the Goldman-Morrow group, the SWP majority specifically ruled out caucuses such as the RFC as a general model, claiming that the left wing could not be built by presenting the masses with a "ready-made" program, but only by working within the existing caucus formations. Since the RFC was led primarily by politically independent secondary UAW leaders, "existing caucus formations" could only mean a policy of entering the major bureaucratic power groupings, which is exactly what the SWP did on its return to activity after the war. Despite the comparative impotence of the trade-union bureaucracy and different nature of the tasks in the early thirties, the Minneapolis experience was cited as an example in defense of a policy that emphasized blocking with sections of the bureaucracy and avoiding the presentation of a program independent of, and counterposed to, the bureaucracy in the unions.

This was the perspective followed by the SWP in the post-war period. In the brief but extensive post-war strike wave—the most massive strike wave in U.S. labor history—the SWP emphasized its enthusiasm for the intense economic struggles and underplayed its alternatives to the bureaucracy. Against the Goldman-Morrowites, the majority explicitly defended a policy of avoiding criticism of UAW leadership policy at the beginning of the 1946 GM strike in order to maintain a common front with the bureaucracy against the company. For a small revolutionary force of only 2,000 (this figure represented rapid growth at the end of the war period) to take such an attitude toward the vast trade-union bureaucracy simply served to weaken the forces which could have built revolutionary leadership by struggling against the inevitable bureaucratic betrayals.

The relative pessimism of 1941 as to the backwardness of the working class gave way in the post-war period to the optimism of "Theses on the American Revolution," the political resolution of the 1946 SWP convention. The "Theses" ruled out a new stabilization of capitalism and saw an unbroken development of the SWP into the vanguard party standing at the head of the revolutionary proletariat. The "Theses" underestimated not only the ability of capitalism to restabilize itself but also the relative strength of the trade-union bureaucracy and of Stalinism. Despite degeneration and decline, the CP still had 10,000 members at the end of the war.

This revolutionary optimism was not matched in the trade unions by the open preparation of revolutionary leadership through "third group" caucuses, however, but by an orientation first toward the more progressive bureaucratic reformists who were leading strike struggles or breaking with their previous allies, the discredited Stalinists. Later, as the cold war set in, the SWP broke with its allies and oriented more toward the Stalinists. As in the late thirties, these orientations tended to be based not on maximum political clarity but on the trade-union issues of the moment. Unlike the late thirties, however, the situation changed rapidly into a general purge of reds and hardening of a conservative bureaucracy, with which no blocs were possible. Furthermore the united fronts of the post-war period tended to take the form of critical support for one faction over another in union elections. Besides having a demoralizing effect on the ranks of the SWP's trade-union cadre, the Trotskyists' failure to present a hard, distinctive revolutionary alternative in the unions in this period thus contributed to the formation of the new bureaucratic line-up and thereby to the eventual cold-war defeats.

Critical Support for Reuther: 1946

Again the UAW is the most important example, since in 1946 in that union the SWP had perhaps its best case for a policy of blocs. After the war, Reuther began a drive for domination of the union with a show of militancy. He led a 113-day strike against General Motors on the basis of the three-point program: open the books to public inspection, negotiations in public and wage increases without price increases. Though he made his basic support of capitalism and the "right" to profits clear, he was able to mobilize militant sentiment with this program, strike a left posture at the 1946 convention and win the presidency of the union from the Stalinist-backed R.J. Thomas.

Reuther, however, made no effort to fight for and deepen the "GM strike program" at the convention. Though he won most of his votes on the basis of this militant strike program, his real program was opposition to the CP. This appealed to militants also, of course, since the CP had been completely discredited by its thoroughly right-wing role during the war (which it had incredibly attempted to extend into the post-war period—the so-called permanent no-strike pledge—on the basis of the Soviet bureaucracy's hopes for post-war peaceful coexistence with its capitalist allies). However, Reuther's caucus also attracted conservative anti-communists such as the Association of Catholic Trade Unionists (ACTU). The *Militant* exposed Reuther's basic conservatism even on trade-union issues by pointing out that he had devised the "one-at-a-time" strategy (isolating strikes against one company at a time); that he had endorsed the introduction of the "company security" clause into the Ford contract and had capitulated to Truman's "fact-finding" panel in the GM strike against the will of the elected negotiating body (23 March 1946). It also pointed out that his written program was no better than the Stalinist-backed Thomas-Addes caucus program "except for language and phraseology" (30 March 1946). Nevertheless, the Trotskyists critically supported his campaign for president because of the fact that the militant workers were voting for him on the basis of the GM strike program.

With skillful demagogy, Reuther had successfully coopted the militant wing of the union, including the earlier Rank and File Caucus (which had dissolved into the Reuther caucus). An approach to this militant wing which would have driven a wedge between the militants and Reuther was needed. In 1944, the SWP had argued that the time was not ripe for the independent drive of the RFC—despite the fact that these "unknowns," only running one candidate and without any serious effort, had secured 20 percent of the vote for president at the 1944 convention (*Fourth International*, October 1944). Yet the SWP had not hesitated to raise programmatic demands on the RFC as it was forming, in order to make its break with the bureaucracy complete. In 1946, however, despite criticisms of Reuther, in the last analysis the SWP supported him simply on the basis of his popularity and without having made any programmatic demands whatsoever on him (such as that he break with the conservative anti-communists as a condition for support).

Critical Support for Thomas-Addes: 1947

An independent stance might have left the SWP supporters isolated at the 1946 convention, but the establishment of such a principled pole would have helped recruit militants by the time of the next convention in 1947. Instead, the SWP simply tailed the militants—or thought it tailed the militants—once again. In the interval between the two conventions, Reuther consolidated his position on the basis of anti-communism—including support for Truman's foreign policy—and bureaucratic reformism. At the 1947 convention, the SWP switched its support to the Thomas-Addes caucus, on the grounds that the militants were already fed up with Reuther and an attempt had to be made to halt the latter's drive toward one-man dictatorial rule. For this bloc, there wasn't even the pretense of a programmatic basis. Despite the shift of Reuther to the right and the phony "left" noises of Thomas-Addes and the Stalinists, however, Reuther's complete slate was swept into office largely because of the discredited character of the previous leadership. Only after this debacle did the SWP put together an independent caucus. If such a course had been unrealistic before, after the 1947 convention it was more hopeless than ever. By that time, however, there was no other choice.

The SWP's course in other unions was similar. In the National Maritime Union, for instance, the SWP supported Curran when he broke from his former Stalinist allies on the basis of democracy and militancy, even though he was already lining up for Truman's foreign policy and letting the Stalinists get to the left of him on militancy. Later, the SWP had to support the Stalinists against his vicious, bureaucratic expulsions.

Cold War and Cochran-Clarke

In 1953 the SWP was racked by a faction fight and split which in part reflected the penetration into the party of the kind of trade-union "politics" it had been pursuing in the unions. What had looked like a hopeful situation in the immediate post-war period had turned rapidly into its opposite. The betrayals and self-defeating policies of the Stalinists had combined with reformist trade-unionist illusions to allow not only the consolidation of a monolithic, conservative trade-union bureaucracy, but the successful purge of reds from the unions and the nurturing of right-wing anti-communism within the working class, which made the international cold-war drive of U.S. imperialism virtually unopposed at home.

The purge and pressure of the cold war caused a section of the SWP trade-union cadre to become disillusioned and give up on the perspective of building a vanguard party in the U.S. This defeatism was organized into a tendency by Cochran, on the basis of liquidation of virtually all public party activity in favor of a "propaganda" orientation which would have left the Cochranites, many of whom were officers in the UAW, free to make their peace with the Reutherite bureaucracy.

The Cochranites made an unprincipled combination with forces in New York around Bartell, Clarke and others who considered themselves the American representatives of the Pablo leadership of the Fourth International. Objectifying the post-war creation of deformed workers states in Eastern Europe and Yugoslavia into an inevitable, world-historic trend, the Pablo leadership proposed, in essence, that Stalinist and reformist leaderships could be forced to the left by the pressure of their mass base into creating more such states in a situation in which the imminence of World War III made the creation of independent Trotskyist parties impossible: the Trotskyist task, therefore, was to liquidate into the Stalinist and social-democratic parties. It was this essentially liquidationist perspective which brought Cochran and Clarke together into a temporary amalgam in the SWP.

While defending the twists and turns of the SWP trade-union policy, Cannon nevertheless indicated that these twists and turns might have had something to do with the degeneration of the cadre into material for Cochranite liquidationist opportunism:

> "Factional struggles in the trade unions in the United States, in the primitive, prepolitical stage of their development, have been power struggles, struggles for office and place, for the personal aggrandizement of one set of fakers and the denigration and discreditment of the other side....
>
> "Cochran's conception of 'power politics' in the party; his methods of conducting a factional fight—come from this school of the labor fakers, not from ours."
>
> —"Some Facts About Party History and the Reasons for its Falsification," *Internal Bulletin*, October 1953

The main cause of Cochranite liquidationism lay in the pressures of the cold war and witchhunt, which had, of course, been completely beyond the control of the SWP. However, Cannon's own documents defending the party against trade-unionist combinationism and liquidationism make clear that the party's position in the trade unions had been insufficiently distinct from "struggles for office and place," just as it had been insufficiently distinct from blocs with progressive Rooseveltians before World War II.

In the course of pursuing a trade-union policy based almost exclusively on making blocs on the immediate trade-union issues, the SWP had gradually adapted to trade unionism and become less discriminating in whom it blocked with and why. Unlike the Stalinists and Shachtmanites, the Trotskyists maintained their class principles by refusing to make unprincipled alliances or by breaking them as soon as they became untenable. (Thus the SWP switched sides in the UAW in 1947 while the Workers Party of Shachtman pursued Reuther et. al. into the arms of the State Department.) In the final analysis, the SWP remained a principled party of revolutionary socialism by struggling against the fruits of its trade-union work internally and accepting the split of 20 percent of its membership in 1953 rather than making further concessions to trade unionism.

Spartacist League: Learn and Go Forward

The policy of making united fronts in the trade-union movement around the immediate issues is not in itself incorrect. What the SWP did wrong was to see this as its exclusive policy for all periods, except those in which no blocs could be made without gross violations of principle, in which case the answer was to do nothing. In any period of normal trade-union activity, blocs can be made around immediate issues. The task of revolutionists is to forge a cadre, within the unions as well as without, armed with a program to break the unions from their role as instruments for tying the workers to capitalism and imperialism. Such a program must go beyond immediate issues and address all the key political questions facing the working class and provide answers which point to a revolutionary policy and leadership.

While the Trotskyists advanced the struggle for revolutionary leadership dramatically with the right united front at the right time, as in Minneapolis in 1934, they more often tended to undermine their own party building with an exclusive policy of blocs, some of which had little or no basis for existence from the standpoint of revolutionary politics. By presuming that it was necessary for a small force to prove itself in action against the class enemy before it could present itself independently to the workers as an alternative leadership, the Trotskyists' united fronts tended to increasingly take the form of promoting someone else's leadership.

The Spartacist League sees as the chief lesson from this experience not the need to reject united fronts, occasional blocs or the tactic of critical support in the trade unions, but the need to subordinate these tactics to the task of building a revolutionary political alternative to the bureaucracy within the unions. A bloc or tactic of electoral support which fails to enhance revolutionary leadership through undermining the bureaucracy as such can only build illusions in reformism. The central conclusion is that there is no substitute for the hard road of struggle to inject a political class perspective of proletarian internationalism into what is normally a narrow, nationalist and parochial arena of struggle. Especially in the initial phases of struggle when the revolutionary forces are weak, it is necessary to make an independent pole as politically distinct as possible, so that the basis for future growth is clear. To this end, the SL calls for the building of caucuses based on the revolutionary transitional program.

Part Three

Organizing the Unemployed in the Great Depression

Fighting for Unity

By Len Meyers and Chris Knox. Reprinted from Workers Vanguard *No. 73, 18 July 1975*

The onset of depression in the early 1930's posed a test of monumental importance for every working-class political tendency and for the labor movement as a whole. Mass unemployment, caused by the capitalist system itself and obviously affected by the political actions of the ruling class and its state, became a political question of the highest order. Today, as millions once again face the prospect of long-term joblessness due to another world-wide capitalist depression, revolutionaries should pay close attention to the political lessons of communist unemployed organizing in the 1930's.

The legions of jobless and homeless were the most dramatic human manifestation of a general economic crisis which was unprecedented in its severity, duration and international extent. Of the major nations, only the Soviet Union, with its collectivised property relations, escaped the dire effects. In the United States unemployment rose continuously, peaking in 1933 at nearly 18,000,000 and creating what was increasingly understood to be a permanent mass of surplus labor. The obtuse administration of Herbert Hoover reflected the quandary of its capitalist masters by seeking to publicly deny the existence of a serious problem as long as possible. Having come to office promising a new era of permanent prosperity, Hoover ended his term in 1933 following a 50 percent decline in industrial production since 1929, with agriculture bankrupt and the entire banking system of the country closed. Lacking any form of unemployment insurance, or even adequate temporary relief, the unemployed faced total destitution.

For labor the question of unemployment was intimately connected with organizing the great mass of unskilled production workers in the big factories into industrial unions. Left to themselves, growing numbers of desperate unemployed provided a ready pool of scab labor for strikebreaking employers. The fear of unemployment alone was sufficient to have a severely depressing effect on the struggles of employed workers: in 1930 the number of strikes was 618, down from 349,400 in 1927, with an equally precipitous decline in numbers of workers involved. Mass organization of both employed workers and unemployed was needed to unite the working class in struggle against a system which by protecting the profits of a few industrial and financial moguls subjected the masses of working people to untold privations.

Leadership of the initial protests of the unemployed fell to the Communist Party, largely because of the default of the official trade-union organizations of the American Federation of Labor. Unprecedented numbers of unemployed were ready to march in political protests as early as 1930, but the hidebound AFL bureaucracy under William Green detested nothing so much as masses of workers in militant action. The AFL's drastic decline in membership (down to three million in 1929 from an earlier peak of nearly twice that), and concentration in the skilled crafts to the exclusion of the overwhelming majority of unskilled workers, only made the union "leaders" all the more cautious and conservative.

At the very beginning of the crisis, the AFL bureaucracy pledged cooperation with the employers: at a 1929 White House conference with business tycoons and the Hoover administration, they pledged not to seek wage advances or strike during the crisis. As late as 1932, the third year of the great depression, the AFL still officially opposed the introduction of federal unemployment insurance. This "alien" scheme, said Green, was an attack on the "freedom" of the American worker.

Early CP Unemployed Organizing

At first the Communist Party dived into the job of organizing the unemployed with vigorous determination and a program which, on paper, reflected the needs of the unemployed by combining reform demands for relief and unemployment insurance with a call to unite the unemployed with employed workers in a struggle to overthrow capitalism. In March 1930 the CP press (with perhaps a bit of exaggeration) reported hunger marches in numerous cities totaling one and a quarter million workers and unemployed—100,000 in New York and Detroit, 40,000 in Boston and Chicago, etc.—under the slogan "work or wages." The marches were met with frenzied violence by the ruling class. In New York the entire police force was mobilized, including mounted patrols and machine gun units, and a ferocious attack launched on the marchers.

In 1931 CP Unemployed Council (UC) organizers led the first hunger march on Washington, with 1,500 delegates from around the country, to present their demands: for unemployment insurance equal to full wages and immediate relief for each unemployed worker, to be paid by government and the bosses; for the seven-hour day without reduction in pay; and for unity of the employed and unemployed in struggle against hunger, wage cuts, mass layoffs and Hoover's "stagger plans." The Communist Party continued to lead militant actions throughout the early 1930's. It must be credited with first arousing American workers from their shock and pressuring enactment of the first large-scale unemployment compensation measures. The heroism, dedication and sacrifice of its cadres was brought home by incidents such as the brutal murder of four marchers, including two young Communists, by police and company thugs during a march on the giant Ford River Rouge plant in 1932.

But in the final analysis the Communist Party pursued an adventuristic and sectarian policy which isolated it from the masses of workers, both employed and unemployed, and disorganized its own movement. After a decade of factional struggle, the CP entered the 1930's as a degenerated caricature of its former self, homogenized into a monolithic instrument of the ruling bureaucratic stratum of the USSR. This parasitic bureaucracy headed by Joseph Stalin, while preserving the economic conquests of the October Revolution, had politically expropriated the working class by eliminating soviet and party democracy in the mid-1920's. Following the Stalinization of the Communist International, the American CP expelled its Trotskyist opposition led by Cannon, Shachtman and Abern, and then its right opposition under Lovestone.

In response to the catastrophic consequences of his earlier rightist policies—and in order to undercut sympathy in Communist ranks for the persecuted Left Opposition—Stalin now embarked on an equally disastrous adventurist and sectarian course. The CP's refusal to fight for a united proletarian front with the Social Democrats against the mounting fascist menace produced a historic catastrophe of monumental proportions in Germany with Hitler's accession to power in 1933 and the consequent destruction of the entire labor movement.

'Soup Consciousness'

The sectarian turn launched by Stalin in 1929 produced a sudden about-face in the U. S. Communist Party's already flawed program and practice, laying the basis for the later sharp right turn embodied in the "popular-front" policies of the late 1930's. Since Stalin's rigid schema presumed an uninterrupted course toward revolution (the so-called "Third Period") was supposed to bring the inevitable demise of imperialism, Leninist tactics of united front and work within the established mass organizations of the workers were completely thrown out. The AFL was denounced as a "fascist" organization, and the rest of the left (such as the Socialist Party and Trotskyists) was dismissed as "social-fascist." The CP for the most part abandoned work in the AFL unions and pulled its relatively small number of supporters out into "revolutionary" dual unions under its own federation, the Trade Union Unity League (TUUL).

Since most unorganized workers still looked to the AFL as the official union movement (many joined the AFL directly through "federal locals"), the "dual" unions stagnated in increasing irrelevancy. When an economic upturn of modest proportions in 1933 coincided with maneuvers by President Roosevelt to enhance the AFL unions (in order to head off the threat of more radical developments), the "duals" served to isolate class struggle militants from intervening in the repeated mass strikes that set the stage for the building of industrial unions. In unemployed organizing, where the key need was for uniting the jobless with the social power of the unions, the CP's turn amounted to self-imposed isolation from the employed workers.

The impotence resulting from this isolation led the Stalinists to capitulate, almost in desperation, to the lowest forms of struggle of the unemployed. After the initial mass demonstrations of March 1930 support for mass protests trailed off considerably, down by more than 50 percent the next year. Seeking to build its own unemployed movement under the leadership of the TUUL and Unemployed Councils [UCs], and lacking a tactical approach toward the official unions, the work of the UCs degenerated to the lowest form of barter and "self-help"—what the Trotskyist paper, the *Militant*, described as the "planned economy of garbage picking." The CP also fell into a one-sided propaganda concentration on its "Workers Unemployment Insurance Bill," as a reformist panacea to the effects of the capitalist economic crisis.

The CP's unemployed work was obviously floundering in early 1931 when Communist Party head Earl Browder called for "the direct caring for starving workers" (*Daily Worker*, 12 March 1931). But four months later he was complaining that the UCs had degenerated to "dragging behind the most miserable bourgeois charity policy" (*Communist*, July 1931). Unable to point to the cause of this impasse—the self imposed isolation brought about by Stalin's "Third Period" policies—Browder did catalogue its effects:

> "In the Unemployed Councils, while we have registered some advances, there are relatively few examples of positive achievements.... they remain narrow cadre organizations which do not have intimate day-to-day contact with the masses, which have not yet established themselves as permanent centers for work among the masses and in most cases, with the removal of 2 or 3 comrades assigned by the party, these organizations would completely collapse."
>
> —*Communist*, October 1931

Socialists and Musteites

Thus Stalinist policy during the "Third Period," despite many mass marches and militant actions, failed to build a broad unemployed organization linked to the established unions. The vacuum left by the CP was partly filled by other organizations with centrist or reformist programs, such as the Socialist Party. Starting out with "self-help" activities and a generally rightist thrust (Norman Thomas supported financier J.P. Morgan's "block aid" plan) the SP gradually grew more militant until after 1933 it became an apparent left-wing alternative to Stalinism. The SP led the Workers Committee on Unemployment in Chicago, its biggest local base, and founded the Workers Alliance of America (WAA) in 1935.

Also occupying this terrain was the Conference for Progressive Labor Action (CPLA), founded in 1929 by A. J. Muste, which later became the American Workers Party (AWP). The CPLA included many left-wing trade-union organizers (the ex-minister Muste had also organized textile workers and formed a labor college) left out of the picture by the CP when the latter pulled out of the AFL unions in the late 1920's. Impressed by the possibilities of mass "self-help" work such as that organized in Seattle by a CPLA member, Muste turned the CPLA in the direction of militant unemployed work as a short-cut to the creation of a "mass labor party" dedicated to establishing a "workers republic."

Lacking a coherent Marxist program for revolutionary social change, the Musteites groped their way leftward only under the persistent blows of experience. Their initial self-help orientation was modified later with the recognition that the scourge of unemployment could not be solved without addressing the question of who holds power and without organizing the working class to seize state power. Yet, capitulating to anti-communist sentiment, they continued to shy away from the conception of the dictatorship of the proletariat.

In their unemployed work, the Musteites adapted to backward sentiment among the masses in order to enhance organizational success. Louis Budenz, the main CPLA theorist who later went over to Stalinist popular frontism, called for an "American Approach" (!) to mass work. But for this capitulation to nationalist prejudices the Musteites paid a heavy price. Their Unemployed Leagues, which were strongest in Ohio and Pennsylvania, became temporary havens for anti-communists seeking to build a bulwark against the CP.

At the 1933 founding conference (on July 4th!) of the National Unemployed Leagues held in Columbus, Ohio, the leftward-moving Musteites were horrified at the display of flag-waving, religious revivalist and even fascist (KKK) sentiment their "American Approach" had netted them. The podium was seized for a time by right-wingers who had to be repulsed, and the Musteites were obliged to silence all criticism, even from left-wing delegates (notably the Trotskyists), in order to maintain control. However, the NUL was founded on a strictly anti-capitalist basis despite stylistic concessions to the "American Approach" in its founding declaration, and the rightists quickly drifted away.

The Musteite-led Unemployed Leagues [ULs] chalked up notable accomplishments. Peaking in membership during 1933, the leagues managed to halt all evictions (which were rampant nationally) in Columbus during the summer of that year. Following the leftward course of the CPLA/AWP, the ULs moved programmatically from exclusive concentration on "practical" reforms to setting the unemployed struggle in the context of the need for "the abolition of the entire capitalist system." Seeing the limitations of unemployed work without links to employed workers, the Musteites led a militant strike struggle in Toledo in 1934, one of the three great labor battles of that year. Their Unemployed League took leadership of the foundering Auto-Lite strike and led it to the point of a city-wide general strike, blazing the way for later sit-down successes in Detroit and the formation of the first mass industrial union in auto.

Early Trotskyist Unemployed Organizing

Prior to the strikes of 1934 and a later fusion with the Musteites, the Trotskyist Communist League of America (CLA) had suffered years of isolation enforced, often violently, by the much larger Communist Party. Attempting to warn the ranks of the official party of the CP's disastrous "Third Period" course, the CLA argued against the sectarian attempt to keep the unemployed movement within the narrow bounds of the TUUL, calling instead for an orientation toward drawing AFL unions into united-front actions around unemployment. The need for a united-front unemployed movement on the broadest possible basis, drawing in all political tendencies, became more and more urgent as the CP, SP and Musteites each developed their "own" unemployed movements. But the CLA never called for unity at the expense of program. It attacked the opportunist errors of the CP (and other tendencies) and gave no quarter to reformist concepts.

The Trotskyists began their analysis by debunking the "Third Period" myth of a final crisis of capitalism: there would be new economic upturns, followed by renewed downturns, until capitalism was overthrown. Trotsky predicted a business upturn before it occurred in late 1933, but pointed out that because of the increasing proportion of constant capital over variable capital—increasing mechanization of industry and rising productivity of labor—unemployment was bound to remain a permanent feature of the economy ("Perspectives of the Upturn," *Writings*, 1932).

Already in 1933, veteran Communist and CLA leader Arne Swabeck, in the pamphlet *Unemployment and the Working Class*, was analysing the CP's swing from sectarian isolation to the opposite extreme of opportunist methods. The CP never conceived of the unemployed movement as "founded upon a united front of the whole working class," and was now abandoning its quixotic "conquest of the streets" adventurism for a crassly reformist program of legalism and dependence upon bourgeois politicians. Instead, the Trotskyists urged a united-front policy and demands which would be "stepping stones to the revolutionary goal."

Among these, Swabeck specified immediate relief and unemployment insurance paid by the employers and the state; a six-hour day, five-day week with no reduction in pay (the Stalinists had earlier elevated this demand to a seven hour day in order to seem more "practical"); and the extension of large-scale credits to the Soviet Union, a concrete expression of solidarity with the world's first workers state. Most important, Swabeck pointed out that the unemployed movement couldn't achieve success in isolation: "Its objectives must be general working class objectives, its struggle part of the general working class struggles for the revolution."

To the best of their ability, the Trotskyists attempted to undertake mass work in the trade unions and among the unemployed even during what James Cannon termed the CLA's "dog days" of isolation and persecution by the Stalinists in the early 1930's. The Trotskyist Gerry Allard was a founding leader of the Progressive Miners of America (PMA), a militant union based on a 1932 revolt of 40,000 miners in southern Illinois against the bureaucratic regime of John L. Lewis in the United Mine Workers. However, the PMA quickly fell under the sway of a new set of "militant" bureaucrats who became indistinguishable from the old Lewis machine. When the UMW ignored the need to organize the unemployed in Illinois, Allard and the Trotskyists played a leading role in building the Illinois Workers Alliance (IWA) which entered the SP-dominated Workers Alliance of America at its founding as the most powerful state section. The IWA soon outstripped the long-established Unemployed Councils as the strongest unemployed organization in the Midwest. It stood for the abolition of capitalism, and in the middle of the decade led militant marches on the state capital against relief cuts.

On the West Coast a patient intervention into the Los Angeles Unemployed Cooperative Relief Association [UCRA] beginning in 1932 gave the Trotskyists leadership of a diverse left-wing bloc. This leadership transformed the UCRA from a "cooperative" self-help movement into an organization which militantly fought evictions, at times roping off whole city blocks to stop dispossessions. In 1933 CLA militant Jane Rose led a protest against the cutting off of free milk distributions to the unemployed by taking over the city council and delivering speeches all day on the "class nature of the unemployed question" (*Militant*, 10 June 1933).

The Trotskyists began to achieve successes in 1933 which increasingly lessened their isolation. Hitler's unopposed march to power, facilitated by Stalin's suicidal sectarianism, had a traumatic impact. Though the CP was heading rapidly toward eventual subservience to Roosevelt's New Deal (formerly seen as "slavery"), its turn temporarily gave the Trotskyists a chance to intervene in Stalinist-led mass meetings.

Stalinists Sabotage the NFUWL

One important opportunity to form a united-front unemployed organization came at the founding conference of the National Federation of Unemployed Workers Leagues [NFUWL] in May of 1933. Chicago, where the meeting was held, had a year earlier been the scene of a successful, broad united-front movement to reverse a 50 percent relief cut. On that occasion, the Stalinists were forced to abandon their sectarianism and unite with "social fascists" around immediate demands. Now they, the SP, Trotskyists, Musteites, Lovestoneites and innumerable other tendencies met and founded the first national unemployed organization having the potential of becoming a truly mass organization.

The Trotskyists led in preventing anti-communist exclusion of the Unemployed Councils from the conference, and succeeded in getting their formulation for a united-front movement passed. This called for the NFUWL to seek "the closest relationship with the *Employed* workers through the trade unions" while guaranteeing "the right of minority expression and freedom of criticism" (quoted in the *Militant*, 20 May 1933). Graphically demonstrating its quandary, the CP delegation supported this conception after having voted against it only a few months earlier at a conference to establish a united front to free jailed labor hero Tom Mooney.

Unfortunately, however, the NFUWL was stillborn because the major tendencies were still determined to build their "own" unemployed bailiwicks in place of any united-front organization. The very next month, Stalinists and Musteites blocked at the Columbus conference of the National Unemployed

Leagues to defeat a Trotskyist motion for affiliation to the NFUWL (*Militant*, 15 July 1933). Since the Trotskyists were still much weaker than CP and SP forces in the NFUWL leadership, they were unable to carry the broad grouping forward themselves. Meanwhile the CP continued to degenerate to the right, so that by the time a united unemployed movement was founded under the name Workers Alliance in 1936 (a year after origination of the WA by the Socialists) it rapidly became a subservient appendage of the Roosevelt government.

Although only a year before they had aided the CP in wrecking the NFUWL and opposing the Trotskyists' efforts to build a broad united-front national unemployed organization, the Musteites' gradual programmatic movement to the left laid the basis for their fusion with the CLA in late 1934. Both tendencies came to the fusion fresh from the field of class battle: the Musteites leading auto workers in Toledo and the CLA at the head of Minneapolis Teamsters.

Although many leading elements of the CPLA/AWP, including Budenz and Muste himself, clung to reformist notions picked up during their checkered political course, the unification was made on the basis of what Trotsky described as a "rigidly principled program." As a result, while Budenz, Muste and others left the WP in a matter of months, the bulk of their erstwhile followers remained. The attendance of 1,200 at the founding convention of the Workers Party of the U.S. represented a significant step in overcoming the Trotskyists' former isolation. The WP now led the National Unemployed Leagues, representing 130,000 unemployed in Ohio, another 25,000 in Pennsylvania, and a strong base in West Virginia.

Trotskyists Lead the National Unemployed Leagues

At once the WP sought to purge the NUL of remaining hangovers from the period when its course was one of limitation to immediate reform issues and opportunist capitulation to backward prejudices among the masses. A "Resolution on the Unemployed Question," passed by a WP National Committee plenum in October 1935 specified that

> "The next step in the development of the unemployed movement must be an increased educational and agitational campaign throughout to root the organizations solidly in the principles of the class struggle."

Analyzing the different unemployed organizations, the resolution noted that the NUL was "the leading organization in the unemployed field," having pursued a policy of mass, class-struggle militancy and "vigorous participation of the rank and file in the life of the organization." Its weaknesses included failure to penetrate major industrial centers and consolidate organizationally, leading to "great fluctuations" in membership. In addition,

> "Nuclei and fractions of revolutionists have not been built systematically within the local leagues. And the organization is not in a genuine sense national in scope."

The resolution called for WP efforts toward solving the two major problems of the unemployed movement, that of achieving a real united front of the numerous unemployed organizations and unity with employed workers. The resolution called for orientation toward the Workers Alliance, which was making overtures to which the Stalinists were responding (and which itself represented leftward development of the Socialist Party).

The NUL also took a serious stance toward the race question and organizing in the South. Symbolic of its concern with the organizing of black unemployed was the selection of E. R. McKinney, a black National Committee member of the Workers Party and former Musteite, as vice-president of the NUL and editor of its weekly paper, *Mass Action*. The NUL adamantly refused to grant charters to segregated locals, and led thousands of blacks and whites in National Unemployed Day marches in 1934 in Gulfport, Mississippi, Ashland, Kentucky and other parts of the South. The NUL recognized "that a local organization may force up relief standards many times, but if it fails to overcome the racial division then it has failed fundamentally and is a menace to the Labor movement" (1934 convention minutes).

The NUL supported certain legislative action, such as the Frazier-Lundeen Workers Unemployment Insurance Bill, but not with the fixation on reformist legislative panaceas characteristic of the CP-led Unemployed Councils. The Workers Party's *New Militant* (1 January 1935) denounced the Stalinists for "making only one demand—the Lundeen Bill—the single issue, [and thereby] dividing the ranks of the unemployed and workers." The WP insisted that the fight for legislative reforms be "a class-struggle fight, not a class-collaboration lobby." However, some slogans used by the NUL and the Illinois Workers Alliance (such as "tax the rich") could have led to the impression that workers' interests lie in reforming the capitalist state apparatus, and should have been left behind with the rest of the Musteite "American Approach" reformist baggage.

Small though they were, during the early 1930's the Trotskyists had made an impressive contribution to communist unemployed work, both on the theoretical and practical levels. While the much larger CP frittered away its influence and opportunities for leadership of the masses by "Third Period" excesses, only to turn later to reformist "popular-front" betrayals, the Trotskyists had provided a correct understanding of Leninist tactics for organization of the unemployed, and realized the goals in the form of mass organization. Concurrently they won over leftward-moving centrists repelled by Stalinist sectarianism as well as by AFL and SP do-nothingism. In their struggle to forge a new revolutionary vanguard party they were in the latter half of the decade to provide additional examples of revolutionary work among the unemployed while the CP sank to the depths of its pro-Roosevelt, pro-war capitulation.

Mobilizing Union Power

By Len Meyers and Chris Knox. Reprinted from Workers Vanguard *No. 74, 1 August 1975*

In the fight to organize the great mass of jobless during the 1930's depression, two key conceptions guided the work of the Trotskyists: the united front and unity of the employed and unemployed. During the early years of the decade the united front was the focus of struggle, as a Stalinized Communist Party refused to cooperate with other left-wing forces (whom it termed "social-fascists") and left the AFL unions in pursuit of its sectarian "Third Period" policies. Then, from 1934 onwards a wave of militant strikes and the organization of mass industrial unions sharply posed the possibility of uniting the unemployed with the employed in a powerful working-class assault on capitalism. However, this opportunity was sacrificed by the Stalinists in the name of their new Messiah: the popular front.

As predicted by Trotsky, U.S. capitalism did not continue to fall steadily deeper into an apocalyptic "final crisis," instead experiencing a limited upturn in 1933 and a general rise in production during 1935–37. Combined with passage of the National Industrial Recovery Act (NRA), the upswing emboldened the masses and led to a flood of unorganized workers into the conservative AFL. But the recovery was hollow and short-lived. With the introduction of labor-saving machinery in industry, unemployment never dropped below 8 million during the "boom" and was probably closer to 11 or 12 million.

Hardly a "return to prosperity" for the masses, the Roosevelt New Deal was a series of conservative, even reactionary, reforms designed to cushion economic crisis and head off labor militancy. Under the wage and price codes of the NRA strikes were broken, incomes fixed and inflation allowed to run rampant. Relief was degrading and difficult to obtain. In addition, local relief budgets were accompanied by sales taxes and other measures designed to throw the burden of the crisis onto the backs of workers and the poor. In some regions there were starvation conditions, as in the South where, according to one CP estimate, relief officials expected a family to survive on as little as $7.09 a month (*Communist*, June 1935).

Accepted at the depth of the crisis as a necessary evil, the NRA was overturned by the Supreme Court in 1935 because its regulatory codes were considered a drag on free enterprise. In the same year, Roosevelt announced the end of all federal aid to relief, although official estimates showed only half the eligible unemployed were on the dole in the first place. Responsibility for maintaining the jobless was dumped back on the virtually bankrupt states and localities (as under Hoover), producing a new round of demonstrations in state capitals protesting the relief cuts.

'Scab or Starve!'

Roosevelt's next move was the establishment of the Works Progress Administration (WPA), which was supposed to compensate for the ending of federal aid by putting the unemployed to work. The WPA never took in more than one quarter of the jobless and consisted largely of useless "make-work" projects. Most important, it was a concerted attack on the living standards of the unemployed (its rates often being below those of local relief) and on union wage scales. WPA projects paid as low as $19 a month in the South and $40 in the North. One federal administrator, challenged by objections to the WPA wage rates, shot back: "Scab or starve!"

The shift in New Deal policies in 1935 was a deliberate attack on the working class, aimed at crippling the mushrooming unemployed organizations and undermining union organization. However, employed and unemployed fought back in massive protests that wrenched important concessions from Roosevelt. Many building trades locals of the AFL struck WPA projects to defend the wage scales of their unemployed members. "Flying squads" were used in New Jersey to shut down WPA sites, and 50,000 WPA jobs went begging in New York City due to an organized boycott. "Progressive" Mayor LaGuardia responded: "Take WPA jobs or go to jail" (*Workers Alliance*, 1 September 1935). Mass marches were called around the country by the Socialist Party-led Workers Alliance demanding $30 minimum for a 30-hour week, and by mid-1936 the administration was forced to grant, on paper at least, the possibility of increased wages according to local standards and the right of union organization on WPA projects.

The fate of the unemployed movement was directly affected by changes in global politics. With the victory of Hitler in 1933, Stalin took fright and ordered foreign Communist Parties to execute an about-face, forming "anti-fascist" alliances with "democratic" capitalist politicians in order to defend the Soviet Union. In the U.S., where the Stalinists and social democrats never came close to the strength they had in Europe, the CP had to be content with one-sidedly supporting Roosevelt, who hardly even bothered to throw it a few crumbs. By 1936 the Communist Party was giving tacit electoral support to the Democrats and leadership of militant unemployed actions fell increasingly to the left wing of the Socialist Party (SP) and the Trotskyists.

Trotskyists Unite Employed and Unemployed

Following fusion with the Musteites and the formation of the Workers Party (WP) at the end of 1934, the Trotskyists led the National Unemployed

League which was particularly strong in the coalmining regions of the Northeast: 130,000 in Ohio, 25,000 in Pennsylvania and a strong base in West Virginia. The Unemployed Leagues organized relief office takeovers to protest cuts, fought evictions with militant tactics and organized workers on federal projects. A strike of government construction sites in Ohio during 1935 saw UL and WP members lead flying squads: "The pickets defied police interference and removed shovels from the hands of reluctant scabs," wrote the *New Militant* (20 April 1935).

The Trotskyists constantly fought for militant unity of the employed and unemployed. When Pennsylvania cut its relief program, a united-front Joint Action Committee composed of the WP-led Pennsylvania Unemployed League, the SP-led Pennsylvania Security League and the AFL Central Trades and Labor Council organized a strike by 7,000 WPA workers throughout the state. The CP's Unemployed Council, which had initiated the Committee, dropped out after the latter adopted the Trotskyists' program for direct action and rejected a Stalinist plan to lobby the state legislature. The strike was victorious and Pennsylvania became the first state forced to grant a WPA wage increase and recognize a bargaining agent (the AFL Council) on the projects (*New Militant*, 12 October 1935).

In Minneapolis the Trotskyists set an example of working-class unity which even the Stalinists found impossible to ignore. Even before the three strikes in 1934 which established the General Drivers Local 574, under Trotskyist leadership, and transformed Minneapolis into a union town, the militant Teamsters sought to organize the unemployed. During the strikes this paid off as many of the 4,000 unemployed workers of the Minneapolis Central Council of Workers (MCCW) militantly defended the truck drivers' picket lines.

The lull in the class struggle following the 1934 strikes brought a sharp downturn in MCCW membership, the kind of fluctuations which plagued all unemployed organizations. Nevertheless, the Trotskyists went ahead with aggressive organizing of the jobless. AFL unions initially refused to cooperate, so Local 574 set up a "Federal Workers Section" (FWS), subordinate to the Drivers Local, but with an autonomous structure and open to all the unemployed in the city. With the power of the solidly unionized truck drivers behind them, the FWS launched a series of struggles which resulted in Minneapolis having one of the highest city relief budgets in the country. FWS organized workers on WPA, and when the project wage of $60.50 per month was found to be less than the dole it forced the city to pay supplemental wages to bring up the WPA scale to the higher level.

As many as 10,000 workers and unemployed were organized by the FWS in this period, through strikes and demonstrations over relief budgets, with the Communist Party for the most part being forced to tail along. The Section's membership expanded with each victory. The FWS also mobilized to support strikes of other unions, so that by 1936 opposition to the Trotskyist-led organizations had largely evaporated in AFL local unions. (Meanwhile the Drivers Local was reinstated into the Teamsters as Local 544.) These new allies proved useful in defeating a city attempt to drive "chiselers" off relief rolls, and the FWS became probably the most stable and well-organized unemployed organization of the decade.

The Workers Alliance of America

Despite the history of sectarian division and continued sabotage by the diehard reactionary AFL leadership, a united national unemployed organization was finally founded in April 1936, under the name of "Workers Alliance of America." The Communist Party was now interested in reconciliation with the Socialist Party; and the SP, reflecting the radicalizing influence of the 1934 strike wave, was impelled to the left. The Trotskyists had fought from the beginning for a united unemployed organization embracing all political tendencies, and despite criticisms of the policies of the Stalinists and social democrats, Max Shachtman wrote in the *New Militant* (18 April 1936) that, "There can be no two opinions about the progressive nature of the merger."

The nearly 700 delegates meeting in Washington, D.C., represented all the major unemployed organizations in the country, including many fresh from WPA picket lines and relief battles. Even the AFL couldn't afford to overlook the unity convention and William Green sent greetings and an official representative. The National Unemployed Leagues, most of which had already merged into the WAA prior to the conference, were represented by 100 delegates. Militant struggles continued following the convention, as Roosevelt had just announced a mammoth cut of 700,000 from WPA projects. The occupation of New Jersey's legislature in Trenton captured nationwide headlines for days and WPA strikes soon gave the WAA bargaining status on New York, New Jersey and Detroit projects.

However, the newly united organization soon came under Stalinist domination and degenerated into a bureaucratic machine to promote the New Deal. Blocking with right-wing Socialists, the CP managed to freeze out left-wingers and Trotskyists. The Unemployed Leagues came away with only three seats out of 25 on the national executive board. A left-SP resolution "not to support the capitalist government of the U.S. in any war it may undertake, regardless of who its allies might be" was defeated. And when a representative of Roosevelt's relief administration addressed the conference, informing the delegates that he "could do nothing for their hungry stomachs," he was politely applauded (*New Militant*, 2 May 1936)!

A year later, at the 1937 convention of the WAA, Stalinist control became total. Full support was voted for the CP's popular-front strategy ("a united front of progress to oppose a united front of reaction"), and the convention even went so far as to remove a clause calling for the "abolition of the profit system" from its founding declaration. Meanwhile uncritical support was given to Labor's Non-Partisan League, the American Labor Party in New York, and other "independent" political formations which helped corral working-class votes for Roosevelt at the polls.

By 1939, CP unemployed organizer and national WAA leader Herbert Benjamin was hailing the estimate that "from 80 to 90 percent of the unemployed favor the New Deal and stand behind President Roosevelt." The Roosevelt "hunger program" (*Communist*, June 1935) was miraculously transformed into "the liberal social measures that have been fostered under the New Deal in the effort to afford some relief to the victims of the capitalist crisis" (*Communist*, August 1939).

From 'New Deal' to 'War Deal'

Communist Party support to Roosevelt in 1936–39 included uncritical support of U.S. war preparations. As it became increasingly clear to all that only a new inter-imperialist slaughter to redivide world markets could "solve" the international capitalist crisis, the "New Deal" rapidly gave way to the "War Deal." Military budgets were drastically increased each year and, despite rising unemployment (approaching 15 million during the precipitous "Roosevelt Depression" in 1937), the administration repeatedly attempted to cut back on "New Deal" measures such as WPA. Thus in the last years of the 1930's, unemployed struggles were directly connected to the war question and the popular front.

The Communist Party's deeply class collaborationist policies turned the Workers Alliance into an instrument for subordinating the struggles of the unemployed to the interests of the capitalist state. Virtually ignoring those unemployed not on federal projects, the WAA degenerated into a pressure group "defending" the WPA against "reactionary attacks on the New Deal." It also served to isolate the unemployed from employed workers in the new CIO unions in order to hold back the stormy development of the class struggle. This was done with the flimsiest of excuses. The national leadership's report to the 1937 WAA convention declared:

> "Preoccupied as they are in other fields, the leaders of the CIO have had no opportunity to give thought to the best means of including our organization within its folds."
>
> —*Communist*, August 1937

The miserable record of the Stalinized Workers Alliance was summed up by the Trotskyists as "company unionism," in which WAA leaders spent their time "fawning before government officials" (*Socialist Appeal*, 24 December 1938). But it was not necessary to rely on Trotskyists for this testimony. Following the Hitler-Stalin pact, when the CP temporarily zigzagged away from the bloc with Roosevelt and called for opposition to imperialist war, none other than Benjamin himself came to the same conclusions.

Admitting that the WAA "has during recent years been without a fundamental program of its own," and that it had drastically lost membership because of the "impression" that it was exclusively a union for the rapidly dwindling number of WPA workers, Benjamin states:

> "The unemployed movement found itself part of this ['progressive people's'] coalition together with the entire progressive labor movement and the Roosevelt Administration. Its relationship to the Administration changed from one of outspoken opposition to that of a critical ally."
> "Clumsy application and distorted interpretation of the policy of cooperation in making the Works Program creditable and successful even led in some instances to the impression that the movement was sort of a 'company union' for the Administration. In any case these circumstances led to an identification of the unemployed movement with the Administration program. The unemployed organization was therefore considered by some unemployed to be partly responsible for the deficiencies of this program."
> —*Communist*, March 1940

While studiously avoiding taking responsibility for this wretched state of affairs, and defending the bloc with Roosevelt as necessary for the period, the head of CP unemployed work here confirmed the Trotskyists' criticisms and described the pitiful results of class collaborationism.

For a Class-Struggle Program

Not long after the Workers Alliance convention of 1936, the Workers Party was dissolved as the Trotskyists entered the Socialist Party in order to reach a new wave of workers repelled by Stalinism who had been attracted by the leftist posturing of the SP. The socialists had shorn themselves of the right-wing "Old Guard," and produced such anomalies as Norman Thomas (whom Trotsky labeled a socialist due to a misunderstanding) attacking the CP's Earl Browder from the left in a debate before a mass audience in Madison Square Garden.

During the year and a half of entry work, the Trotskyists more than doubled their forces, ripping away the left wing of the SP and thereby removing an important stumbling block for the development of the revolutionary party. Unfortunately, however, the period of entry reduced the effectiveness of Trotskyist work in mass arenas such as the unemployed movement. Even with the necessary limitations imposed by SP discipline and the absorbing factional struggle, Trotskyist leader James Cannon pointed out that "we neglected to do as much mass work as we might have done." In particular opportunities were missed during the early months of the CIO. But the entry also strengthened the Trotskyists' position to undertake mass work in the future by providing them with new openings in the trade unions.

After their expulsion from the SP in late 1937, the Trotskyists founded the Socialist Workers Party in 1938. The new party determined to continue and intensify its work in the Workers Alliance despite the fact that the latter had become Stalinized and in effect "an adjunct of the Roosevelt Administration." Resolving to "press for relief committees in the unions and work for unification of trade union and WAA committees," the SWP made collaboration of the unemployed movement with the new CIO unions a central goal.

The Trotskyists also recognized that the organization of mass industrial unions "has suddenly replaced trade union problems with political problems in the theater of the class struggle...." The new party declared that "organizations without an adequate program will be useless," and called for idle factories to be nationalized and operated under workers control. They also demanded that all war funds "be turned over to the unemployed."

Stalinists Sabotage WPA Strikes

While still in the SP, the Trotskyists initiated the organization of progressive caucuses within the Workers Alliance. These groups immediately came under bureaucratic attack by the Stalinists, who were intent on making the WAA utterly loyal to Roosevelt. Seventeen locals which quit or were expelled from the New York Workers Alliance went on to form the Unemployed and Project Workers Union, with 5,500 members. The Stalinists admonished the WAA ranks to "ignore this corrupt group of Trotskyites," and "remain faithful to the Alliance which is recognized and respected by our President and our Mayor" (quoted in *Socialist Appeal*, 8 October 1938). "Our Mayor" happened to be the same LaGuardia who earlier said "take WPA jobs or go to jail"!

As for the "respectful" president, following 1938 congressional elections he ordered *one and a half million* workers dropped from WPA rolls. The Stalinists continued to whine that the new downturn was all the fault of "Wall Street" trying to make "progressive government" and the New Deal look bad. In the midst of mounting protests against Roosevelt's massive WPA cuts, the CP sponsored a National Right to Work Congress featuring Eleanor Roosevelt, who declared that WPA workers were government employees and therefore could not be permitted to strike against the government. The next month (July 1939), however, there was a nationwide WPA strike against the cuts.

Protest actions against Roosevelt's post-election cuts in late 1938 included some in which the unemployed successfully linked up with the new industrial unions despite Stalinist sabotage. The Roosevelt depression had thrown many newly organized young workers in CIO unions onto the unemployed heap, and they were anxious to continue the struggle for industrial unionism. Wherever possible the SWP pushed for organization of the unemployed directly within the new unions. In Detroit, the WPA division of the United Auto Workers soon gained a membership of 15,000. In December 1938, this UAW-WPA section threatened a city-wide general WPA strike in order to win reinstatement of fired stewards.

In reaction to mounting protests against WPA cuts in the spring of 1939, the Roosevelt regime shifted gears and attempted to achieve the desired effect by abolishing prevailing wage rates and specifically requiring skilled workers to put in as much as 130 hours in order to earn what they would have previously in 75. Known as the "Woodrum Bill" after its Democrat sponsor, this measure understandably angered building trades workers and sparked a largely spontaneous nationwide WPA strike in July. The strike was strongest in Minneapolis, where the Federal Workers Section continued its class-struggle leadership of the unemployed, and in other centers of organized militancy, but embraced hundreds of thousands across the country. The Workers Alliance played a strikebreaking role, deliberately setting a delayed date for the action *after it had already begun*, and defending Roosevelt's injunction against striking against the government. The strike was defeated because of the absence of a national class-struggle leadership.

The 1939 WPA strike was the closing action in a decade of unemployed struggles in which many of the most basic lessons of the class struggle were sharply drawn. The unemployed had to learn that their destitution was not a personal failing of their own or a temporary condition, as claimed by the ruling class, but a permanent feature of capitalism which could only be eradicated with the overthrow of capitalism itself. Unemployed organizers had to learn that by themselves the unemployed are difficult to organize into a stable formation and are prey to right-wing ideologies and tempted to scab on employed workers. Leadership in the unemployed struggle must ultimately fall to the employed workers, who can utilize the economic power and organization derived from their position in capitalist production.

The commanding role of politics in the class struggle was clearly demonstrated by the disastrous effect produced by the Stalinists with their early sectarian and later popular-frontist betrayals, as well as by the positive effects of leftward motion in the Musteites and the Socialist Party during the middle 1930's, and by the Trotskyists' exemplary leadership of the Minneapolis Teamsters and of the National Unemployed Leagues. Militant class-struggle policies clearly had the greatest impact on organizing the unemployed when they emanated from within the trade unions, as in Minneapolis.

The conditions of the 1970's are by no means identical to those of the Great Depression. The leadership of the industrial unions has long since become an entrenched, ossified bureaucracy, utterly incapable of unleashing militant strike action to fight mass layoffs. Socialist forces, in turn, are far weaker numerically. But as cyclical downturns produce millions of jobless, taxing the meager reforms of the 1930's to the breaking point, revolutionists, through militant and effective organizing of the unemployed, can win supporters for the struggle against capitalism. In doing so, they would do well to study the class-struggle record of the Trotskyists in this earlier period, with their untiring struggle for the united front and employed-unemployed unity combined with thorough-going programmatic clarity.

Part Four

Spartacist Trade Union Work in the 1970s: Selected Readings

National Maritime Union

10 Percent of Seamen Vote for Class-Struggle Opposition
Militants Make Big Gains in NMU Elections

Reprinted from Workers Vanguard *No. 209, 16 June 1978*

One thousand members of the National Maritime Union (NMU) cast their ballots in the recent NMU elections for candidates of the Militant-Solidarity Caucus (M-SC) running for the union's two top national positions. While the NMU bureaucracy pads its totals with the ballots of unrelated shoreside workers, the militant challengers to the reactionary Shannon Wall regime won fully *10 percent* of the vote among deep sea, river and Great Lakes NMU sailors. Not only is maritime a strategic industry, but this impressive showing is the first time since the 1940's that a genuine class-struggle opposition has won such significant support in a national union election. The results of the April-May balloting register the fact that the M-SC has become the generally recognized opposition in the NMU.

Caucus candidates Gene Herson and Jack Heyman won 995 and 1,067 votes respectively for the offices of NMU president and secretary-treasurer. Both came in second, well behind the incumbents but *ahead* of more traditional would-be bureaucratic "reformers." Herson received more than twice as many ballots as Eli Wier, a former supporter of Jim Morrissey, the liberal dissident who garnered wide publicity in the late 1960's for his court suits against long-time NMU president Joe Curran. Moreover, in key East Coast, Gulf and West Coast ports where the Caucus' program and its ten-year record of consistent struggle are well-known, the M-SC candidates received a significantly higher percentage than the national average. *Thus in the Port of New York, Herson won 316 votes for president against 1,485 for Shannon Wall—16 percent of the port total for the M-SC against Wall's 76 percent.* In San Francisco, New Orleans, San Pedro (Los Angeles) and Port Arthur, Texas—ports where the M-SC publication, *The Beacon*, was distributed during the campaign—the Caucus candidates received up to 12–17 percent of the vote.

As a *Beacon* supplement dated 12 June noted, the M-SC's strong vote—triple the total received by Herson when he ran for president against Wall five years ago—came "despite a sustained barrage of red-baiting directed at our Caucus throughout the union." Even though a significant level of anti-communism persists in the union as a residue of the red purge of the late 1940's and early 1950's, *"one seaman in ten voted for candidates who were persistently labeled 'communists and left-wingers'"* by the NMU tops. The

M-SC candidates did not pull their punches in the face of these McCarthyite smear tactics, running on a full class-struggle program including demands for an industry wide maritime strike, repudiation of protectionism in favor of international organizing, defense of busing, labor/black defense guards against Nazis and KKK, and "No support to Democrats, Republicans—for a workers party based on unions, and workers government."

Storm Over Contract Sellout

A further confirmation that the M-SC is now seen as *the* opposition in the union, by ranks and bureaucracy alike, came at a June meeting of the Port of New York where a tumultuous rank and file booed, shouted and voted down by almost a two-to-one margin the sellout contract which Wall & Co. are trying to claim was "approved" by the membership. This year's settlement followed the same course as previous contracts, trading off a modest increase in wages against a failure to provide any defense against a massive company onslaught against jobs through automation and runaway shipping that has decimated the ranks of the union. A major complaint at the NY port meeting was the way the companies are cutting back on jobs by continually reducing manning scales, not just on the automated container vessels but even on many of the older boom ships, without a peep of resistance by the NMU officers.

A particularly unpopular item in the new contract was the pension clause. Only six years ago NMU seamen could retire at any age after 20 years service at $250 a month. But the precipitous decline in jobs has greatly weakened the union pension fund: some 14,000 pensioners are supported by 13,000 active seamen sharing 6,500 deep sea jobs. The result has been one cutback after another in pensions, so for anything over the minimal $250-a-month benefit, 25 years' service is required; moreover, seamen cannot collect payments before age 55. The new contract was another slap in the face to the NMU membership (average age 51) for whom the pension is of prime importance. For each additional $20 monthly increase in pension benefits, seamen would be required to work an extra year. In effect the seamen, not the maritime companies, paid for even the minimal pension increases contained in this contract ("The Contract Stinks! Vote It Down! Tie 'Em Up!" M-SC leaflet, 5 June).

Prior to the June ratification meeting at the Port of New York the M-SC had undertaken a vigorous campaign for rejection of the new sellout deal. A caucus leaflet emphasized that there was an alternative:

> "The contract of the SIU [Seafarers International Union], West Coast seamen, and West Coast longshoremen (ILWU) all expire next month. This provides a powerful opportunity to take a major step forward. Together, seamen and longshoremen can shut down the docks and win a major victory against our common enemy, the shipowners."
>
> —*Beacon* supplement, 22 May

By the time the meeting began the ranks in New York were furious. The Caucus mobilized supporters and active union members to defeat the sellout. Speaker after speaker rose to denounce the contract while the few members who attempted lamely to defend the agreement were angrily booed down. An

M-SC leaflet described the scene:

> "Caucus member Jack Heyman led off the discussion in the June 5 special meeting on the contract, pointing out that the proposed agreement offers no real gains and in fact keeps seamen far behind the rest of unionized labor. When another Caucus member, Bill Savery, got the mike he stressed that a joint strike of all maritime unions is the only way we can secure the things we need.
>
> "The Caucus members received enthusiastic applause along with other members who rose to condemn the sellout pact Wall's crew was pushing for the companies. The few flunkies of the officials who tried to speak in support of the contract could not conclude their remarks without being interrupted by loud booing and jeering from the rest of the membership. Having tested the waters, not one union official dared take the floor to discuss the contract—except for N.Y. Agent Rich, who had to make the report.
>
> "After discussion was abruptly ended, one of the bureaucrats' typical razzle-dazzle mayhem-type vote counts was taken, with patrolmen shouting out arbitrary numbers from non-specified 'sections' of the auditorium. This in itself simply provoked a din of angry protest from the membership as they watched the engineered confusion to swindle them out of jobs, hard cash, benefits and conditions. The vote, by a show of hands, was unquestionable: overwhelmingly opposed to the contract, by a margin of almost two to one.
>
> "Agent Rich was noticeably nervous as he barely reduced some of the irate clamor to announce his phony tally: '136 in favor and 123 opposed'!! When the officials admit such a close vote it always means they were thoroughly defeated; but this vote was *ridiculously* absurd. An outcry exploded from the membership. Gene Herson, prepared for the officials' tricks to try for a sudden adjournment, jumped to the microphone, holding it with one hand, while holding the plug in the outlet with the other hand, and called for 'a division of the house,' denouncing the false vote.
>
> "The master-at-arms was right behind Herson yanking at his arm to unplug the mike while 'recording secretary'/patrolman Zeidel prepared to kick Herson in the head. The Caucus and supporters leapt to Herson's defense while demanding a recount. The national officers, including Vice President J.C. Hughes and Secretary-Treasurer Martinez, quickly moved into the fray, which in turn brought the rest of the membership and officers down the aisles as utter bedlam broke loose. As the shouting subsided the officers declared that the meeting was adjourned, while the Caucus and the overwhelming majority of members declared the contract was voted down.
>
> "A petition for a special meeting for a full discussion and fair contract vote was circulated by the Caucus and other active members....
>
> "What is significant is that the membership demonstrated it has the capacity to fight. It is this potential for *membership action* that the Caucus seeks to lead along the lines of a class-struggle program to win lasting gains for NMU seamen."
>
> —*Beacon* supplement, 12 June

A Caucus of a New Type

Since the hotly contested union election of 1973, the Militant-Solidarity Caucus has been the only organized opposition inside the NMU. Convinced that its chances of getting into office were nil, the much larger Morrissey grouping evaporated after that vote. With the brief spurt in shipping (prompted by the Vietnam War) winding down and thousands of additional jobs lost due to the lay-up of passenger ships, the beleaguered seamen faced massive unemployment with a reactionary union leadership unwilling to defend the seamen's interests. Concerned only with his lawsuit against the NMU officers and treasury, Morrissey disappeared altogether after winning a settlement of more than $100,000 in 1977. Only the M-SC continued to fight against the betrayals of the leadership.

The M-SC did not merely seek to articulate the anger of the ranks but also put forward a fighting alternative to the defeatism of the Wall regime, whose program for jobs was limited to stealing them from other workers—raiding other unions and support for protectionism. The Caucus demanded jobs for all through a shorter work period at no cut in pay and organizing the runaway flag ships. In the current elections and contract period, the Caucus candidates demanded a real fight against the capitalists, calling for an industry wide strike of seamen and longshoremen against the bosses and pointing to the need to expropriate the parasitic shipowners with no compensation.

In contrast to the usual union "reform" caucus, which comes to life only at election time to fight over cushy jobs, the M-SC has fought to lead seaman in struggle, both on internal union issues and broader social questions. In the early 1970's the Caucus led demonstrations of seamen against the lay-up of passenger ships and discrimination against lower-seniority (Group 2) seamen. It has intervened vigorously against racial discrimination, calling on the NMU (which has a high percentage of black and Spanish-speaking members) to initiate a labor/black defense to protect school children being bused in Boston. During the recent dramatic 110-day coal strike it exposed the bureaucracy's willingness to allow coal to be carried on NMU contract vessels on the rivers and called for hot-cargoing of scab shipments. Stressing the need for international solidarity, it called for U.S. out of the Panama Canal and independence for Puerto Rico.

Caucus chairman Gene Herson, 35, who has been shipping NMU for 14 years, founded the *Beacon* in 1968 as an outgrowth of a dispute which erupted in Morrissey's Committee for NMU Democracy. Morrissey had tried to censor articles on the Vietnam War, racism and the Democratic Party, thus producing the split. Morrissey's entire campaign oriented to currying favor with the liberal bourgeois press, and pursuing the unprincipled practice of calling on the capitalist government to intervene in the NMU against the union bureaucracy, a la Arnold Miller in the Mine Workers. In fact, during the 1973 NMU presidential election campaign Miller came to New York to hold a press conference endorsing Morrissey; sitting like Edgar Bergen between the two competent "reformers" was Democratic Party bigwig lawyer Joe Rauh, who masterminded both operations and particularly their common reliance on the capitalist government.

While the Caucus has untiringly fought against the opportunist perspective that shipwrecked the large opposition movement in the NMU in the late '60's and early '70's, the other "dissident" candidates who ran in the current elections were at best capable of nothing more than serving up warmed-over Morrisseyism. One such candidate was Roy Rydell who received over 1,000 votes in union-wide balloting for New York patrolman (equivalent to a business agent). Rydell was backed by *Labor Today*, published by Trade Unionists for Action and Democracy (TUAD) which is politically supported by the Communist Party (CP). The Communist Party itself has a long history in the NMU. At one time effectively the leadership of the union, its class-collaborationist policies—particularly during World War II when its support for the war led it to vigorously support the no-strike pledge and even turn in militants to the government in order to suppress any outbreak of struggle—paved the way for the demagogic Curran to launch a red purge which led to the expulsion of hundreds of leftists from the union. In the 1973 elections Rydell and TUAD backed Morrissey although Morrissey had earlier been a hatchet-man for the bureaucracy in the red purge and refused to oppose the union's anti-red clause.

Rydell ran a thoroughly opportunist campaign in which he simply endorsed popular demands such as more vacation days and restoration of the 20-year no-age pension. He systematically ignored any controversial issues such as the union's steady-man system, under which a minority of seamen "homestead" a ship for seven or eight months while the majority of seamen are mostly unemployed surviving on relief jobs. This system encourages sweetheart deals with management, leading to the erosion of union conditions and is justly resented by militants. Following in the footsteps of Morrissey (whom he has never repudiated), Rydell failed to oppose racism, demand support for busing and school integration, mention a word of criticism of the capitalist parties or oppose the bureaucracy's vicious support for protectionism. To cap it all off, Rydell claimed to run as an "independent" yet confined his "criticisms" of Wall & Co. to such milquetoast verbiage as complaining that they took the "wrong approach."

Although Rydell (a charter member of the NMU) is well aware that the maritime unions were built through militant struggles against the companies, he has consciously opposed any call for strike action against the bosses. During the contract negotiations Rydell pandered to widespread anti-strike sentiment in the ranks, many of whom are fearful that any militant action undertaken by the present corrupt leadership would end in disaster. The M-SC has answered this legitimate concern not by giving up but instead calling for democratic election of a contract/strike committee to prepare for an industry wide strike embracing all the maritime unions. Rydell's answer to Wall's sellout deal was to send it back for "renegotiation"—thus implying that the reactionary Wall regime is capable of "persuading" the companies to grant seamen what they need—without engaging in any struggle!

NMU Elections and the Left

For the most part the American left has simply sought to ignore the decade of principled struggle by the Militant-Solidarity Caucus in the National

Maritime Union. In the 1973 elections most of the left backed the liberal Morrissey against Wall, sneering that the M-SC was too small and insignificant to merit any support. In fact, what they really believe is that it is impossible to achieve any influence in the labor movement by building a principled, programmatically based opposition. Instead the fake lefts have consistently thrown in their lot with big-name reformist oppositionists like the Millers, Morrisseys and Sadlowskis.

The large vote for the Militant-Solidarity Caucus in the recent NMU elections demonstrates that you don't have to be opportunist to win authority with the ranks. And yet, with the exception of *WV*, the left ignored the NMU election. This is not because the M-SC is "too small" to warrant the attention of outfits like the CP, the ex-Trotskyist Socialist Workers Party (SWP) or the social-democratic International Socialists (I.S.). It is because the M-SC's principled struggle is directly counterposed to the reformists' defeatist line—and exposes it—that the CP/SWP/I.S. *et al.* refused to support the caucus candidates.

The successful campaign of the Militant-Solidarity Caucus is a verification of the revolutionary program pursued uniquely by the Spartacist League: building a left-wing opposition in the unions which draws a hard programmatic dividing line between itself and all wings of the trade-union bureaucracy. In 1973 most of the left, reformists and centrists alike, whined that the M-SC was dooming itself to irrelevancy, isolating itself from the ranks of seamen by refusing to support the liberal union-suer Morrissey. In fact just the reverse was true. When Morrissey showed his true colors, the prestige and authority of the Caucus increased markedly. It won real respect for telling the truth and refusing to surrender principles.

It must be noted that because of the absence of social struggle in this section of maritime, hard-hit by demoralizing job losses, the Caucus has not yet had an opportunity to demonstrate in practice that its leadership and program are capable of winning real victories over the class enemy. It is also necessary to go beyond willingness to vote for a class-struggle candidate to actual demonstration of support for its program by active participation before it can be said that the M-SC has built a mass base in this union. But the successful campaign and the consistent course pursued in the NMU by the Militant-Solidarity Caucus point the way forward for all class-conscious workers, demonstrating, in a modest fashion, the possibility of winning support on the basis of a hard fight against all brands of trade-union reformism.

United Auto Workers

Elections in Chicago UAW Harvester Local

Reprinted from Workers Vanguard *No. 43, 26 April 1974*

CHICAGO, April 19—More than any other U.S. union the United Auto Workers has the responsibility to provide leadership for a working-class response to the second Nixon recession and the phony "energy crisis." Sharper hit than any other section of the industrial workforce by the wave of layoffs, auto workers are currently at center stage of the domestic class struggle. This situation sharply poses the question of what kind of leadership the UAW must have not only to defend its membership, but to point the way forward. With a convention coming up in June the UAW provides an opportunity for militant opposition groups to put forward their programs in elections for convention delegate.

In Local 6, representing International Harvester's Melrose Park plant outside of Chicago, thirty-five candidates on five separate slates are running for eight convention delegate seats. The Local has a militant tradition as well as sharp internal political divisions. In the last Local elections Norman Roth, a supporter of "Labor for Peace" and the Communist Party-backed "Trade Unionists for Action and Democracy" (TUAD), defeated Dick Egan, the red-baiting, racist incumbent, with whose ex-supporters he now shares the Local leadership.

The right wing has now regrouped under the anti-communist shop chairman Bob Stack, leaving Egan out in the cold. While Stack's "Defense Coalition" red-baits Roth, Egan eagerly splits the right-wing vote by denouncing Stack's slate as "opportunist" and "vigilantes." This might leave a clear field for the opportunist Roth and his Solidarity Caucus were it not for his left-wing competition!

Stalinist Brand of Labor Reformism

Typical of the type of trade-union reformism the Stalinists support, Roth is the perfect liberal. He opposed the Vietnam war, favors impeachment of Nixon and eulogizes Martin Luther King in his column in the Local 6 paper. Roth has also come out for opening the books of the corporations, an end to wage controls and an end to labor participation on Nixon's wage-controls boards. He presents nice-sounding lists of reform demands to the Local in the guise of general program and writes articles in *Labor Today* (the TUAD newspaper) advising militants on how to deal with bureaucratism in their union meetings.

But at the same time, Roth stays fully within the bounds outlined for him as a member of the tightly monitored Woodcock bureaucracy. How are UAW members to express their outrage over wage controls, for instance? Not through strike action. Roth suggests they write their congressmen! Furthermore, he calls for "genuine" price and profit controls ("like there were during World War II," says Roth—has he forgotten the fraud of war-time controls, in which inflation soared ahead of frozen wages?).

Roth soft pedals his differences with Woodcock, as over the last contract, by restricting opposition to a few verbal gestures and presenting the International position as a *fait accompli*. Woodcock's latest atrocity, "dealing" with layoffs through pleas for government handouts and quota limitations on imports, is characterized by Roth as "a start."

Most importantly, Roth's agreement with the CP's "anti-monopoly coalition" (otherwise known as supporting "lesser-evil" Democrats) keeps him in the same capitalist political ball park as Woodcock. Once this political "principle" of picking and choosing among capitalist politicians is established, differences on trade-union policy necessarily become minor differences of emphasis—how much and when to apply "pressure" for crumbs from the ruling class. Roth, with an eye on ensuring his bureaucratic future, has already announced his intention to endorse Woodcock's re-election at the convention!

Fake-Left Syndicalists

A contradictory grouping to the left of Roth's Solidarity Caucus, but existing in a symbiotic relationship with it, is the Workers Voice Committee, a syndicalist formation which has spawned the Workers Slate for the elections. The bulk of the WVC's activity consists in enthusiastic support for the day-to-day struggles of the workers. This enthusing is interrupted from time to time, however, by the need to take positions on broader issues. Thus during last year's Local elections, the WVC announced, "We are not running a slate. We think that the development of *struggle by the workers* on the shop floor is the key to solving our problems" (*Workers Voice,* Vol. IV, No. 5 [1973]). Its leaders Mike Goldfield and Roger Stromberg issued a leaflet, however, which gave very obvious backhanded support to Roth.

In the present contest, the Workers Slate raises slogans which the WVC has never raised in the course of its work, including demands for a shorter workweek at no loss in pay and a labor party. The Slate leadership, however, puts out leaflets which don't mention these demands. Furthermore, despite the inclinations of some of its more left-wing supporters, the WS fails to actually call for a break with the Democratic Party. The labor party demand is thus an empty abstraction. Reuther and Mazey were long-time supporters of such abstractions.

The WS also says nothing about government intervention in the labor movement and the use of courts against unions. The WVC has in the past supported suing the unions in the capitalist courts over unfair labor practices—a "tactic" which in this period of massive government intervention into the unions poses the threat of the final strangulation of the unions as independent workers' organizations.

The "leftism" of the Workers Slate reflects only episodic desires on the part of a thinly-disguised reformist leadership around Goldfield to distinguish itself from the CP-supported bureaucratic reformism of Roth. At bottom they are the same. The WS is a contradictory swamp which cannot last long.

Militants Launch Class-Struggle Slate

In contrast to this sorry opportunist spectacle, a Militant Action Slate of three candidates, Judson Jones, Marc Freedman and Chuck Marino, is running on the basis of a program calling for a reorientation of the labor movement toward a perspective of class struggle rather than class-collaborationist reformism.

The Militant Action Slate is a more recent grouping, composed of several individuals who have been attempting to raise class-struggle demands in Local 6. One of the militants who helped form MAS put forward a motion last fall in the Local calling for reinstatement of fired wildcat strikers in Detroit. More recently, it was one of the MAS candidates who introduced a motion calling for financial support to British miners and "hot-cargoing" of scab goods going to Britain during the British miners' strike. Seeing no harm in adding this demand to his verbal stockpile, Roth supported the motion, and it passed. Naturally, Roth did nothing concrete to implement it.

These militants were not satisfied with the hypocritical verbal militancy of Roth's Solidarity Caucus and the syndicalist Workers Voice Committee and sought to go further. The program of MAS specifically calls for a break with the Democratic Party, as well as calling for a labor party based on the trade unions. Unlike Roth or the WS, MAS calls for specific action instead of platitudes to deal with layoffs—a nationwide strike which would shut down all of auto (including plants the employers want to keep running) in order to reverse layoffs, through a shorter workweek at no loss in pay.

MAS also calls for impeachment, but without relying on Congress or Gerald Ford as do Roth, Woodcock and the CP. Instead, it calls for labor strikes to force new elections and "the running of a militant labor candidate for president to oppose the candidates of business." MAS also calls for ending discrimination through union control of hiring on a first-come, first-served basis with no preferential treatment for any group. It calls for international workers' solidarity, international strikes against international corporations and strike action against imperialist wars. The MAS program is clearly aimed at the very basis of the capitalist economic system; MAS urges auto workers to break with reformism by struggling for their demands without regard to the ability of capitalism to survive. MAS calls for the expropriation of industry under workers control and for a workers government "which can defeat the corporations once and for all."

Prospects for victory in the election look best for Stack's "Defense Coalition," with its majority support of the Shop Committee, its incumbent position and straight pro-Woodcock line. This is all the more reason *not* to place any faith in fake lefts like the Solidarity Caucus or Workers Slate: their reformist illusions and false promises only feed Stack's anti-communist business unionist fires.

The Spartacist League calls for support to the Militant Action Slate which, if it continues past the election, is bound to set an example for militants throughout the Chicago area and UAW nationally. Given its solid programmatic foundation, with the proper steadfastness in building and recruiting a base in the plant, the militants grouped together in the MAS can hope to participate fully in the construction of an alternate pole of class-struggle leadership in the labor movement. They can rest assured, however, that this is only the beginning of a difficult road, and the real content of their program and leadership must be tested in action before they can hope to win the support of the majority of the workers.

Black Family Firebombed in Chicago

UAW Local Sets Up Labor/Black Defense Guard

Reprinted from Workers Vanguard *No. 67, 25 April 1975*

CHICAGO, April 18—C. B. Dennis, black UAW union member, has been trying to move into the white neighborhood of Broadview. His house was firebombed and stoned repeatedly. But tonight, like every night for the past week, the Dennis family home is being protected by an integrated defense guard of his union brothers. Local 6 of the United Auto Workers, International Harvester, voted unanimously at the membership meeting Sunday to set up the defense guard.

At a time when there is a dramatic increase in racist terror against blacks all across the country, the UAW local's action is a powerful example of what can be done to stop the night riders. And it is the best possible answer to those who preach reliance on the bourgeois cops by hiding behind the despairing lament, "workers won't defend blacks against racist attacks—there's no solution except to call on the troops"!

The attacks, which have caused thousands of dollars' worth of damage to the house and prevented the family from moving in, are part of a pattern of terror against blacks in white areas here, where right-wingers have been trying to stir up race hatred. In another neighborhood on the Southwest Side, four black families have been forced to live under a virtual state of siege, with the National Socialist White People's Party (Nazis) all but taking direct credit for the firebombings (see article in this issue).

The first volunteers from Local 6, including Local president Norman Roth, were at posts outside the damaged house within hours of the union meeting. C. B. Dennis, who is a repairman at the Melrose Park IH plant and has been working there for 15 years, was interviewed at the house by *Workers Vanguard.* He said he had been unable to get adequate police protection.

"They said they would come by 20 minutes out of the hour. But that's no protection at all," Dennis told *WV,* observing that patrols had been by only once in two hours that night. "This is the best thing we could do," he said, referring to the volunteer guards, "I was really proud of the union today. I think it's a good thing." An older black worker who was listening agreed, saying he could recall no similar action by the Local in its history. He likened it to the defense activities of the anti-eviction campaigns in which he had participated in the 1930's.

The UAW Local's defense action received considerable attention in Chicago. Articles appeared in both daily papers on Monday, and Dennis and Local 6 officers were interviewed on two television stations Monday evening. At least three radio reports were also made.

On the second night, the union guards were heckled by passers-by in the area, and a neighbor two doors down shouted at them to "get the hell out" of there. Another white resident, however, had earlier come over to talk to Dennis for 20 minutes, expressing sympathy and pointing out that some of the rocks had hit his house as well.

It is clear that the racial polarization runs deep but the entire neighborhood has not been terrorized. Local 6 defense volunteers speak in terms of the need to prevent another Boston-type racist mobilization in Chicago. There have been no new attacks as the teams of union volunteers have been guarding the house daily. Members vow the guards will remain "as long as necessary" to ensure that the family is safely moved into the house.

The attacks on black families have mounted during an organizing offensive by fascist and racist groupings in Chicago. Besides the attacks on four black families on the Southwest Side, there were earlier attacks on other families in Broadview. The Nazi Party ran candidates for alderman in five wards in the last elections, and the Ku Klux Klan has also been actively organizing lately.

These scum thrive on the despair generated by heavy inflation and unemployment in the working class, and their efforts to divide the workers along race lines can only benefit the employers. Resolute action such as that undertaken by Local 6 could, if followed through and adopted by the rest of the labor movement, prevent future attacks and quickly lay the tiny but deadly dangerous fascist movement in the grave where it belongs.

The third attack on the Dennis house, which occurred two days prior to the union meeting, particularly incensed many members of the Local. The motion to set up the volunteer union defense guards was made by a member of the Labor Struggle Caucus, which had distributed a newsletter in the plant before the meeting calling for a militant response to the wave of racist terror. The Labor Struggle Caucus is a grouping in Local 6 with a class-struggle program which has recently been active in successful struggles against a company leafleting ban in the plant and against a move to extend terms for local union officers to three years. Its resolution at the Sunday meeting supported the "struggle for integration of blacks in housing, education, and jobs," as "vital interests of the entire working class," and denounced reliance on the police, who "serve the employers and cannot be depended upon to defend the rights of blacks or of the trade unions." The motion also called for defense activities to be extended to the black families on the Southwest Side, as well as Broadview.

Following the meeting, the Local issued a special number of its newsletter. Although this was reportedly not very well distributed, a special meeting held Tuesday night for volunteers was attended by 25 members from all political groupings in the Local, as well as by a television crew, which filmed the entire proceedings. President Roth chaired and took a lot of criticism for the inefficient distribution of the special Local newsletter which, it was said, kept the meeting from being larger.

He also relented under pressure on his earlier objection to the formation of a special committee to organize the defense guards. A steering committee was then set up under the chairmanship of the by-laws committee chairman. It includes two members of the Labor Struggle Caucus, a member of the syndicalist Workers Voice group, and other Local members. Members of the steering committee immediately began signing up volunteers in the plant.

Support for the defense activity was forthcoming, at least verbally, from the UAW officialdom in the area, including regional director Robert Johnston. The special Local newsletter asserted, "These efforts are in accord with our UAW principles and policies."

On the other hand, the UAW officials seemed primarily concerned to get government officials to intervene, thereby relieving the union of its responsibility. At the Dennis house on Sunday night, Roth told *WV* of his intention "to exert every political pressure possible to try to get the authorities to do something." He further claimed that "In some instances, the police have given some protection."

Roth, who is a prominent supporter of Trade Unionists for Action and Democracy, the trade-union group backed by the reformist Communist Party, not surprisingly places confidence in the bosses' state. Yet neither courts, cops, troops nor National Guard will protect blacks against racist victimization. This can be clearly seen in the Boston situation, where the courts are conciliating the racists and have taken a giant step backward on the busing plan.

In Boston there have been two sharply counterposed lines on how to defend the endangered blacks from racist attack. On the one hand there are the liberals, joined by the Communist Party and Socialist Workers Party, who have called for federal troops. Against this dead-end reliance on the armed forces of the capitalist state, the Spartacist League has called for integrated working-class defense. Both in Chicago and Boston or elsewhere, labor/black defense guards could quickly eliminate racist terrorists, neutralize wavering elements in the white population and eventually defuse racist mobilizations.

The Local 6 action could be the start of a general initiation of militant, class-struggle response to racist terror in the Chicago area, but only if the whole Local, leadership included, works to undertake it seriously and spread the idea to other locals. If the Local 6 leadership instead spreads illusions in the state, the way will be left open for a worsening racial polarization. The guard must not be ended prematurely, on the advice or promise of the cops or city officials that defense will be provided by the state.

The recent action of the Local 6 members stands as an inspiring example for all trade unionists and black militants: black and white workers *can* unite and organize to fend off racist terror. It will take an all-sided fight for class-struggle policies and leadership throughout the labor movement to turn this example into the rule. But an important beginning has been made.

Labor/Black Defense Continues in Chicago

Class-Struggle Candidate Polls 17% at Harvester—Woodcock Forces Sweep Local 6 Elections

Reprinted from Workers Vanguard *No. 69, 23 May 1975*

CHICAGO—Recent elections in UAW Local 6, at International Harvester's important Melrose Park plant on Chicago's West Side, produced a sweep for the right-wing, business-unionist pro-Woodcock slate. The results were a stern indictment of the reformists who hide their politics in unprincipled coalitions and disguise their opportunism with phony "militant" phraseology. But they also showed strong support for the one candidate who actively built the Local's on-going labor/black defense guard as a main focus of his campaign.

A month ago the Local voted unanimously for a resolution presented by the Labor Struggle Caucus resulting in the formation of a defense guard to protect a black member's house, which had been repeatedly attacked (including firebombing) in an attempt to prevent him from moving into the predominantly white neighborhood of Broadview. These attacks were part of a wave of terror against blacks in white areas of Chicago. On the Southwest Side, Nazis have all but taken direct responsibility for similar incidents.

Despite foot-dragging by the Local 6 leadership and silence from most of the candidates in the recent election, the defense guard continues to operate and has thwarted new attacks on the house. Support for the defense has reportedly been received from UAW Local 688 (Broadview Parts Depot), boilermakers Local 1257 and the Bulk Mail Center local of the Postal Workers

Union. Resolutions of support have been raised in at least three other local unions, including Steelworkers Local 65, at U.S. Steel's Southworks.

Red-Baiters Denounce 'Dream Schemes'

The across-the-board winners in the election were the candidates of the Positive Action Leadership (PAL) slate, consisting of the incumbent administration under retiring shop chairman Robert Stack. The PAL launched a no-holds-barred red-baiting attack on its main opponents grouped together in the Rank and File Coalition (RFC). Echoing a classic J. Edgar Hoover line, Stack wrote in his regular Local newsletter column inveighing against "anarchistic, revolutionary elements" who "used and exploited the plight of minority members of the union" (*Union Voice,* 25 April). The opposition, said PAL, was a "catch-all coalition of militant visionaries" who would "present their 'dream-schemes' for world revolution to the Company as your views." PAL, in contrast, promised "responsible" unionism with "a team of experienced leaders."

The opposition, which included Local 6 President Norm Roth running a losing battle for shop chairman, was indeed a catch-all coalition, but that was the only accurate point in Stack's diatribe. The RFC grab-bag was no more capable of presenting a program for "world revolution" than PAL, but the few so-called "revolutionaries" within it opened themselves up to vicious red-baiting with their own well-practiced and incurable opportunism.

Roth, who has a long-standing individual following in the plant, is a leading member of Trade Unionists for Action and Democracy and helped found the short-lived Auto Workers Action Caucus (AWAC), both of which are supported in the press of the reformist Communist Party. AWAC was touted by the CP as the answer to the United National Caucus (UNC), which it considered too oppositional. CP-supported elements, including Roth, backed Woodcock for UAW president at the union's last convention.

The RFC also included left social-democratic elements and received the support of the International Socialists. The IS, however, is a chief backer of the UNC—despite the latter's support for protectionism and its attempts to exclude socialists at UNC demonstrations—and criticizes the CP's support for Woodcock. Thus about all the RFC could agree on was a low-level program of shop-floor militancy. At a time when massive layoffs and racist violence are the main issues facing the membership, the RFC concentrated its campaign fire on speed-ups. While mentioning six hours' work for eight hours' pay in its program, the RFC also endorsed the current sellout contract whose bankruptcy in the face of layoffs is demonstrated by the collapse of GM and Chrysler SUB funds.

No effective answer to PAL's sophisticated red-baiting could possibly be mounted by a group so divided on fundamentals that one half of it praises "détente" as the answer to unemployment (the plant happens to be operating largely on Soviet tractor orders) while the other half capitulates to anti-communist "Buy Americanism"! Since the RFC offered nothing beyond a slightly frenzied version of the same business unionism as PAL (one plank in the RFC program was a vague call for "total non-cooperation" as the answer to speed-up), the membership, logically enough, opted for the "experts."

Defense Guard Must Be Strengthened

Meanwhile, the Labor Struggle Caucus, a group of Local 6 militants putting forward a class-struggle program, reduced its number of candidates from three (in the 1974 elections) to one this year, largely because of the LSC's heavy involvement in building the Local defense guard. Its candidate for executive board member-at-large was Marc Freedman, who is also secretary of the Civil Rights Defense Committee.

A recent incident at the Dennis house drove home the need for the entire Local to strengthen this defense committee, a point which the LSC has been making for some time. Last week five whites drove up to the home, yelling racial epithets and making threatening moves toward a car in which two unionists on duty at the time were sitting. No violence resulted, but the failure of the union leadership to mobilize for the guard has heightened the danger of renewed racist violence.

One of the two campaign leaflets issued by the Labor Struggle Caucus attacked the other candidates for ignoring the guard and ran a "box score" showing who had served guard duty and who hadn't. In a capitulation to racism in the plant, the entire PAL slate had not served once. While Roth and a few candidates for lesser office on the RFC slate had helped guard the house, these "militants" remained silent about the defense squad in all their campaign literature.

In addition to supporting labor/black defense as part of a militant, integrationist program to fight racism with united working-class action, the LSC was alone in proposing an effective response to the layoffs (of 200 to 250 workers) which were announced for the plant just prior to the election. On this key question, which is plaguing the auto union and the entire working class, Roth proposed "détente" and paid lip-service to the old UAW slogan of a shorter workweek at no loss in pay. The Labor Struggle Caucus made the issue quite concrete by proposing a resolution for a strike to stop the layoffs, "extended throughout the Harvester chain and backed up with the full power of the International union."

The LSC also rejects class collaborationism and called for opposition to the parties of big business (Democratic and Republican), and for the building of a workers party which would "fight for a workers government to reorganize our society to do away with unemployment and racism."

Unable to mount a serious challenge to the main slates with only one candidate, the LSC nevertheless scored a victory for the labor/black defense effort and its class-struggle program by winning 441 votes, or 17 percent of those voting, for its candidate. This is more than double the highest vote received by a candidate of the Militant Action Slate (which subsequently became the LSC) a year ago. The program and determined struggle of the LSC point the way forward to victory for a class-struggle leadership of the workers movement in the future.

Militants Fight Layoffs in West Coast Auto

Reprinted from Workers Vanguard *No. 60, 17 January 1975*

SAN FRANCISCO, January 11—A demonstration was held yesterday in front of the Federal Building here against a lawsuit which seeks to give preferential treatment against layoffs to women (regardless of their seniority) at the Fremont General Motors assembly plant. The demonstration, which numbered about 30, included workers from the plant, coming to protest the suit. Among these were members of the Committee for a Militant UAW (CMUAW), which has been opposing the suit in the plant.

The protest was called by the Spartacist League to coincide with a hearing before Judge A.J. Zirpoli in federal district court for an immediate injunction to stop layoffs for women workers in the plant. The judge refused to grant an injunction.

Also yesterday, over 2,300 workers at Fremont worked their last day for an indefinite period. Given the depth of the layoff (going back 12 years in seniority) many will undoubtedly lose recall rights before GM restores the second shifts to auto and truck production lines at the plant.

The demonstrators demanded, "Drop the Suit, Save the Seniority System!" and "No Layoffs, Jobs for All!" An SL leaflet announcing the demonstration had called for the union to fight discrimination against women and minorities, and for a union fight against layoffs.

Other demands of the demonstration were, "No Government Interference in the Unions!" "No Lawsuits Against the Unions!" and "The Union Must Fight Racial and Sexual Discrimination!" A counterdemonstration, composed primarily of supporters of the Maoist October League and CLUW, defended the "women's lawsuit."

The SL demonstration was given more attention by the media than the hearing itself. Channel 7 broadcast a film clip of the SL speaker, while Channel 2 noted that the demonstration, as opposed to the counterdemonstration, was in favor of jobs for all, through a shorter workweek at no loss in pay and a union hiring hall to combat discrimination. Both television channels, as well as local papers, have been covering the events surrounding the Fremont layoffs, reflecting the nervousness of the bourgeoisie over the prospect of militant working-class response to the mass layoffs and mounting unemployment nationally.

While trade-union leaders both locally and nationally have been meekly accepting the layoff announcements and mouthing the capitalists' own excuses for their "inevitability," groups such as the CMUAW at Fremont have been indicating the direction a true class-struggle response to layoffs could take. "WE ARE NOT HELPLESS IN THE FACE OF LAYOFFS," emphasized a recent (11 December) issue of the group's paper, *The UAW Militant:* "One of the most powerful of labor's weapons comes from the UAW's own tradition: the sit-down strike."

Counterposing union struggle against all layoffs and plant closures to impotent court "remedies" which protect some workers at the expense of the rest, the CWUAW advocates a sit-in demonstration in the plant "to set an example to other plants" and lay "the basis for a nationwide campaign for a shorter work week at full pay." This campaign has stirred widespread interest in the plant and union (Local 1364), as has the group's opposition to the "women's lawsuit."

At the court hearing, in addition to denying the request for a temporary restraining order preventing the company from laying off women, Judge Zirpoli postponed a hearing on the full suit to March 14. The suit was filed against General Motors last August by eight women assembly workers as their answer to large-scale layoffs at Fremont. The suit denounces the seniority system as the "vehicle" of GM's discrimination against women, and calls for "population parity" for women in the plant.

According to spokesmen for the Committee for a Militant UAW, backers of the suit have been lying about its real aims to the workers in the plant. One leaflet distributed in the name of "the women who filed the suit and their supporters," claims,

> "We are *not* asking for 50 percent women in the plant within four years. Is it true that men will lose their jobs? In cases like this one, no court has ever ruled that men be bumped out of their jobs. Nothing in our lawsuit calls for this to happen."

This is a clear and direct falsification. Although argumentation in the body of the suit disavows any desire to see men laid off, the main intention is made clear:

> "such affirmative action plan shall have as its goal permanent population parity for female employees at GMAD Fremont..., that is population parity *without regard to workforce size at any time.*"

Lawyers present at yesterday's hearing, not surprisingly, interpreted "population parity" to mean just what it says. that the plant must have as many women as in the surrounding population, i.e., about 50 percent. And one judge in a similar case *has* in fact ruled that workers *may* be laid off to make way for minorities with less seniority (see *WV* No. 59, 3 January 1974).

This Lawsuit Is Dangerous!

A victory for this suit could become part of a nationwide precedent doing nothing to stem layoffs or unemployment, but enabling employers to break the seniority principle in order to give special treatment to minorities. The seniority principle is a major gain of the labor movement. Although often implemented in a discriminatory fashion, seniority protects all workers from arbitrary victimization by the employers. The suit also hands the courts the right to rule on working conditions, a question central to all union contracts.

The International Butts In

The danger of the suit is so great that even the UAW International has belatedly shipped an official delegation to the scene to block the remedies proposed in the suit. The International, however, expressed no interest in opposing the court's power to rewrite the contract. Instead, it has entered the case with a "friend of the court" brief proposing an "alternative": women who can "prove" they were discriminated against in hiring can get back pay but not super-seniority.

The judge ruled that the UAW could not enter the case as a neutral "friend of the court," but only as a defendant, since it is a party to an agreement (the contract) upholding seniority, which is what the suit opposes. This should have come as an eye-opener to the suit's backers, who have been vigorously insisting that the suit is aimed only against the company, not the union and seniority!

Commenting on the International's court brief, a CMUAW press release (7 January) says:

> "Our Committee is fighting to have the suit *dropped*, not changed or added to. We do not recognize the right of the courts to rule on whether our contract terms will stand or fall. Further, it is the height of hypocrisy for the International to come into the case at this late date. Not only has the International never taken up a fight against discrimination as it has been carried out by the auto companies, but it has never waged even a token struggle against massive layoffs now sweeping the industry...."

Inside the plant over 650 workers (more than half of whom were women or minority men) signed a petition circulated by the CMUAW calling for the union-busting suit to be dropped because it will weaken the union and open the door to government intervention. Addressed to the union, the petition demanded "that the union fight all forms of discrimination, and mount a campaign to end layoffs...."

Stalinist Goon Attack

The CMUAW's principled and well-received opposition to the women's suit has understandably caused intense frustration among Maoist backers of the suit. While the suit's initiators and October League backers have resorted to lying, the left-posturing but equally right-Maoist Revolutionary Union (RU) fell back on its time-worn tactic of Stalinist gangsterism. At a small demonstration for "Jobs or Income Now" held by the Local's Unemployed Committee and well-attended by RU supporters, one of the latter tried to steal stacks of leaflets being distributed by CMUAW members. When two supporters of the CMUAW sought to recover the leaflets, a bunch of these hooligans jumped them. The CMUAW supporters fought back and a brother from the plant floored one of the two-bit Maoist thugs. The CMUAW was outnumbered but TV cameras closing in on the fight discouraged the Maoist back-alley boys, who prefer to do their dirty work in secret. (This is not the first time members of Local 1364 have run into the RU's policy of goon attacks. In October 1973 the union passed a motion upholding workers democracy and the right of various labor-socialist groups to distribute literature outside the plant. This was in response to attacks at Fremont GM on salesmen of *Workers Vanguard* and the *Bulletin* by RU supporters.)

Aside from continuing its history of attempted physical suppression of the left, the RU's answer has been the "jobs or income" demand. This demand accepts the fact of layoffs and the capitalist business cycle and dissipates the struggle for jobs.

The stance of the Local 1364 officials in the face of the layoffs has been completely passive. At first they refused to support CMUAW's position against the lawsuit, later tried to claim credit for the anti-suit petition and finally backed the International's brief. On January 4 they held a half-hearted demonstration against layoffs with Local President Vern Dias and Shop Chairman Earlie Mays leading 150 marchers to an isolated park in Fremont, where Dias offered a few platitudes about how "we need jobs or income for American people" without presenting any strategy for a union fight for jobs. The International, meanwhile, limits itself to "moral persuasion" and plans for a march on Washington in February to pressure Congress.

Speaking at the rally, Joan Putnam of the CMUAW said that auto workers need *jobs,* not a dole. "GM wants us on the street, not in the plant," she said. The answer is sit-down strikes in the factories, where the strength of organized labor lies. She denounced the "women's court suit" as an attack on the union and the seniority system and criticized a banner calling for a shorter workweek but neglecting to add the demand for no loss in pay. Putnam ended with a call for workers control of the factories, expropriation of industry and a workers government.

A Sit-Down to Focus the Struggle Against Layoffs

When the present layoffs were announced, the Committee immediately began agitation, demanding that "The union must stage a sit-in demonstration inside the plant to protest the layoffs and force the Company to negotiate with us" (CMUAW leaflet, "Sit Down: The UAW's Oldest Weapon," 19 December). The Committee called on the Local leadership to hold a mass meeting inside the plant to adopt the sit-down tactic and democratically determine tactics regarding publicity, defense and negotiations.

Recognizing that layoffs cannot be reversed in just one plant, it put forward the following demands for local negotiations: "No reprisals—unlimited recall rights," "Unlimited, unconditional unemployment benefits from Company assets for all laid-off workers—make the government take over SUB payments when the fund runs out." Their stated aim was to use a local sit-in demonstration, attracting immediate nationwide and worldwide attention, as a launching pad for similar actions elsewhere which would lay the basis for a nationwide campaign against all layoffs and plant closures.

In late December it was rumored that the Shop Committee of Local 1364 had seriously considered the group's proposal. The rumor was confirmed at the December 22 special membership meeting when President Dias, in an attempt to justify having ruled the CMUAW motion for a sit-in out of order, said that the leadership had conferred with union lawyers on the subject and were told that such an action would be "illegal" and therefore unfeasible. If Vern Dias had consulted "union lawyers" in the 1930's, he would no doubt have been told that sit-down strikes were "illegal." Had auto workers followed such advice then, there would be no UAW today!

Proponents of the "women's lawsuit" cravenly capitulated to the cowardice of the Local leadership by opposing the sit-in and red-baiting the CMUAW. The Maoist supporters in Local 1364, having supported the present Brotherhood Caucus leadership when it came to power at Fremont in 1973, thus continued their role as water-boys for the reformist bureaucracy. They have been thoroughly discredited by their dishonest support to divisive and reactionary use of the courts against the labor movement.

Only the CMUAW, with its class-struggle program, pointed the way forward in the context of the massive layoffs which have now swamped the entire auto industry as a result of the deepening economic crisis. The soaring unemployment is already making employers bolder and more aggressive in their war against the unions.

The increased threat of scabbing and the labor bureaucracy's complete passivity in the face of what they themselves call "depression" conditions can only have a demoralizing effect on the union ranks. The key to success is the question of leadership, that is, the need to oust the present sellout, defeatist union bureaucracy and replace it with a militant class-struggle leadership which can point the way forward. Caucuses like the CMUAW at Fremont which put forward a full class-struggle program, including the need for working-class political independence from the capitalist parties, are urgently needed throughout the UAW and the rest of industry.

Fremont Newspaper Interviews Committee for a Militant UAW

Reprinted from Workers Vanguard *No. 60, 17 January 1975*

Two members of the Committee for a Militant UAW at the Fremont General Motors plant, Darlene Fujino and Ruth Ryan, were interviewed by the Fremont-Newark *Argus* (22 December) in a full-page feature article on the opposition to the "women's lawsuit." After listing the reasons why Fujino and Ryan (both of whom are being laid off) oppose this union-busting attack on seniority, the article gives the CMUAW's alternative:

> "They wouldn't rely on seniority alone to protect workers. What they have in mind involves more than that: institution of 30 hours work for 40 hours of pay and nationalization of the auto and energy industries without compensation were two of the parts of the program they emphasized.
>
> "Other goals of their program: no restrictions on political expression in the union; industry-wide strikes against layoffs, workers control of industry; change the union leadership; a workers party fighting for a workers government; keeping police, employers and courts out of the union; and elimination of discrimination by means of a union hiring hall."

The interviewer asked "if unemployed workers wouldn't prefer a more immediate solution," to which Ryan replied, "There are no shortcuts."

Communication Workers of America

MAC Leads Struggle
CWA Convention Rejects Gag Rule Amendment

Reprinted from Workers Vanguard *No. 24, 6 July 1973*

A vicious assault on union democracy, spearheaded by California local bureaucrats of the Communication Workers of America, was defeated by a close vote at the CWA convention in June. The local officials, headed by the "militant" Kirkpatrick of San Francisco, proposed to give Joe Beirne's die-hard anti-communist International bureaucracy the constitutional power to persecute "reds" and "disrupters" in any local of the union, thereby greatly expanding the International's disciplinary powers. The defeat of this red clause constitutional amendment was a victory for all union militants.

A crucial role in stopping this atrocity was played by the Militant Action Caucus (MAC) of Oakland Local 9415. MAC initiated a "No on 19-2C" Committee which was joined by other oppositional groupings and individuals, and attended the convention in order to muster support against the proposal.

While the red clause was drafted by Kirkpatrick, it was eagerly supported by the other California local bureaucrats. One of their chief targets was MAC, which had recently defeated a lame attempt by discredited bureaucrats in the Oakland local to bring some of its members up on phony charges of "bringing the union into disrepute" (see *WV* Nos. 16 and 17, February and March 1973). These elements and others like them wanted a new club with which to beat down oppositions which exposed their rotten role. So armed, they hoped to be able to cling to office no matter what. Most delegates correctly saw this as a threat to them, however, since it could be used by the International to stifle any opposition.

Anti-Communism and Class-Collaboration

The posh Fontainbleau Hotel in Miami Beach was the scene of CWA's 35th annual convention—an appropriate setting for bureaucrats to ignore the pressing problems of the membership. While some of the 2,600 delegates had been elected by the membership of CWA, most attained delegate status merely by virtue of their positions in the local hierarchy. Thus the Militant Action Caucus waged a pre-convention struggle within Local 9415 for elected delegates, but bureaucratic manipulation prevented the issue from coming to the floor.

While profuse lip service was paid to democracy and freedom of expression for all points of view, the convention reeked of the vicious anti-communism of the CWA bureaucracy and its staunch support for the capitalist system in general and the cold-war liberals in particular. Telegrams from Senators McGovern and Humphrey, leading supporters of government wage controls and compulsory arbitration, as well as from other similar "friends of labor" were read from the rostrum, while awards were given to those CWA members who had raised the most money for the Democratic Party through the CWA's Committee on Political Education (COPE).

In discussing Nixon's wage freeze, a violation of every union contract in the United States and an attack on the union's position as sole bargaining agent for its members, CWA President Joseph Beirne, who has publicly called for Nixon's impeachment, commented only that the controls should be fair! The CWA bureaucracy has never taken up a struggle against the wage freeze and, in fact, the AFL-CIO executive board, of which Beirne is a Vice-President, actually called for wage controls even before Phase I was announced. Until the spring of 1972, Beirne also sat on the government's Productivity Advisory Board, which concerned itself with devising new and more efficient ways to exploit workers, and it was not until February of this year that the *C.W.A. News* called for an end to the Economic Stabilization Act—Beirne and the rest of the labor bureaucracy helped to create this act and now Beirne asks that the controls be "fair"!

One of the gravest threats facing the membership of CWA at this time, as it is facing the working class as a whole, is increasing automation, which under capitalism, because of the widespread unemployment it engenders, must take the form of a curse instead of a blessing. Not one of the resolutions placed before the membership even touched upon this critical problem. The delegates were instead encouraged to discuss and vote on such issues as year-round daylight saving time, testimonials to the memory of Presidents Truman and Johnson and support for Radio Free Europe.

The politically most controversial convention discussion centered on the "anti-red" amendment, clause 19-2C of the International Constitution.

According to the proposal originally put forward by Kirkpatrick, union members could be fined, suspended or expelled by trial set up by the International (most offenses are handled locally) for:

> "Wilfully supporting or assisting any and all corrupting influences or the undermining effects of Communist agencies or others who are opposed to the basic principles of our democracy and free and Democratic Unionism."

Known for his supposed "opposition" to Beirne, Kirkpatrick claimed he was the only president in his district who opposed the last contract settlement (1971), calling it a "sellout." This "militant" wanted to hand Beirne a hatchet with which to chop any oppositionist whose *ideas* were considered subversive—such as the idea that Beirne's contracts are sellouts! Beirne has split many locals and helped blacklist local leaders for just such ideas carried a bit too far for his liking.

The Constitution Committee found Kirkpatrick's wording a little too reminiscent of the witchhunting of the 1950's, however, so it proposed language of its own. In its version:

> "Wilfully engaging in activities for the purpose of disrupting Local meetings; wilfully publishing untruths about any Local or its elected officers; or wilfully filing false charges under the Union Constitution or Local Bylaws against any member of the Union."

That its intentions were identical to Kirkpatrick's, despite the tidied-up language, was revealed in the Committee's motivation for the amendment:

> "There are, however, small groups of persons who have occasionally during the history of Labor convinced themselves that they know better than the membership itself, that because they contend the members are incapable of making proper decisions about their own lives, that the Democratic procedures must be vacated and that any means to their end are the proper ones. The result, when this kind of situation is permitted to continue, is a flaunting of the members' desires, the destruction of Union Democracy, and the subversion of Local Unions to the private purposes of special interest groups."

The Constitution Committee, moreover, printed both versions of the amendment in its report, making clear the purpose of the final wording, and objecting to the original version only on grounds that it was "far too broad in scope."

But the fact is that it is not the militant oppositionists but precisely the bureaucrats who have been guilty of "flaunting the members' desires, the destruction of union democracy, and the subversion of Local Unions to the private purposes of special interest groups." In Local 9415, it is the bureaucrats who have adjourned meetings against the will (and vote) of the membership. It is the bureaucrats who refused to support a wildcat in 1971 despite its overwhelming support by the membership. It is the bureaucrats who published in the local's *Labor News* a cowardly and vicious, red-baiting, sex-baiting, "anonymous" slander letter directed against members of the Militant Action Caucus. It is the bureaucrats who involved themselves in physical attacks on union members. And it is the bureaucrats who for months have prevented the election of shop stewards despite the fact that this was voted for by the vast majority of the membership last November!

In Kirkpatrick's Local 9410, it was President Kirkpatrick himself—this splendid champion of union democracy—who declared at a meeting last month that only "over my dead body" will the members get the right to elect their own stewards.

Nothing could be more ludicrous than the claim of this rotten union leadership, which refuses to fight for even minimal contract demands and which has never shirked from violating any democratic procedure which stood in the way of its own appetites, that its concern is the preservation of union democracy and the protection of the membership from "corrupting influences."

No! The real concerns of the bureaucrats are to keep the membership ignorant and quiet, unable to protest one betrayal after another by their "leaders." Some elements of the bureaucracy wanted to begin laying the groundwork for the upcoming 1974 contract fight by getting rid of all the troublesome opposition within the union. As they gear up for another great sellout in the Beirne tradition, they are acutely aware that their ability to consummate a deal with the bourgeoisie and force it down the throats of the membership will depend on their ability to silence militancy in the ranks, preferably through physical expulsion. And the time to start is now.

The Militant Action Caucus, *Yellow Pages* (San Francisco), *Bell Wringer* (Oakland) and the United Action Caucus (New York) backed a "No on 19-2C" Committee in order to fight this amendment. The Committee circulated a petition against the amendment and raised money to send two representatives to the convention to leaflet, petition and persuade delegates to vote against the amendment. Members of the MAC initiated the Committee and carried the brunt of the work from the outset, while others in the Committee took a more or less passive attitude. Of the $125.00 which the Committee raised to help send representatives to Miami (both members of the MAC), *Yellow Pages* supporters contributed only $5.00. The United Action Caucus in New York refused to take part in the struggle at all, beyond a pro-forma endorsement. Another opposition group, the Traffic Jam caucus (San Francisco) showed up for one meeting of the "No on 19-2C" Committee and left after about a half hour with no explanation. Faced with direct attack on the very right to opposition, launched by the president of their own local, they do nothing at all. Nor have recent issues of the newspapers of the Revolutionary Union, Progressive Labor or the International Socialists, who support these caucuses, seen fit to campaign against this witchhunting attack.

The two representatives of "No on 19-2C" did find support at the convention, however, particularly from some CWA members from Washington, D.C. and Atlanta, Georgia. The Atlanta phone workers had, like the members of the MAC, been brought up on charges within their local for "bringing the union into disrepute" (i.e., criticizing the local leadership).

A leaflet was issued against 19-2C and all parties who wished to participate in the struggle were encouraged to distribute it and to contact potentially sympathetic delegates. By aggressively pushing the issue other CWA members were found to help distribute the leaflet and numerous delegates were contacted, several of whom later spoke on the floor against the amendment. Overall the Committee's intervention had a noticeable impact. The failure of the amendment to win approval is due in large part to the efforts of this group and, even more, to the MAC, which had initiated the fight on the West Coast and had carried it through with persistence and determination. The final rejection of 19-2C was the act of a majority of CWA delegates. The delegates had been assured repeatedly—by Beirne (!) particularly—that the CWA was the most democratic union in the world. It was to this tradition that those opposing what was essentially a gag rule successfully appealed in their remarks during the debate (which took up most of one day). Local leaders had their own reasons to oppose the amendment, however. They were faced with certain contradictions: while it would have been nice to get rid of the militants, it would have given the International leadership an added handle to intervene in local affairs (since trial bodies under the amendment would be selected by the International).

Moreover, Beirne himself played a relatively passive role in the discussion. From his point of view there was no need to antagonize the local bureaucrats at this point by pushing the amendment through, there was the desire to project a liberal image and also a certain reluctance to deal with the flood of charges and counter-charges which would certainly engulf the International following adoption of the amendment. Much better to let the local leaders clean their own houses. Nevertheless, his concluding speech attempted to console those who had fought for the amendment and to gear them up for a fight against the militants (whom he called "commie bastards") in the coming period.

The defeat of the amendment was an important victory for all militants in CWA. The Militant Action Caucus, which led the struggle against 19-2C, has continually pointed out the need for a full political program to fight the CWA bureaucracy. This is borne out by the current red-baiting and the 19-2C amendment. The union leadership is firmly wedded to the capitalist system and will do everything necessary to protect it, from supporting wage-freezes and expelling militants on trumped-up charges to sponsoring secret CIA-funded operations (as Beirne did for years). To fight the bosses and their agents in the unions down the line the MAC calls for nationalization of the phone company under workers control, full union democracy, ousting the bureaucrats and building a labor party based on the trade unions to fight for a workers government. An integral part of this program is the need for a united-front defense of victimized militants and opposition to witchhunting in the unions. MAC put this section of its program into practice by initiating the "No on 19-2C" Committee and by taking the fight to the delegates at the CWA convention itself.

For MAC, the convention experience was important also because it exposed their program and strategy to other militants throughout the entire country and indicated the need for a national Militant Action Caucus within CWA. In the immediate future, the caucus is planning a series of forums to discuss the CWA convention, as well as MAC's program and strategy for trade-union struggle in general. A regular newsletter is also planned. More information concerning these activities, as well as MAC literature, can be obtained by writing to: Militant Action Caucus, P.O. Box 462, El Cerrito, California 94530.

Class-Struggle Opposition in Oakland CWA Local

Reprinted from Workers Vanguard *No. 46, 7 June 1974*

The Militant Action Caucus (MAC) in Oakland CWA Local 9415 ran a candidate, Kathleen Burnham, in elections for convention delegate this spring, on the basis of its class-struggle opposition to Beirne's bargaining plan and many other issues, including its call for expropriation of the phone companies and oil industry under workers control, for a general strike to oust Nixon and force new elections and for a workers party and a workers government.

The Caucus has a four-year history of struggle for its program in the Local. MAC fought last summer for a united labor defense for the Farm Workers against the Teamster/grower alliance, including demands clearly counterposed to the pacifism and liberalism of the Chavez leadership of the UFW: MAC called for "hot-cargoing" of struck goods by other unions and a California-wide general strike to defend the Farm Workers.

MAC has also been in the forefront of the struggle against racial and sexual discrimination. Its campaign program called for putting an end to discrimination through the struggle for a shorter workweek at no loss in pay to end unemployment and for equal access to all jobs and promotions through non-discriminatory, union-controlled hiring. MAC counterposed this program to divisive "Affirmative Action" quota systems, which do not make more jobs and invite government intervention to undermine unionism.

During the recent "Operation Zebra" program, in which San Francisco Mayor Alioto instituted a racist round-up of black males in the city, MAC raised a motion condemning this "vicious attack" which was "designed to fan racist hysteria." The motion passed overwhelmingly in the Local.

MAC injected another issue into the campaign, which it alone has been raising in the union. The Beirne regime has been notorious as a major supporter of anti-communist union-busting operations by the AFL-CIO in foreign countries, particularly Europe and Latin America. A Caucus leaflet issued during the Local campaign points out:

> "The American Institute for Free Labor Development is supposedly a private organization to support the development of 'free unions' in Latin America. Joe Beirne was the brains behind the idea of AIFLD and its treasurer. ...George Meany is its president. Its Board of Directors, however, reads like an international investors list—representatives of ITT, Kennecott and Anaconda Copper, Chase Manhattan Bank—22 corporations in all. With such a board of directors it should be apparent what kind of 'free unions' AIFLD wants—those free of workers control."

The leaflet goes on to expose AIFLD's activities in Chile. "Unions" affiliated to AIFLD in Chile include an organization of the same naval officers who were instrumental in leading the reactionary military coup that overthrew the Allende government, and a hodge-podge grouping including shopkeepers and professionals, some of the officers of which are leaders of "Patria y Libertad," a Chilean fascist organization. MAC demands the immediate severing of all ties with this reactionary, CIA-backed organization.

During her campaign, Burnham pointed out that Beirne's support to AIFLD and other schemes of Jay Lovestone's AFL-CIO International Department is simply a reflection of the same class collaborationism which led to the "national bargaining" scheme: Beirne and his cronies are committed to defend capitalism, whatever the inevitable conflicts this position produces with the real interests of the workers.

During her campaign, MAC's candidate for delegate debated three other candidates, most of whom had little or nothing to say in counterposition to MAC's program. One of them was Manja Argue, whose views often reflect those of the reformist International Socialists. (For instance, she is for militant defense of the UFW—but within the confines of Chavez' pacifist, defeatist policy and without any criticism of the latter.) Argue had more to say than others, but when pressed as to her differences with the MAC program, she said she had none. She objected instead that MAC supposedly refused to get involved in day-to-day problems and work of the union. At that point a MAC shop steward who was in the audience got up and exposed Argue's phony objection. She added that Argue's presence on the Local legislative committee without waging a constant fight for a break with all capitalist politicians was lending a left cover to the rabid supporters of the Democratic Party who ran the committee.

Burnham received 103 votes, or 15 percent of the total vote, for her class struggle program and MAC received support from many union members who hadn't previously supported the Caucus. (The top vote-getter got 233, and the other winner for the two open posts got 192, out of 673 votes cast. Argue got 28.) Thus while the vote was not enough to elect Burnham to the convention, the campaign introduced the Caucus to new members of the union and made a strong impact in the Local. MAC represents the only kind of opposition capable of accomplishing the replacement of Beirne's reactionary bureaucracy, by creating an alternative leadership based on a full class struggle program.

OUTRAGE!
Carter's Secret Service Drags CWA Delegate Off Convention Floor!

Spartacist League press release, reprinted from Workers Vanguard *No. 236, 20 July 1979*

DETROIT, July 16—in front of hundreds of stunned delegates, U.S. Secret Service agents this afternoon grabbed union official Jane Margolis, handcuffed her and dragged her protesting off the floor of the 41st Annual Convention of the Communications Workers of America (CWA). Shortly before President Jimmy Carter was scheduled to speak before the body, agents surrounded Margolis, 32, an elected delegate and member of the executive board of CWA Local 9410 (San Francisco), as she was standing with her delegation. Without warning they rushed her from the hall and locked her in an adjoining room. When outraged delegates rushed to the speakers' microphones to protest this criminal assault, the mikes were abruptly turned off.

White House officials at first denied that anyone had been detained, but changed the story after a CBS newsman reported accidentally finding Jane Margolis in a back room to which she had been abducted by the agents. This is the first known time that the Secret Service has invaded a union convention and seized a union officer. Margolis has announced that she intends to seek maximum legal redress for this outrage.

Out of sight of the convention delegates federal agents manhandled Jane, threatening to hold her incommunicado for days—on the basis of "reports" from unidentified "sources"—for suspicion of threatening the life of the president. While she was being subjected to interrogation and refused access to a lawyer, Detroit police told Margolis she was under arrest on unspecified charges. Thirty-five minutes later she was released, without explanation, but subjected to continued intensive surveillance by the Secret Service even after returning to the convention floor.

Jane Margolis is a spokesman for the Militant Action Caucus, an opposition group in the union which has repeatedly protested government interference in the labor movement, particularly by the CIA in Latin America. Earlier in the day she was prevented by the chair from presenting a motion that the union convention not allow itself to be used as a platform for the anti-labor strike-breaking policies of the Democrats. Clearly, a key purpose of the ham-fisted, blatantly illegal action by the Secret Service was to keep union delegates from registering any dissent against Carter and his energy speech.

In New York, James Robertson, National Chairman of the Spartacist League/U.S., immediately issued a vehement protest upon learning of the seizure of Margolis, an SL supporter and long-time personal friend. "What the Secret Service did to Jane is an outrage against organized labor," he said. "We don't have kings here. According to the laws, every citizen is supposed to have equal rights. But Jimmy Carter's personal goons simply march into a union convention and mug a woman who is an elected union official! Furthermore, Jane Margolis was in that meeting by right—Jimmy Carter was an invited guest."

"We demand that Jane Margolis be released immediately," said Robertson, so that she can resume her place with her delegation carrying out union business. And we demand that this Jimmy Carter apologize in his speech, both to Jane and to the entire CWA membership, for his unprecedented attack on the union. Jane Margolis never shut down any gas pumps!"

Jane Margolis: 'One Critic Carter Didn't Hear'

Reprinted from Workers Vanguard *No. 236, 20 July 1979*

"I'm going to reach out," said Jimmy Carter in his Sunday night sermon, and reach out he did. Through the long arm of his Secret Service goons, he "reached out" and mugged class-struggle militant Jane Margolis right on the floor of the Communications Workers of America (CWA) Convention (see accompanying Spartacist League Press Release). The fact that Margolis was an elected delegate to the convention with the right and responsibility to present her views was obviously a matter of no concern to Carter. For the capitalist class which this peanut baron represents, the rights of working people and the integrity of their labor organizations can be violated at their whim. Carter himself, on the other hand, is protected by a host *of lèse majesté* laws which give his armed thugs the right, among other things, to grab all "suspicious" persons for preventive detention.

Jane Margolis was suspected of planning to do something which was absolutely intolerable to Carter—exercise her democratic right to speak out on the floor of the convention of her trade union and expose his little energy confidence game for the cheap hustle that it is. So, she was subjected to "preventive" gagging. But the only "weapon" that this trade-union militant had pointed at the heart of the president was the simple *truth* that the energy crisis is not a crisis of confidence or faith or prayer or the rest of Carter's empty "born again" hokum, but a crisis of *capitalism.* And it is *real;* not in our hearts and minds but in the streets!

Carter had said, "I'm listening to the voices of Americans," but, in the words of the *San Francisco Examiner* (July 18) headline, Jane Margolis was "One critic Carter didn't hear." Carter is so manifestly unpopular, his support so shallow and his program such an obvious con game that he can't risk the slightest encounter with the truth. What if this trade unionist had punctured Carter's hot air balloon?

Jane Margolis has the right to say what she went to the convention to say, and the working people have the right to hear it. WV asked her for the statement she would have made, and we publish it [below].

What the Secret Service Wouldn't Let Jane Margolis Say

Brothers and Sisters,

Jimmy Carter came here today to get approval from the working people for his energy program—the program that blames *us* for the energy crisis because of our "greed," our "gas guzzling" and our "self-indulgence." While they hop around the country in their Lear jets and limousines, the capitalists would like to convince us that it is our duty to make sacrifices for the good of the country, to settle for the 7 percent guideline while the cost of living soars at 14 percent.

The present oil shortage is a well-known ripoff for Big Oil. The problem is that this rotten system delivers the profits to the peanut bosses, the oil magnates and the Ma Bells while we cannot even get enough gas for our cars.

The CWA convention must not be turned into a platform for the racist anti-labor Democratic Party of Jimmy Carter. I want to remind the delegates how in 1978 when the heroic miners shut down the coalfields for the right to strike and for adequate health and safety protection Carter invoked the slave-labor Taft-Hartley injunction to break their strike. Let's remember how in the face of soaring black unemployment and desperate ghetto poverty, Carter's callous response was simply that "life is unfair." Nor have we forgotten how he threatened to break our own proposed CWA strike in 1977 and how he will undoubtedly try to again if we prepare for the solid coast-to-coast phone strike we need next year!

I came to this convention on the platform—"Not a dime, not a vote for the strikebreaking Democrats and Republicans!" This is the program I ran on. This is the program on which I was elected to my local Executive Board and on which I have twice in a row been elected a delegate to this convention. In Carter's speech last night he told us to "stop cursing and start praying." *We say it's time to start fighting!* And our fight must be to break labor's ties to the bosses' parties and to form a powerful workers party to lead us as we struggle for a workers government.

International Longshoremen's and Warehousemen's Union

Militant Elected to ILWU Local 6 Exec Board

Reprinted from Workers Vanguard *No. 58, 6 December 1974*

OAKLAND, November 25—Bob Mandel, a seven-year militant in the ILWU, has been elected on a class struggle program to the executive board of Local 6 (warehouse division) from the East Bay. He got 636 votes (the top vote-getter received 691). Banned by undemocratic Local regulations from publishing any campaign literature except one short statement in a special official election bulletin, Mandel took his program to the membership by campaigning at warehouses and retail outlets throughout the Oakland area.

In his election statement, Mandel advocated industry-wide strikes against layoffs and a shorter work week at no loss in pay to meet spreading house closures and "runaways" in ILWU-organized warehouses as well as layoffs in the longshore and Hawaiian sections of the union. He also demanded that militant international labor solidarity be revived "through tactics like the recent boycott of cargo to Chile in defense of workers struggling against the junta."

Mandel condemned the ILWU's support for the "racist Alioto" as "a defeat for the movement of workers and oppressed," and called for an independent workers party. He also called for workers control and for a workers government "to end the cycle of inflation, recession, racial and sexual discrimination" through the "nationaliz[ation of] all industry without compensation" to the present owners.

Finally, Mandel underlined the betrayals of the present union leadership, which include disarming the workers in the face of every kind of employer attack (layoffs, blacklisting of militants who fight company attacks, armed strike-breakers in the ILWU Borax strike, etc.). "An opposition caucus must be built throughout the union," he declared, to fight for this class struggle program.

Mandel ran eighth in a field of 12 candidates for the 10 positions open on the executive board. He narrowly missed being elected delegate to the International convention as well, losing by only 30 votes (eighth out of 14 contenders for 6 positions).

Mandel established his reputation as a militant defender of hard-won union gains through his campaign for sympathy-strike support by ILWU warehousemen to the 1971 longshore strike and, more recently, through his initiation of struggle against blacklisting and for implementation of boycotts of Chilean ships and goods. He has also served on union committees and as steward.

It is significant that in a union with a strong Stalinist current in its background Mandel got more votes than many Communist Party-backed candidates despite vicious Stalinist denunciation of him and his program, particularly during the anti-blacklisting campaign earlier this year.

Mandel's victory is a victory for a class-struggle program and the future class-struggle leadership of the labor movement. It is an answer to the many fake-left organizations which insist that it is necessary to support bureaucrats running on totally reformist programs (such as Arnold Miller), abandoning working-class principles in order to gain influence in the working class.

Longshore Militants Confront I.S. at 'Rank And File' Conference

Reprinted from Workers Vanguard *No. 60, 17 January 1975*

OAKLAND, January 6—A conference on "Building the Rank and File Movement" sponsored by the International Socialists (IS) ran into trouble with rank-and-file unionists here yesterday. The largest and most authoritative grouping of militant rank-and-file leaders at the conference denounced the sponsors' reformist trade-union policies, especially IS' support for Stanley Weir's court case against ILWU Local 10.

In an interview with *Workers Vanguard* the militants, members of the West Coast longshore union, told of the shabby, bureaucratic treatment they received from the cynical "left" talkers who organized the conference. Howard Keylor, a member of the ILWU's longshore division for over 20 years, most of that time as an active oppositionist, was invited to be on a panel during the morning session. Keylor had opposed the original deregistration of 59 lower-seniority B-men, the object of Weir's court action against the union, and has actively defended their rights ever since. While opposing the lawsuit, he calls for action by the union ranks to force reinstatement of the victimized B-men with full rights.

Keylor is now a candidate for the Local 10 executive board on a program highlighting a call for six hours' work at eight hours' pay, and the need for a workers party and a workers government. On the panel he spoke about his experience battling the Bridges machine in the ILWU. He stressed that years as an oppositionist and trade unionist had taught him the deeply unprincipled character of appealing to the bosses' courts against the union.

Further, he declared the necessity to build opposition around a full program of class struggle. In that way opposition to the incumbent union misleaders would not be sidetracked into campaigns for just another set of slicker bureaucrats to preside over the same old sellouts. Two recent cases of such out-bureaucrats' running for office, both supported by the IS, were Arnold Miller of the United Mine Workers and James Morrissey in the National

Maritime Union. According to Keylor a class-struggle program must include demands for a sliding scale of wages and hours, nationalization of industry without compensation, running industry under workers control and a workers party to fight for a workers government.

Keylor reportedly concluded his remarks by addressing two questions to the organizers of the conference: (1) Will the International Socialists continue to support Stan Weir's lawsuit against the ILWU? and (2) How can the IS, which in its press claims to support at least some elements of a class-struggle program, justify its support for two out-bureaucrats like Miller and Morrissey, who both ran on programs of "democracy" enforced by the federal government?

In the lively and often heated discussion that followed, supporters of IS' social-democratic policies became increasingly embarrassed. A rank-and-file Teamster and founding member of the IS-supported Fifth Wheel caucus asked what he should do about a suit in his local brought by a Chicano who had been the victim of gross discrimination. Should the suit against the union be dropped while the suit against the company continued? John Larson, member of Teamsters Local 70 and Fifth Wheel supporter, answered that there was no question of principle involved in suing the union; other IS supporters defended the Weir suit.

Supporters of IS policies did their bureaucratic best to avoid substantive political questions. But Stan Gow, a militant with 18 years in the ILWU, took the floor and pinned them down. Gow, a Local 10 executive board member, is running for re-election on a joint program with Keylor. He demanded to know why the IS refused to support Gene Herson, candidate of the Militant-Solidarity Caucus of the National Maritime Union, who in 1973 ran for president of that union on a class-struggle program calling for a workers government. Instead the IS supported Morrissey in that election.

Finally forced to reply, IS supporters said that the M-SC's Herson ran on "only a paper program" while Morrissey had "real support" in the union. (In fact Morrissey has no organized support whatsoever in the union. His real support came from the U.S. Departments of Justice and Labor.) They said this despite the fact that Herson received more votes by far than the IS has members.

Then Bob Mandel, who was recently elected to the executive board of ILWU Local 6 on just such a "paper program," attempted to take the floor. This was more than the IS could bear. Mandel was surrounded by four IS goons determined not to let him speak. They backed off, however, when Mandel's union brothers stood up to make it clear that they would insist that the meeting continue in democratic fashion.

After some tense moments, the IS was obliged to grant an unscheduled second round of discussion. Mandel commented that he was used to fighting for the floor at meetings of his own union local, but that the IS behavior was even more bureaucratic than the usual behavior of the labor bureaucracy.

In the afternoon session Mike Parker confirmed the cravenly opportunist appetites which lay behind the IS' reformist trade-union policies. He explained that although there had been a lot of talk at the conference about organizing in trade unions around a full class-struggle program, such a program was not needed. Rather, what was needed was "a program that points to a full program." In clear contradiction to Lenin's call for a vanguard party to bring socialist consciousness to the masses of the workers (expressed in *What Is To Be Done?*), Parker declared that "simple wage demands lead to socialist consciousness." He then said what everybody already knew—that the IS was not the revolutionary party. The IS would await the rank-and-file upsurge which would create the revolutionary party. Then, presumably, a full program would be appropriate.

By the end of the conference the IS, unable to pass off its warmed-over New Left social-democratic reformism in the face of the class-struggle politics of the six ILWU militants (who together represented more than 70 years of trade-union experience), resorted to a bureaucratic exclusion. The militants were officially disinvited from a "mulled wine party" that was scheduled to conclude the conference. Genuine working-class militants are, it seems, too much for IS stomachs!

Labor Solidarity Halts Union-Busting in Oakland Strike

Reprinted from Workers Vanguard *No. 61, 31 January 1975*

OAKLAND, January 28—Mass picketing initiated by militants in the warehouse local of the International Longshoremen's and Warehousemen's Union has stopped a union-busting drive which could have been the spark for a similar assault on all of Bay Area labor. The employer, KNC Glass Company in Union City, had sought to repeat the crushing blow delivered to ILWU Local 30 by U.S. Borax last fall.

In that strike, management used several hundred scabs to keep its mine in Boron, California, operating. Borax also sent a warning letter to its striking employees, threatening them with permanent replacement if they didn't return to work immediately, without a contract. The threat worked because AFL-CIO craft unions crossed the picket lines and the ILWU International failed to organize solidarity actions, even within the union itself. Thus, ILWU longshoremen in Los Angeles were forced to ship scab borax. As a result, hundreds of workers were thrown out of their jobs and other union gains were sacrificed.

The Boron strike was held up as an example to all employers by a feature story in the December issue of *Fortune* magazine. The pattern is familiar—scabs, cops and the passivity of the trade-union bureaucracy—but this open union-busting is a sharply increased danger in the present period, as unemployment swells the pool of potential strikebreakers.

The KNC strike looked like it would become a Boron in the Bay Area, paving the way for a general anti-labor assault by the Distributors Association (the warehouse employers' group) during contract negotiations approaching in the next few months. The company kept its offer low, hired notorious strikebreaking guards and sent a Boron-style ultimatum to the strikers: go back without a contract or be fired. The ILWU leadership under Local 6 president McLain also followed the pattern, by failing to respond with militant union action to stop the scabbing.

However, a class-struggle program raised by three warehouse militants, Bob Mandel (a member of the Local 6 executive board), John Dow and Pete Farrugio, pointed the way forward. Denouncing the do-nothing policy of the union leadership, they demanded mass picketing and a "hot-cargoing" labor boycott of material going to and from the plant. Response to their leaflet was impressive: hundreds of workers from surrounding ILWU shops joined the picket lines over a period of days. Local 6 and even International leaders were forced to show up.

Teamster officials—themselves feeling the pinch of employer union busting through increased owner-operator trucking—turned out despite their bureaucratic rivalry with ILWU officials over warehouse and longshore container jurisdictions. And militants from several other unions also appeared, including members of the Militant Action Caucus of the Communications Workers and the Committee for a Militant UAW from the Fremont GM assembly plant.

Mass picketing by 75–100 workers and union officials on January 9 stopped the scabs, but the company sought an injunction to put an end to picketing. This had been anticipated by Mandel and the other militants, who tried to get the Local 6 stewards council to defy the injunction. But members of the stewards council influenced by the Communist Party and Revolutionary Union helped the ILWU bureaucracy table Mandel's motions.

Nevertheless, sentiment among the ranks for defying the injunction—and thus confronting the leadership's class collaborationism head-on—mounted rapidly. ILWU members from the Local hiring hall, from the longshoremen's local and from shops such as Associated Grocers and St. Regis Paper continued to man picket lines, keeping out scabs in defiance of the injunction. Emboldened by the court action the professional strikebreaker guards became increasingly vicious, waving guns and unleashing dogs. In response, members circulated petitions in a number of Local 6 houses demanding shop meetings with union officials to organize defense. At Associated Grocers workers voted to walk off their jobs if necessary to defend the strike.

The mass support for KNC strikers impressed both employers and the union leadership, neither of which had any desire to see it spread and influence upcoming disputes. The company backed off from its attempt to break the union while union leaders hastily accepted a slightly improved management offer. Despite a personal show of militancy on the picket line, and despite his complaints about the ILWU International's failure to wage a militant defense of the Boron strike, when the chips were down in his own local McLain refused to further mobilize the members for the achievement of lasting gains in the KNC strike. Thus this plant is still saddled with a substandard contract which holds down the wages of other Local 6 members. Furthermore, it has no cost of living provision whatsoever and no attempt was made to give KNC a contract termination date together with the majority of Local 6 agreements.

Workers Vanguard interviews with KNC workers revealed the important lessons that were learned during the strike. It was the solidarity of other workers in the union, and of other locals and industries, which made the limited victory possible. A subsequent Local 6 meeting showed that the leadership had also learned something from the strike. While John Dow (one of the militants who had initiated the mass picketing) was criticizing the inadequate terms of the KNC settlement, the microphone was seized from him by a supporter of the leadership. In addition, according to a leaflet distributed at East Bay warehouses today, at the end of the meeting ILWU International secretary-treasurer Lou Goldblatt "warned" Mandel that a move was afoot to expel him from the union.

The class-collaborationist ILWU officialdom, like the rest of the union bureaucracy, is committed to the conception that management and labor must live in harmony. These defeatists and professional capitulators argue that if labor fails to make peace with the employers it will be crushed by them and their government. Not only must class-struggle oppositionists therefore be silenced, but the workers must be mobilized in support of the interests of the employers.

Thus Goldblatt spoke at length at the meeting on the theme that "foreign" money is "turning the U.S. into a colony." This is a bald-faced attempt to whip up national chauvinism in preparation for inter-imperialist trade rivalries and wars in which all workers will be the losers. Moreover, the immediate effect of Goldblatt's line is to drive a wedge within the Local 6 membership itself, portraying Spanish-speaking workers (such as the KNC strikers) as the "enemy within"!

Only the building of a new class-struggle leadership, counterposed to the class collaborationism of the Bridges, Goldblatts and McLains, can spread the militant methods of the KNC strike, in order to stop future "Borons" and strengthen international labor solidarity.

Workers Vote for Class-Struggle Candidates in ILWU Local 10

Reprinted from Workers Vanguard *No. 61, 31 January 1975*

SAN FRANCISCO, January 25—While a major longshore contract betrayal loomed in the background, elections for officers and executive board members held recently in the Bay Area waterfront local of the International Longshoremen's and Warehousemen's Union failed to provide a way out of the impasse facing the union. With about two thirds of Local 10's 2,400 members voting, key offices were divided between supporters and opponents of ILWU president Harry Bridges.

Support for the anti-Bridges forces in the Local slipped somewhat from last year's elections, in which an entire slate of oppositionists under Mills and Stout had been elected. In addition, questions were raised in the minds of some members over the handling of the election when a key Bridges supporter was elected by only one vote and an outspoken opponent of both wings of the Local leadership was maneuvered out of a seat on the executive board after having tied for last place.

Local 10 has been the center of resistance to the International leadership over the last four years as Bridges has allowed automation to drastically erode jobs and working conditions. Recently he has also attempted to force the sale of the Local's hiring hall to commercial developers aligned with his friend, S.F. mayor Joe Alioto.

The Mills-Stout regime, although a nuisance to Bridges, was completely unable to lead the Local in a qualitatively different direction. It folded under pressure instead of mobilizing the ranks to defend a spreading boycott of work on automated LASH barges (owned by Alioto's shipping company) which had been worked by non-longshore labor. It also capitulated to Bridges' demands for an immediate contract settlement (six months ahead of schedule!) at the recent December meeting of the Coast Longshore Caucus. And it bowed to a new plan by the International to railroad hundreds of B-men (second-class members) out of the union, despite a contractual clause requiring their elevation to full membership this year.

Increasing support for a class-struggle alternative was revealed, however, in the votes for two militants, Stan Gow and Howard Keylor, for executive board. Gow and Keylor, who between them have 37 years on the West Coast docks, ran as a team counterposed to both the pro- and anti-Bridges wings in the Local leadership.

The two militants called for resistance to the impending contract sellout, a sliding scale of hours to make more jobs with no loss in pay and immediate full membership status for all B-men. They also denounced the leadership's alliance with Alioto, calling for a break with the Democrats and Republicans and the building of a workers party to fight for a workers government. Gow, who was a member of the outgoing executive board, was re-elected with 239 votes, an increase over his vote last year. Keylor tied for last place, ahead of 19 other candidates, with 221 votes (also an increase in his showing in Local elections).

Keylor came into the union in Stockton in 1953. He helped lead opposition to the first purge of B-men in 1963. (Bridges at that time singled out 82 working longshoremen, who should have been full members, for firing because they had been critical of the union leadership.) Some of the victims subsequently took the union to court, a move that Gow and Keylor now point out was an error which will only hurt the union.

Gow came into the ILWU in 1959 in Local 10. Both he and Keylor were at one time supporters of Longshore Victory, a now-defunct opposition group, and initial backers of Mills and Stout. Experience has shown, they point out, that simple honesty and good intentions are not enough—it is program that is decisive.

Gow and Keylor campaigned on a program "to make the ILWU defend its members' real interests and to put the working class in control of society." They called for international working-class solidarity, including use of labor boycotts to support the struggles of Chilean workers, farm workers in the U.S., etc. They demanded nationalization of the longshore-transport industry, without compensation, and called for workers control.

Their joint program also called for a struggle to build a workers party based on the unions, a struggle directed at ousting—not simply pressuring—the present pro-capitalist labor bureaucracy. Finally, they denounced appeals to the courts against the union, such as the B-men suit and a Mills-Stout suit to stop Bridges' hall-grabbing.

> "The question of B-men and the hall has to be fought out within the union. To rely on the government to come in and do it for us is worse than futile.... Opening the door to the government is opening the door for it to smash us. The worst enemy of the ILWU and of all labor is the capitalist government."
> —"Defend the ILWU—Stop Bridges' '75 Contract Sellout,"
> 31 December 1974

The new officers quickly made a ruling which kept both Keylor and the other candidate tied for last place off the executive board. Formerly it had usually been the practice that the five full-time offices (president, secretary-treasurer, business agents, etc.) are filled by members who also run for executive board. Since officers sit on the executive board ex-officio, those that are elected to both positions have been replaced on the board by the five candidates who received the next highest votes.

Application of this principle has varied in the past, however, thereby creating an opportunity for bureaucratic abuse by the officials. In this case, instead of calling a run-off election to resolve the tie for last place, the new officers decided to leave the vice president on the board. Thus Local 10 officials were relieved of an opponent on the executive board, and the membership was deprived of the right to choose its representatives.

The new president of Local 10 is Larry Wing, a business agent in the previous administration. Wing was brutally beaten last September by a goon squad of Bridges supporters who were demanding that the leadership turn over its keys to the Local's hiring hall. It was also Wing who first authorized and then called off the "hot cargo" boycott of LASH barges belonging to Alioto's Pacific Far East Lines. The boycott by Local 10 members was in solidarity with the Stockton Local, which had been denied longshore work on the barges.

Perhaps because of his reputation as the most militant member of the Mills-Stout team, Wing received the highest vote—850—of any candidate in the election (his pro-Bridges opponent got 753). Wing's lack of an alternative program for the union was shown, however, when he called off the boycott while it was still going strong. Moreover, he has done nothing to oppose the new move to deregister (and thus fire) those B-men with the least hours worked in 1973.

Besides Wing, the chief business agent is also an anti-Bridges member. The other three officers, however, are pro-Bridges. In the key race for secretary-treasurer—who signs the checks for payments to the Local's separate hiring hall ownership corporation—a Bridges man with a notoriously unreliable reputation was elected by a single vote, 761 to 760. The winner, Carl Smith, played a prominent role in the first purge of B-men in 1963. Smith may now be in a position to force sale of the hall by simply refusing to make payments necessary to meet hall expenses.

The executive board was divided between the various factions in the Local. Marshall, one of the International supporters accused of participating in the goon attack on Wing, was elected with 362 votes. Archie Brown, a well-known supporter of Communist Party positions, was elected by 416 votes and also returned to the Publicity Committee, where he runs the Local's news sheet.

At the Local meeting following the election, in an apparent reference to rumors of irregularities, Brown made a token attempt to question the election committee's report certifying the election as proper. However, he did not pursue the subject, thereby "making the record" while avoiding a serious attempt to track down rumors.

At the first meeting of the new executive board yesterday, the new leadership already revealed its bankruptcy in the face of mounting attacks jointly engineered by the International and the employers' Pacific Maritime Association. In the face of the Coast Caucus' capitulation to Bridges, who has already stated his willingness to arbitrate any differences in order to ram through a hurried-up contract, the PMA began openly provoking the union by ordering "steady men," who are only supposed to do maintenance and other specified work, to work in the holds of ships. (Steady men, who work regularly for one employer rather than being assigned jobs through the hall, were first allowed by Bridges in the 1966 contract.) Instead of acting against this threat to the union hiring hall, the executive board voted, 20 to 7, to refer the question to the International.

Meanwhile, star chamber proceedings have been scheduled by a joint union-management labor relations committee to "hear" the cases of B-men threatened with deregistration. These men, who should be full members and who have met contractual requirements of availability for work, are now supposed to testify as to why they should not be fired!

Gow and Keylor had prepared motions for an immediate mobilization against this attack: for an immediate halt to deregistration proceedings, for granting full "A" hiring status to B-men immediately and for full union membership for B-men. However, their motions were shoved to the last place on the agenda, and consideration of them conveniently avoided through adjournment. An immediate fight must now be taken to the membership to stop this illegal and undemocratic railroading of working longshoremen and union members.

In their last leaflet issued before the election, Gow and Keylor made their position clear on the question of support, critical or otherwise, to the "militant, democratic" opposition to Bridges.

> "Many brothers in Local 10 have asked us if we are supporting some of the anti-International candidates like Wing, George Kaye or Archie Brown. No. None of them offer any real alternative program to Bridges. We went through it once with Stout and particularly Herb Mills and learned that in relation to events like the goon squad and the monitorship [semi-receivership of the Local instituted by Bridges], being honest and democratic isn't enough....
>
> "Those of us that have been around long enough remember that Archie Brown actively supported the deregistration of the B-men in '63 and that he threw his full prestige behind the treacherous M&M contract....Then, just before the 1973 contract, Brown retreated from his previous total opposition to 9.43 [a contract clause providing for "steady men"] and made a resolution for an equalization of hours formula."

The leaflet called for the formation of a caucus on a class-struggle program, to construct a union leadership which will not capitulate to capitalist politicians like Alioto, to the bosses' anti-labor laws, which outlaw militant actions such as labor boycotts, or to the employers' drive to maximize profits. It is precisely the lack of a class-struggle program which causes immediate capitulation to the companies and the class-collaborationist policies of the union bureaucracy by even those militants who begin with honest intentions to fight for the rank and file's interests.

Gow and Keylor made clear that they would base the struggle for such a program on the mobilization of the membership (as over the boycott of Alioto's barges) rather than reliance on the bureaucracy of the International or on "militant democrats" (no better than Stout-Mills-Wing in Local 10) in power in other locals such as Los Angeles. They have thus begun to lay the basis for the building of an alternative, class-struggle leadership throughout the ILWU. This struggle within the unions is a vital support to the building of a revolutionary vanguard party which alone can lead the working class to victory over capitalism.

Interview with a Participant

Communist Tactics in the Trade Unions
Class Struggle on the Waterfront

Reprinted from 1917 *No. 4, Autumn 1987*

On July 19 we interviewed Howard Keylor, a longtime trade-union militant on the waterfront in San Francisco. Brother Keylor is on the Executive Board of International Longshoremen's and Warehousemen's Union Local 10 (longshore division) and is the editor of *Militant Longshoreman*. Keylor's record of over three decades in the ILWU and his break from Stalinism to Trotskyism give him a unique perspective on the fight for a class-struggle leadership in the American labor movement.

In the 1970's, as a supporter of the then-revolutionary Spartacist League, Keylor played an important role in organizing several small but successful actions on the waterfront in defense of the victims of South African apartheid and the Chilean junta. In the last several years, in addition to playing a leading role in several waterfront strikes, Keylor initiated two larger and more important actions in solidarity with heroic black workers battling the racist Botha regime. These actions provided a concrete alternative to the liberal moralism prevalent in the campus-based anti-apartheid movement and provide a model of how a communist opposition in the unions should act as the tribune of the oppressed.

1917: Let's start with your history in the ILWU. How did you come into the union?

Keylor: The hard way. I started in 1953 as a casual. That means just picking up extra work by standing around in the dispatch office. It means no stable, registered or even recognized status. I was lucky enough to know a couple of older activists in the union—one of whom belonged to the CP, another was an old Wobblie—who were friends of mine and used a bit of influence and got me on a casual list. It wasn't until 1959 that I got recognized status in the ILWU.

1917: But you were a member of other unions before?

Keylor: Yes, as a matter of fact in 1953 I had been fired from the job I worked for two years in a paper mill. I belonged to the papermakers' local union. I was active in that union in a limited way.

1917: You were a supporter of the Stalinist Communist Party for over 25 years. How were you won to Trotskyism?
Keylor: I had always been something of a secret dissident, I guess you could have called me a left-Stalinist. I was quite unhappy most of the time during the McCarthy period with the Communist Party trying to hide what seemed its own limited, but at least formally revolutionary ideology. I was never too happy with the policy of primarily trying to form alliances with bourgeois or petty-bourgeois formations. I guess I was an unreconstructed Third Period Stalinist.

I had my own somewhat secret, actually very secret, theory about the Soviet Union as a workers state in which the bureaucracy had seized power from the working class and suppressed working class dissidents. I knew that was the case, but I'd never been able to generalize my political differences.

1917: So how did you come to Trotskyism? Did you read a book by Trotsky or did you meet people that called themselves Trotskyists?
Keylor: I never read anything by Trotsky or any of the main writings about Trotskyism or met a Trotskyist until the 1971–72 longshore strike when I came in contact with Asher Harer, a member of the union who was a well-known supporter of the Socialist Workers Party and is today with Socialist Action. I collaborated with him in writing a leaflet during the 143-day strike in 1971–72 and I wasn't too happy with the collaboration because, while some of what we were asking for programmatically seemed to make sense, he was very adamant on not criticizing the international union bureaucracy and their conduct in the strike. He was the only ostensible Trotskyist I had ever had any contact with.

It wasn't until about August 1974 that I ran into an old tattered copy of Deutscher's *The Prophet Armed* [the first volume of a three-part political biography of Trotsky]. I took it home; stayed up all night reading it and then went to a library the next day and got the rest of the trilogy, read it and walked around in a daze for a couple of weeks. It wasn't until I came in contact with the Spartacist League in the fall of 1974 that I began doing some consistent reading on Trotskyism and was won over painfully.

1917: You eventually became a supporter of the Spartacist League?
Keylor: Yes, I became a supporter of the Spartacist League, which as you know, at that time had a serious orientation to trade-union work—something which is no longer the case. Actually, initially I became a member of the SL-supported Longshore/Warehouse Militant Caucus, and in April of 1975 became an organized supporter of the Spartacist League.

1917: This is the thirteenth consecutive year you have been elected to the Executive Board of ILWU Local 10 on an openly socialist program. How have you managed to win a base for your politics in the union?
Keylor: There are really two separate questions. Getting elected to the Executive Board was initially rather difficult. There was a lot of competition for

Executive Board posts in the earlier period. Having transferred from the small up-river port of Stockton to San Francisco in 1970, I was a relatively "new boy" on the block. Also, I was white and the San Francisco longshoremen were, and are still, about 70 percent black. Initially it was not easy to get elected and running on an explicitly socialist, transitional program made it even more difficult.

By December 1974, when I first ran on this program as a member of the Militant Caucus, socialists had mostly been identified with the Communist Party in Local 10. The Communist Party had to a large extent been discredited because of their support to the international union's bureaucratic sellout of the workers interests. In the first period some of our support came from militants who thought we were uniquely honest in saying what we stood for, and because we were projecting a positive program and were not afraid to criticize all levels of the bureaucracy. That was rather unusual because almost all other figures, even minor ones in the Local at that time, were identified with either one of two main bureaucratic factions—the [ILWU President Harry] Bridges faction or the large, amorphous anti-Bridges faction.

We stood outside these formations and acted as a very small, hard left political pole, and nothing like that had been done for a long, long time. I particularly suffered some difficulty, because in moving toward an explicitly socialist program based on the Transitional Program, I had to break with the whole anti-Bridges bloc that I had worked with for almost four years—some of whom were my close friends.

1917: So in the union you ran on the Transitional Program. One of the criticisms which we often hear of this approach by groups like Workers Power in Britain is that raising a full socialist program amounts to "ultimatism." Their idea is that demands like the call for workers defense guards or for a workers government are too advanced for the present consciousness of the class. How would you respond?

Keylor: I would respond that the failure to raise the whole Transitional Program as applied to the particular trade-union milieu or trade-union situation amounts to misleading the workers, because all points or aspects of that program sometime or other, sooner or later, relate to immediate questions facing the union. It is impossible to build a class-struggle opposition that can lead workers, even to defend themselves, without educating at least a section of the activist workers—the most advanced ones—about the social and political reality in which they are operating.

For example, in the mid to late fifties, the union started to get very deeply involved in Democratic Party politics in San Francisco. Actually earlier in Hawaii, the bulk of the union became intertwined with the Democratic Party to such an extent that the interests of the various coalitions they were backing ran directly counter to the interests of the workers. To oppose support to the Democrats you have to explain the class nature of the capitalist state, and that automatically raises the question of the workers government—just like any serious picket line situation poses in embryo the necessity for some kind of workers defense guards.

The bottom line is that you can't build a pro-socialist wing in the unions by hiding your politics—that's always a sign of adaptation to the present backwardness of the class. You've got to be upfront about what you stand for and try to apply your program in a creative way to address the concrete questions which arise. To pick out a few of the demands of the Transitional Program that might be more popular at a given moment, and just run on them, in effect destroys the whole purpose of the program—which is to connect the immediate, felt needs of the workers to the necessity of a political struggle for power.

1917: From time to time there have been oppositional formations in the ILWU that ran on a program of "more militancy" and "more democracy," similar to Ed Sadlowski in steel or Arnold Miller in the coal miners union, or the Teamsters for a Democratic Union [TDU]. Many leftists see these campaigns as a step forward because they oppose the incumbent bureaucrats. How do you look at such a lesser-evil approach to union work?

Keylor: It's not very practical. Even when they succeed in throwing out the existing bureaucrats the results are usually disastrous. Even assuming you've got honest, well-meaning elements leading these oppositional groups—and not just another gang of would-be bureaucrats—when they get into power, they find themselves up against the same opposition from the government, the same legalistic restrictions and the same nasty, brutal repression from the employers. And lacking an understanding—a political class understanding—of how to break out of those restrictions, those leaders will end up acting like Miller, Nixon's candidate in the mineworkers. They will become brutal bureaucrats themselves and suppress the rank-and-file.

In longshore there was a big, broad oppositional grouping to the Bridges leadership in the late sixties, based in part on new people who had come into the union. When Bridges finally retired, various elements of this opposition came into power, especially in the major longshore locals. They didn't do any better in defending the interests of the workers than the Bridges machine. The only real alternative is to pose class-struggle oppositional formations, which stand as a political alternative to all varieties of business unionism.

1917: What would distinguish such caucuses from formations like the TDU?

Keylor: They are distinguished primarily by their program. When they get elected in a given section of a union they are predictable in terms of what they will do. When oppositional groupings that are not programmatically based win leadership in a union, they usually don't remain intact. The only glue that holds them together is the fight for power. Once they get in, they quite frequently split or dissolve into their components, fighting over crumbs; or they become cynically co-opted into the bureaucratic system. The very best of such formations will simply degenerate into nickel-and-dime economism or social-democratic maneuverism. An opposition based on a coherent program of class struggle can win workers to a political understanding and the necessity to fight for it. In learning to apply that program to all aspects of the union's life, as well as in the whole of society, they become committed to that program.

Individuals can betray or fall away but the betrayal will be quite conspicuous. One of the virtues of running on a clear class-struggle program is that the workers know where you stand on all major issues or can figure out which side you are going to come down on regarding the issues facing the union.

1917: When is it correct for Trotskyists in the unions to support other groups or individuals for union office? What should be the conditions of that support?
Keylor: Given the extremely degenerate condition of the American trade-union leadership, one has to be extremely careful about offering even critical support to individuals or groupings running for office. Even the smallest committee in the union will be dealing with questions that have to do with the power of the employers over the workers or questions of class-collaboration. So the criteria that one has to apply must be based on program.

While it will vary from time to time in practice, there are certain minimum positions we would generally want to see publicly taken by individuals running for office before we would think of voting for them. There are three interconnected questions that I can think of. One is no support for the top trade-union bureaucracy. There isn't a single major union in this country in which all the components at the top have not been at least complicit in major betrayals of the workers interests. Only people that are prepared to openly break with all sections of the trade-union bureaucracy, and criticize it, can have sufficient independence to merit support.

Another absolutely minimal programmatic aspect is the defense of the independence of the workers movement, especially the unions, from the capitalist state. This usually comes up over the question of lawsuits against the unions or government intervention into the internal affairs of the unions.

1917: Or defying injunctions?
Keylor: Yes, that is another aspect of the same thing. Anyone who runs for office in a union and will not take a position on the necessity to defy injunctions or court orders emanating from the capitalist state, is simply not able to defend workers interests.

And then there is the question of a break with the Democratic and Republican parties, the twin bourgeois parties. While we always call for a break with the Democrats and Republicans and for a workers government that will expropriate industry without compensation, in some cases we have given critical support to candidates for office who simply called for breaking with the Democrats and Republicans and forming a workers party.

In general though, "critical support" in union elections is an application of the united front. Lenin compared it to that which a rope gives a hanged man. What he meant was that an important aspect of critical support is exposure, in practice, of the inadequacies and contradictions of a reformist program. You cannot expose a reformist unless he or she runs on a platform that in some fashion represents a real break from class-collaborationism. Every out-bureaucrat will promise "more militancy" and "more democracy"—it's cheap. If you vote for somebody on that basis you are really just voting for one reformist because he's more popular than the other.

It's always a concrete question, but if a reformist oppositionist is running at the head of a real rank-and-file movement, and is seriously committed in the eyes of his base to fight for some programmatic plank which is really opposed to pro-capitalist business unionism, then class-struggle elements could consider offering him critical support, despite the reformist limitations of the rest of his platform. At the same time, it is necessary to warn those who follow such a candidate that his platform as a whole contradicts this particular demand. That way, if and when he betrays this demand, those who supported him because of it will begin to understand that only the consistent class-struggle elements in the union are capable of really fighting for their interests.

1917: In 1984 you initiated a united front for the political strike which boycotted the South African cargo on the Nedlloyd Kimberley in San Francisco. A lot of the workers involved in that action had very different politics than yours, right?

Keylor: That is correct. The initiating committee and the committee that implemented the boycott after it was approved, was composed of individuals who had not only widely different political views, but who had often been in very sharp, antagonistic disputes in the union and even outside the union.

1917: On the eleventh day of the cargo boycott, when a federal court injunction came down, the bloc split. What happened?

Keylor: When the federal injunction came down the local union leadership, which had been giving passive support, and in some cases rather active support to the boycott, called a special meeting of the local executive board. After extensive debate the board voted eleven to five to comply with the injunction. In the course of that debate the bloc split with most of the members, who were either one-time adherents or supporters of the Communist Party, various Maoist groupings or who could be characterized as something like black nationalists, went along with the union bureaucracy in advocating an end to the boycott and complying with the injunction.

The local executive board voted to end the boycott and voted down my proposal to call a mass, stop-work membership meeting at the pier to make the decision. I called for this because a meeting of a couple of thousand longshoremen at the pier would have amounted to a mass picket line and could well have led to successfully defying the injunction. At any rate, my proposal was voted down. So then, I, along with a number of other militants in the union and supporters from outside the union, attempted to put up a picket line and continue the boycott and defy the injunction. Initially we closed down the pier and stopped the trucks for an hour and the longshoremen did not work. But eventually the Stalinists, the adherents of the Communist Party, helped the cops to break the action by escorting the trucks through the picket line and creating fear among those participants who were not part of the union that they would go to jail for long periods of time for defying the injunction.

1917: Recently there has been an important strike on the waterfront by the Inland Boatman's Union [IBU], an affiliate of the ILWU. I understand you have been active in promoting cooperation between the IBU and the longshore division to stop scabbing. Was there any defiance of injunctions in this strike?
Keylor: Not defiance of an injunction specifically, but there was an invasion of "private property" when the employers took three barges that had been stopped through joint IBU/ILWU action in Oakland to Redwood City and began unloading them with non-longshoremen. This was seen as a direct incursion of longshore jurisdiction, as well as an attempt to weaken and break the IBU strike. All the longshoremen, clerks and walking bosses in the Bay Area then left their jobs and traveled to the pier to protest the scabbing. This was an "illegal" action because, according to federal law, we were violating our contract. In fact, members of the longshore division and the striking boatmen went onto the pier and "illegally" chased off the scabs.

There have been many injunctions in the IBU strike which have largely strangled it, because they have been adhered to by the leadership of the IBU and the ILWU. The lesson that class-conscious militants in the unions have to constantly hammer home to the membership is that even a minimal defense of the union requires actions that are illegal under some section or sections of federal law. Whether defiance of an injunction, or even the most minimal stop-work action, the Taft-Hartley law makes it all illegal.

1917: Gompers-style "business unionists" argue that unions should concern themselves simply with the wages and working conditions of their members. In the long run the interests of the longshoremen are tied pretty closely to the interests of the class as a whole, including the unemployed. How can this connection be made?
Keylor: One of the problems we ran into in longshore is the parochialism, growing out of the fact that longshoremen, by the nature of their work, even though they are small in numbers, have an unusual economic power. Ports and port facilities can't be moved easily. But the union could not have been formed in the first place or defended against employer attacks, especially in the early decades, without the support of other workers and especially other maritime workers. There is an unusually rich history of this in longshore which has almost been lost, but which the class-struggle militants went back to and used as illustrations.

For example, it is not well known, but in 1934 when scabs were loading ships in San Francisco harbor and some other west coast ports, the longshoremen in Chile, even though they were under a quite repressive government, refused to handle scab cargo. Longshoremen in Australia and some other countries did the same. That kind of international support was one of the factors that helped win the strike. Of course it was the massive San Francisco general strike and the threat of extending it to the rest of the west coast that finally won the establishment of the longshoremen's union in 1934. Today we call for using the union's full power to organize the unemployed in waterfront areas. That should make a lot of sense to any trade-unionist—it's elementary self-defense.

As for the unemployed, rather than accept a shrinking workforce in longshore, for example, we call for a shorter work shift with no loss in pay to the point where not only all present workers are kept working, but additional workers can be added. This is how the Transitional Program proposes to solve unemployment—by dividing the available work among the available workforce, at no loss in pay.

It is also important to start organizing the unemployed directly by the unions, similar to what was done in the 1930's especially in the mass organizing of auto workers. That's part of the lost history of the labor movement. It would have been a lot harder to organize those auto plants if they hadn't been organizing the unemployed along with them. A lot of the pickets that surrounded and sealed off the auto plants were composed of unemployed auto workers organized in unemployed leagues close to the union.

1917: Historically, the most important single obstacle to class consciousness among white workers in America has been the deeply embedded racism in this country. How can socialists in the unions take up this problem?

Keylor: Socialists first of all have to confront the problem where it exists. Even in the longshore union division racism existed in the form of restrictions against blacks coming into the union in a number of locals. The issue has to be confronted directly in terms of hiring, especially in hiring of blacks, Asians and other minority workers. In the longshore division that battle has been largely won for now. But the overall threat to the union by divisions among workers growing out of racism is a very real one.

Several years ago when a black longshoreman in my local moved into an area of the suburbs that was largely white, he was subject to direct threats and even attacks on his house by the Ku Klux Klan. At that time we Trotskyists fought for a defense guard composed largely of longshoremen to defend that worker's home in conjunction with black community groups. We fought this issue out in the union. We lost the fight but in the process we made some gains in terms of educating workers in the necessity of not depending on the bourgeois state for defense against racist, fascist groups like the Klan.

1917: As I understand it, the union bureaucracy decided to hire private security guards instead.

Keylor: That is correct. The interesting thing is that we won the fight in the sense that the union bureaucrats had to concede that it was not realistic to simply rely on the police to defend this threatened worker. But their solution was to hire private security guards around the clock to protect his home.

1917: Finally, how do you see the possibilities for the creation of a class-struggle current in the unions in the coming period?

Keylor: The potential is great but the difficulty is that in the short run there are not sizable political groupings in place that can initiate and give rise to indigenous class-struggle formations which can pose a quantitatively significant alternative on a national level. It is not going to happen spontaneously. It didn't happen that way in the high points in North American trade-union history in the past. The obstacles to an alternative class-struggle leadership being built are in some ways even greater today, so that the necessity to bring forward the hard-won lessons of working-class struggle in initiating and building such formations is even more critical.

Part of the reluctance of workers to struggle and to go on the offensive is a lack of confidence in their present leadership. In fact, I wouldn't say part of the reason, I'd say the overwhelming obstacle to a working-class offensive against Reagan is that the union ranks don't trust their leadership to lead them in struggle.

There is among American workers a very profoundly felt hunger and need for labor unity in struggle. This was clearly expressed around the PATCO strike. Many workers have told me, even the most conservative workers, that the only thing that could have saved that strike, and stopped Reagan's union-busting was a nation-wide general strike, or at least regional general strikes where the airports were. That was a very deep-felt need of workers at that time. Unfortunately there were not the political groupings in place within the unions with the will and the authority to have raised those demands in such as way as to force some action. So we saw a defeat.

The key is to build a revolutionary organization with a real, organic connection to the working class. That is why I am a supporter of the Bolshevik Tendency. Because I think the Bolshevik Tendency has learned these lessons best and can show the way to build such formations in the working class. At this point, the question is one of the struggle for political clarity in the construction of the nuclei of the future leadership of the class.

There is today a growing awareness on the part of the more advanced workers that their problems can't be solved on a national basis. I have been surprised at how aware workers are that capitalist interests can move their money around pretty freely from country to country. They recognize that it isn't possible even to wrest lasting gains in this country because the capitalists can always move their money to where the rate of exploitation is higher than it is here.

There is a really deep felt need for international solidarity among workers. We found this was true in longshore when we raised demands for the defense of workers in other countries: South Africa, Chile and others. And when there was a possibility of acting, even in a small and symbolic fashion, to build solidarity with workers internationally, I have found through my own experience on the waterfront that the workers are quite open. And that's why you can remain optimistic about the future. In the last analysis though, it all comes back to the question of available alternatives—the question of the crisis of working-class leadership.

Militant Longshoreman Program

The following text is reprinted from Keylor's union publication circa 1987

1. **DEFEND OUR JOBS AND LIVELIHOOD**—Six hour shift, no extensions, at eight hours pay. Manning scales on all ship operations, one man—one job. Weekly PGP. Full no-cap C.O.L.A. on wages. Joint maritime union action against non-union barge, shipping and longshore operations. No ghost riders or witnesses. No long-term contracts.
2. **DEFEND THE HIRING HALL**—Use regular gangs on container ships; no dispatch of "unit gangs." Call all 9.43 men back to the hall. Stop-work action to defend the hiring hall and older and disabled men.
3. **DEFEND UNION CONDITIONS AND SAFETY THROUGH JOB ACTION**—Stop PMA chiseling on the contract. Eliminate "work as directed," "no illegal work stoppage," and arbitration sections from the contract. Mobilize to smash anti-labor injunctions. No employer drug or alcohol screening.
4. **DEFEND OUR UNION**—No Class B or C longshoremen. Register directly to Class A. Keep racist, anti-labor government and courts out of the union and BALMA. Support unions' resistance against court suits and government "investigations." Union action to break down racial and sexual discrimination and employer favoritism on the waterfront. Organize for a coastwide strike to get what we need—no concessions—no give-backs.
5. **BUILD LABOR SOLIDARITY**—Against government/employer strikebreaking. No more defeated PATCO or HORMEL strikes. Honor all class-struggle picket lines—remove phony, racist, anti-working class picket lines. Don't handle struck or diverted cargo. No raiding of other unions. Organize the disorganized, and the unemployed. Defend IBU-ILWU (INLAND BOATMEN) against Crowley union busting.
6. **STOP NAZI/KLAN TERROR** through union-organized labor/black/latino defense actions. No dependence on capitalist police or courts to smash fascists.
7. **WORKING CLASS ACTION TO STOP REAGAN'S WAR-DRIVE**—Labor strikes to oppose U.S. military actions against Cuba, Nicaragua or Salvadoran leftist insurgents. boycott military cargo to Central America. Build labor action to smash the apartheid injunction.
8. **INTERNATIONAL LABOR SOLIDARITY**—Oppose protectionist trade restrictions—For a massive trade-union program of aid to help non-U.S. workers build unions and fight super-exploitation by the multinational corporations—Defend undocumented workers with union strike action.
9. **BREAK WITH THE DEMOCRATIC AND REPUBLICAN PARTIES**—Start now to build a workers party based on the unions to fight for a workers government which will seize all major industry without payment to the capitalists and establish a planned economy to end exploitation, racism, poverty and war.

Part Five

Revolutionary Continuity and Transitional Demands

Transitional Demands: From the Comintern to the Fourth International

In 1939, Marceau Pivert, a prominent French socialist, disparaged the Fourth International for fetishizing the "dogmas" of the Communist International of Lenin's time. Leon Trotsky responded:

> "Only continuity of ideas creates a revolutionary tradition, without which a revolutionary party sways like a reed in the wind.
>
> . . .
>
> "Pivert either refuses or is unable to understand that our invincible strength lies in our theoretical thoroughness and irreconcilability. 'Trotsky allows in his organization,' writes Pivert, 'only those members who accept as dogma (?), and consequently without discussion (?), a systematic reference to the principles elaborated in the first four congresses of the Communist International. Our conception of the party is altogether different'....
>
> "In the Bolshevik Party differences arose *after* the first four congresses of the Comintern, whose decisions were elaborated with the most direct participation of the future leaders of 'the Left Opposition.' A sharp turn toward opportunism was sanctioned by the Fifth Congress. Without renouncing the revolutionary tradition, the greatest in the annals of history, we have nevertheless not made the first four congresses more than *our starting point*, nor have we restricted ourselves to them."[1]

The Communist (or Third) International was launched in 1919 by the leaders of the Bolshevik Revolution as an agency of world proletarian revolution. It is well known that Trotsky played a prominent role in the Third International in its early years, but the direct political continuity between the first four congresses and the Fourth International is less widely appreciated.

The *Death Agony of Capitalism and the Tasks of the Fourth International* (commonly known as the *Transitional Program*) was adopted as the program of the Fourth International at its founding conference in September 1938. In it Trotsky fused the programmatic conceptions of the revolutionary Comintern with the subsequent contributions of the Left Opposition (particularly on Stalinism and fascism). The 1938 program is chiefly noted for its inclusion of a series of "transitional demands" (a sliding scale of wages and hours, workers' control of production, workers' defense guards, etc.) aimed at mobilizing the working class to struggle for power. It is often supposed (even by many ostensible Trotskyists) that the idea of a "transitional" program (as opposed to the minimal/maximal program of the social democrats and Stalinists) was devised by Trotsky as a sort of gimmick to distinguish his new inter-

1 Leon Trotsky, "'Trotskyism' and the PSOP," *Leon Trotsky On France* (New York: Monad Press, 1979), pp 242–43

national. But anyone taking the trouble to read through the major documents of the early years of the Comintern can plainly see that the transitional demands in the Fourth International's 1938 program came directly from the resolutions of the first four congresses of the Third International.[2]

In the turbulent years following World War I, the "World Proletarian Revolution" seemed a very immediate prospect. Between the First Congress of the Comintern (1919) and the Fourth (1922), European capitalism was shaken by a series of revolutionary and near-revolutionary upheavals. In a July 1921 speech in Moscow, Trotsky recalled the mood at the first two congresses:

> "...it is unquestionable that in the era of the First Congress (1919) many of us reckoned—some more, others less—that the spontaneous onset of the workers and in part peasant masses would overthrow the bourgeoisie in the near future. And, as a matter of fact, this onset was truly colossal. The number of casualties was very large. But the bourgeoisie was able to withstand this initial onset and precisely for this reason regained its self-confidence.
>
> "The Second Congress in 1920 convened at the breaking point. It could already be sensed that by the onset alone the bourgeoisie would not be overthrown in a few weeks or in one, two or three months; that needed more serious organizational and political preparation. But at the same time the situation remained very acute."[3]

Factory committees and Workers' Control

The Second Congress had addressed the importance of the struggle for leadership of the mass organizations of the working class:

> "The indecision of the working masses, their intellectual irresolution, their susceptibility to the specious arguments of the opportunist leaders, can be

2 Jean van Heijenoort reported:

> "In February 1933 in Prinkipo [Trotsky] had asked Pierre Frank and me to put together all the theses and resolutions adopted by the first four congresses of the Communist International. His plan was to use them exactly as they were, so that they would constitute a kind of chart for the international Trotskyite organization. Once the texts had been collected, it became obvious that, besides dealing with broad political perspectives, they covered so many narrow, out-of-date problems that it would be impossible to use them unchanged for a new program. The project had to be abandoned."
>
> —*With Trotsky in Exile* (Harvard University Press, 1978), p 63

Trotsky did not entirely abandon the project, as is evident from the programmatic "chart" he produced five years later for the Fourth International. His attachment to the traditions of the Leninist Comintern is also reflected in his remarks on selecting a name for the new revolutionary international, as reported by van Heijenoort (p 54) from a 27 July 1933 discussion:

> "There is the secondary and subordinate question of a name. Fourth International? It is not very pleasant. When we broke with the Second International, we changed our theoretical foundations. Now, no; we remain based on the first four congresses [of the Communist International]. We could also proclaim: the Communist International is us! And call ourselves the Communist International (Bolsheviks-Leninists). There are pros and cons. The title of Fourth International is neater. This may be an advantage as far as large masses are concerned."

3 Leon Trotsky, "The School of Revolutionary Strategy," *The First Five Years of the Communist International*, Vol. 2, (New York: Monad Press, 1972), p 8

> overcome only in the course of the sharpening struggle, to the extent that the broadest strata of the proletariat learn from their own experience, from their victories and defeats, that it is no longer possible within a capitalist economic system to get human conditions of life, to the extent that the advanced communist workers learn to act, in the economic struggle, not only as heralds of the ideas of communism, but as the most determined leaders of the struggle and of the trade unions. Only in this way will it be possible to get rid of the opportunist union leaders. Only in this way can the communists get at the head of the trade union movement and make it an organ of revolutionary struggle for communism...."[4]

The resolution called for forming "factory committees" to implement "workers' control of production" in order to counter the effects of capitalist economic irrationality and sabotage:

> "The economic disorder which is enveloping one country after another shows even the backward workers that it is not enough to fight for higher wages and a shorter working day, that with every day the capitalist class is less and less able to restore economic life and to ensure for the workers even the standard of life they enjoyed before the war. From this growing recognition arise the efforts of the working masses to create organizations which can take up the struggle to rescue economic life by workers' control, exercised through the control of production by factory committees...."[5]

The creation of factory committees and the imposition of workers' control (dual power on the shop floor) are "transitional" measures that clearly pose the question of state power:

> "The struggle of the factory committees against capitalism has as its immediate general object workers' control over production....The committees in the different factories will soon be faced with the question of workers' control over entire branches of industry and industry as a whole. But since any attempt by the workers to supervise the supply of raw materials and the financial operations of the factory owners will be met by the bourgeoisie and the capitalist government with the most vigorous measures against the working class, the fight for workers' control of production leads to the fight for the seizure of power by the working class...."[6]

These ideas, subsequently reiterated by both the Third and Fourth Congresses, feature prominently in the *Transitional Program*.

'Conquest of the Masses'

The Third Congress took place in 1921 in the midst of a series of setbacks for the international workers' movement:

> "During the year that elapsed between the II and III Congress of the Communist International a series of working-class uprisings and battles have resulted in partial defeats (the Red Army offensive against Warsaw in August 1920;

4 "Extracts from the Theses on the Trade Union Movement, Factory Councils, and the Communist International," *The Communist International 1919–1943 Documents*, Vol. 1, (London: Frank Cass and Company, 1971), p 147

5 *Ibid.*, p 148

6 *Ibid.*, p 149

> the movement of the Italian proletariat in September 1920; the uprising of the German workers in March 1921).
>
> "The first period of the revolutionary movement after the war is characterized by the elemental nature of the onslaught, by the considerable formlessness of its methods and aims and by the extreme panic of the ruling classes; and it may be regarded by and large as terminated."[7]

The Third and Fourth Congresses attempted to solve the problems posed by the transition from a period of working-class offensive to one of relative capitalist stabilization. In a report on the Fourth Congress, delivered on 28 December 1922, Trotsky recounted how, in the aftermath of the German Communist Party's abortive March 1921 uprising:

> "The International issued a warning: 'You must conquer the confidence of the majority of the working class before you dare summon the workers to an open revolutionary assault.' This was the lesson of the Third Congress. A year and a half later the Fourth World Congress convened.
>
> "....The Fourth Congress developed, deepened, verified and rendered more precise the work of the Third Congress, and was convinced that this work was basically correct."[8]

The "Theses of the Third World Congress on the International Situation and the Tasks of the Comintern," drafted by Trotsky, and adopted on 4 July 1921, proclaimed:

> "The fundamental task of the Communist Party in the current crisis is to lead the present defensive struggles of the proletariat, to extend their scope, to deepen them, to unify them, and in harmony with the march of events, *to transform them into decisive political struggles for the ultimate goal.*"[9]

RILU's 'Program of Action'

The "Program of Action" for the Red International of Labor Unions (RILU—also known as the Profintern), adopted by the Third Congress, addressed the same question:

> "17....Red unions should remember that these problems cannot be lastingly settled within the framework of capitalist relations....They must use every action, every local strike, every conflict, however minor, to argue their point. They must draw the lessons from the experience of struggle, raising the consciousness of the rank and file and preparing the workers for the time when it will be necessary and possible to achieve the social revolution and the dictatorship of the proletariat."[10]

7 "Theses of the Third World Congress on the International Situation and the Tasks of the Comintern," *Theses, Resolutions & Manifestos of the First Four Congresses of the Third International*, (London: Ink Links, 1980), p 184

8 Leon Trotsky, "Report on the Fourth World Congress," *The First Five Years of the Communist International*, Vol. 2, (New York: Monad Press, 1972), pp 312–13

9 "Theses of the Third World Congress on the International Situation and the Tasks of the Comintern," *Theses, Resolutions & Manifestos of the First Four Congresses of the Third International*, (London: Ink Links, 1980), p 202, emphasis in original

10 "The Communist International and the Red International of Trade Unions—The Struggle

The "Program of Action" addressed the problem of layoffs and unemployment as follows:

> "5....In no circumstance should factory owners be allowed to throw workers out onto the streets without bearing any of the consequences. They ought to pay full redundancy pay. The unemployed and, to an even greater extent, the employed workers should be organized around this question. They should be shown that the problem of unemployment cannot be solved as long as capitalist relations exist and that the best method of beating unemployment is to fight for social revolution and the dictatorship of the proletariat."[11]

The call in the *Transitional Program* for a sliding scale of wages and hours is more elegant, and more clearly anticipates how work is organized in a planned economy. But the intent of the RILU program is the same: to unite the employed and unemployed in common struggle to make the bosses bear the costs of labor-displacing technological innovation and "downsizing."

The RILU program proposed to respond to capitalist threats to cut hours or close down operations by opening the books. This demand was clearly linked to the imposition of workers' control and workers' management of production:

> "6....The unions must fight the closure of factories and demand that the workers have the right to investigate the reasons behind the closure. Special control commissions to deal with raw materials, fuel and orders must be established to carry out on-the-spot checks of the raw materials in stock, the materials essential to production and the bank balance of the factory or institution. Specially elected control committees must undertake a thorough investigation of financial relations between the concern in question and other concerns—this raises in a practical way the need to open the books.
>
> "7. Factory occupations and work-ins are also forms of struggle against the mass closure of factories and wage cuts. In view of the prevailing lack of consumer goods, it is particularly important that production be maintained and unions should not permit the deliberate closure of factories....The administration of factories occupied by workers should be placed in the hands of factory committees and union representatives specially picked for the purpose."[12]

Workers' defense guards, another key transitional demand, was also raised in the RILU program:

> "12....Every important strike, for example, needs to be thoroughly prepared. Furthermore, from the outset the workers must form special groups to fight the strike-breakers and combat the provocative action of the various kinds of right-wing organizations which are encouraged by the bourgeois governments. The Fascists in Italy...have as their object the destruction and suppression of all working-class activity, not only by providing scab labour,

Against the Amsterdam (scab) Trade-Union International," *Theses, Resolutions & Manifestos of the First Four Congresses of the Third International*, (London: Ink Links, 1980), p 273

11 *Ibid.*, p 270

12 *Ibid.*, pp 270–71

> but by smashing the working-class organizations and getting rid of their leaders. In such situations the organization of special strike militias and special self-defence groups is a matter of life and death."[13]

Third Congress 'On Tactics'

The resolution "On Tactics" adopted by the Third Congress (1921) was drafted by the Russian delegation led by Trotsky and Lenin. Of particular interest is the section entitled, "Single-Issue Struggles and Single-Issue Demands," which outlines how communists connect the immediate struggles of the working class to its historic interests:

> "By putting forward a militant programme urging the proletariat to fight for its basic needs, they can show the backward and vacillating masses the path to revolution and demonstrate how all parties other than the Communists are against the working class. Only by leading the concrete struggles of the proletariat and by taking them forward will the Communists really be able to win the broad proletarian masses to the struggle for the dictatorship.
>
> "All the agitation, propaganda and political work of the Communist Parties must start from the understanding that no long-term improvement in the position of the proletariat is possible under capitalism....*This does not mean, however, that the proletariat has to renounce the fight for its immediate practical demands until after it has established its dictatorship.*
>
> "Even though capitalism is in progressive decline and is unable to guarantee the workers even a life of well-fed slavery, social democracy continues to put forward its old programme of *peaceful reforms* to be carried out on the basis and within the framework of the bankrupt capitalist system....The social democrats are thus retreating to their *minimum programme*, which now stands clearly revealed as a counter-revolutionary fraud.
>
> . . .
>
> "The Communist Parties do not put forward minimum programmes which could serve to strengthen and improve the tottering foundations of capitalism. The Communists' main aim is to destroy the capitalist system. But in order to achieve their aim the Communist Parties must put forward demands expressing the immediate needs of the working class. The Communists must organize mass campaigns to fight for these demands regardless of whether they are compatible with the continuation of the capitalist system."[14]

Unlike reformists, revolutionaries do not limit themselves to what the capitalists can afford to concede:

> "If the demands put forward by the Communists correspond to the immediate needs of the broad proletarian masses, and if the masses are convinced that they cannot go on living unless their demands are met, then the struggle around these issues becomes the starting-point of the struggle for power."
>
> . . .
>
> "The Communist Parties should make certain that the demands they put forward not only correspond to the demands of the broad masses, but also draw the masses into battle and lay the basis for organizing them. Concrete slo-

13 *Ibid.*, p 272
14 "On Tactics," *Theses, Resolutions & Manifestos of the First Four Congresses of the Third International*, (London: Ink Links, 1980), pp 284–86, emphasis in original

> gans that express the economic need of the working masses must lead to the struggle for *control of industry*—control based not on a plan to organize the economy bureaucratically and under the capitalist system, but on the factory committees and revolutionary trade unions. Only the creation of such organizations and their co-ordination within the different industries and areas makes possible the organization of a unified struggle of the working masses....The present epoch is revolutionary precisely because the most modest demands of the working masses are incompatible with the continued existence of capitalist society, and the struggle for these demands is therefore bound to develop into the struggle for Communism."[15]

Many demands from the old social-democratic minimum program remained relevant, but the Comintern posed them not in a reformist spirit, but in ways that promoted awareness of the necessity for workers' power:

> "In place of the minimum programme of the centrists and reformists, the Communist International offers a struggle for the concrete demands of the proletariat which, in their totality, challenge the power of the bourgeoisie, organize the proletariat and mark out the different stages of the struggle for its dictatorship. Even before the broad masses consciously understand the need for the dictatorship of the proletariat, they can respond to each of the individual demands. As more and more people are drawn into the struggle around these demands and as the needs of the masses come into conflict with the needs of capitalist society, the working class will come to realize that if it wants to live, capitalism will have to die. This realization will be the main motivation in their struggle for the dictatorship of the proletariat. The tasks of the Communist Parties is to extend, deepen and unify the struggle around these concrete demands."[16]

Fourth Congress Endorses 'Transitional Demands'

The Fourth Congress was supposed to discuss and adopt a program for the Comintern. Three draft programs were prepared for discussion: one by the Bulgarian party, one by the Germans and one by Nikolai Bukharin on behalf of the Soviet leadership. While the adoption of a program was to have been one of the main political tasks of the Fourth Congress, the delegates felt that they lacked the time to properly consider the drafts and voted to postpone a consideration of the question to the next congress.

(The question was again postponed by the Fifth Congress in 1924. Finally, at the Sixth Congress in 1928, where Trotsky was expelled, the Stalinized Comintern adopted a very different program, also written by Bukharin, in which the task of organizing the World Revolution was replaced with that of building "Socialism in One Country." Trotsky's critique of this program is contained in his book *The Third International After Lenin*.)

In place of adopting a program, the presidium of the Fourth Congress proposed a motion on the question which was introduced by Grigory Zinoviev. This short five-point motion, which passed unanimously, indicates

15 *Ibid.*, pp 286–87
16 *Ibid.*, p 286

the centrality of the concept of transitional demands in Lenin's time. It thus vividly illustrates the political continuity between the Third and Fourth Internationals:

> "3. The programmes of the national sections must clearly and decisively establish the necessity of the struggle for transitional demands, making the necessary reservations about the dependence of these demands on the concrete circumstances of time and place.
>
> "4. The theoretical basis for all transitional and partial demands must be clearly stated in the general programme, and the fourth congress likewise decisively condemns the attempt to depict the inclusion of transitional demands in the programme as opportunism, as well as all attempts to gloss over or replace the fundamental revolutionary tasks by partial demands.
>
> "5. The general programme must clearly explain the basic historical types of the transitional demands of the national section, in accordance with the basic differences in the economic and political structure of the different countries, for example England on the one hand, and India on the other."[17]

In terms that were later echoed in Trotsky's 1938 draft program, the "Theses on Comintern Tactics" approved by the Fourth Congress declared that world capitalism had:

> "...fulfilled its mission of developing the productive forces and...reached a stage of irreconcilable contradiction with the requirements not only of modern historical development, but also of the most elementary conditions of human existence. This fundamental contradiction was reflected in the recent imperialist war....
>
> . . .
>
> "Capitalism to its very end will be at the mercy of cyclical fluctuations. Only the seizure of power by the proletariat and a world socialist revolution can save humanity from permanent catastrophe, caused by the existence of the modern capitalist system.
>
> "*What capitalism is passing through today is nothing other than its death throes. The collapse of capitalism is inevitable.*"[18]

The "death throes" of world capitalism have proved considerably more protracted than either the Comintern or the Fourth International anticipated. But, as the current "globalization" offensive by capital against the past gains of the working class reminds us, "if [the working class] wants to live, capitalism will have to die."

17 "Resolution of the Fourth Comintern Congress on the Programme of the Communist International," *The Communist International 1919–1943 Documents*, Vol. 1, (London: Frank Cass and Company, 1971), p 446

18 "Theses on Comintern Tactics," *Theses, Resolutions & Manifestos of the First Four Congresses of the Third International*, (London: Ink Links, 1980), pp 388–89, emphasis in original

Index